TEACHING BION

The Harris Meltzer Trust Teaching Series

Teaching Meltzer: Modes and Approaches
edited by Meg Harris Williams

Teaching Bion: Modes and Approaches
edited by Meg Harris Williams

TEACHING BION
Modes and Approaches

edited by

Meg Harris Williams

with Antonello Correale, Angel Costantino,
Gertraud Diem-Wille, Charles W. Dithrich, Michael Eigen,
Dawn Farber, Dorothy Hamilton, Martha Harris,
Robert Harris, R. D. Hinshelwood,
Luiz Carlos Uchôa Junqueira Jnr., Howard B. Levine,
Chris Mawson, Claudio Neri, Lee Rather,
Igor Romanov, and Leandro Stitzman

published for

The Harris Meltzer Trust

by

KARNAC

Published for The Harris Meltzer Trust by
Karnac Books Ltd, 118 Finchley Road, London NW3 5HT

British Library Cataloguing in Publication Data
A C.I.P. for this book is available from the British Library

ISBN 978 1 78220 119 9

Edited, designed and produced by The Bourne Studios
www.bournestudios.co.uk
Printed in Great Britain

www.harris-meltzer-trust.org.uk
www.karnacbooks.com

CONTENTS

Antonello Correale graduated in medicine and psychiatry at the Sapienza University of Rome, then trained in psychoanalysis with the Italian Psychoanalytic Society. He is former head of Area II of the Mental Health Department of Roma BASL (the Italian national health service). His edited books include *Il Campo Istituzionale, Quale Psicoanalisi per le Psicosi?*, (with L. Rinaldi), *Psicoanalisi e Psichiatria* (with G. B. Ceroni), *Borderline* (with A. M. Alonzi, A. Carnevali, P. Di Giuseppe, & N. Giachetti), *Il Gruppo in Psichiatria* (with V. Nicoletti), and *Il Soggetto Nascosto: Un Approccio Psicoanalitico alla Clinica delle Tossico Dipendenze* (with F. Cangiotti and A. Zoppi). His latest book is *Area Traumatica e Campo Istituzionale* (Borla, 2006).

Angel Costantino is a full member of the IPA and practises psychiatry and psychoanalysis in Buenos Aires. He completed his postgraduate training in 1971 at Araoz Alfano Hospital under the direction of Mauricio Goldenberg and proceeded to supervise psychoanalytic and psychiatric work at San Isidro Hospital, in collaboration with Enrique Pichon Rivière. He supervises the clinical work of candidates of ApdeBa and other psychoanalytic and psychotherapy organisations. From 1997 he has conducted study groups and workshops in Argentina mostly focused on Bion, but also on the works of Klein, Segal, Money Kyrle, Meltzer, and Betty Joseph.

Gertraud Diem-Wille is a professor of psychoanalysis in education at the University of Klagenfurt, Austria. She is a training analyst for children, adolescents, and adults at the Viennese Psychoanalytic Society and the International Psychoanalytic Association. She has pioneered and supported the training in Austria in psychoanalytic observational approaches to psychoanalytic training and in the educational field. She has published *The Early Years of Life: Developmental Theories according to Freud, Klein and Bion* (2011) and *Young Children and Their Parents: Perspectives from Psychoanalytic Infant Observation* (Karnac, 2015).

Charles W. Dithrich, PhD, is a personal and supervising analyst and faculty member of the Psychoanalytic Institute of Northern California, San Francisco. He has taught and lectured extensively on Bion. His practice is in Oakland, California.

Michael Eigen, PhD, is author of twenty-five books, including *Contact With the Depths, The Sensitive Self, Emotional Storm, Feeling Matters, The Psychoanalytic Mystic, Kabbalah,* and *Psychoananalysis and Faith.* He teaches and supervises for the National Psychological Association for Psychoanalysis and the New York University Postdoctoral Program in Psychotherapy and Psychoanalysis. His private seminar on Bion and Winnicott and his own work has been ongoing for over forty years.

Dawn Farber is a personal and supervising analyst at the Psychoanalytic Institute of Northern California; a faculty member; and past chair of PINC's Outreach and Public information Committee, 2001–15. She has a private practice seeing individuals and couples in Oakland; teaches and consults widely in the community; and runs ongoing case consultation groups in Oakland. She enjoys writing poetry, book and film reviews and has published in psychoanalytic and literary journals.

Dorothy Hamilton is a training therapist and supervisor, a Professional Member of the Association for Group and Individual Psychotherapy and member of the College of Psychoanalysts. She is an Honorary Fellow of the UKCP and a member of its Psychotherapy Council. She teaches in the fields of metapsychology, transference, and Bion, and is pursuing studies in the apprehension of beauty in a variety of disciplines.

Martha Harris (d. 1987) was a training analyst at the British Institute and worked closely with Klein and Bion For many years she was responsible for the Child Psychotherapy training at the Tavistock Clinic in London, developing a model of psychoanalytic training based on Esther Bick's infant observation and on Bion's work-groups. In the 1970s she invited Bion to give the talks subsequently published as *The Tavistock Seminars*. Her writings are collected in: *Your Teenager* (2007), *The Story of Infant Development* (2007), *The Tavistock Model* (2011), *Thinking about Infants and Young Children* (2011), and *Adolescence* (2011). Students' experience of her as a teacher is documented in *Enabling and Inspiring* (2012), ed. M. H. Williams.

Robert Harris is a group analyst and writer based in London. He has a special interest in the development of group analysis internationally, taking into account different cultural settings, and is currently helping to develop group analytic training institutions in Russia, Kazakhstan, Kalmykia, and Albania. He teaches and supervises at the Institute of Group Analysis (IGA) in London and other locations in the UK, and is a member of the IGA International Courses Committee. He integrates Bion's thinking into much of his teaching and supervisory work, and amongst other papers and publications, contributed a chapter to *Bion's Sources*, ed. R. D. Hinshelwood and N. Torres (Routledge, 2013.)

R. D. Hinshelwood is Professor at the Centre for Psychoanalytic Studies, University of Essex, and previously was a consultant psychotherapist in the NHS for 20 years, and Clinical Director at the Cassel Hospital, London. He is a Fellow of the

British Psychoanalytical Society and of the Royal College of Psychiatrists. He founded the *British Journal of Psychotherapy* and *Psychoanalysis and History*, and authored *A Dictionary of Kleinian Thought* (1989) and other books and articles on Kleinian psychoanalysis. *Observing Organisations* (2000) was edited with W. Skogstad and applies psychoanalytic observation to social science. *Suffering Insanity* (2004) is about the treatment of schizophrenia in psychiatric institutions. In 2013 he published *Research on the Couch: Single Case Studies, Subjectivity and Psychoanalytic Knowledge* (Routledge) and edited (with N. Torres) *Bion's Sources: The Shaping of his Paradigms.*

Luis Carlos Uchôa Junqueira, Jnr. trained in medicine at the University of São Paulo) and worked as a psychiatrist with the Brazilian Psychiatric Society. He is a training analyst and past president of the Brazilian Psychoanalytical Society of São Paulo. He is chair of the 'Biennial Meetings' of the SBPSP and editor of the corresponding books. He is the author of *Sismos e Acomodações: A Clínica Psicanalítica como Usina de Idéias* (Rosari, 2003).

Howard B. Levine is in private practice in Brookline, Massachusetts. He is on the faculty at the Psychoanalytic Institute of New England East (PINE) and on the editorial Board of the *IJP* and *Psychoanalytic Inquiry.* He has authored numerous articles, book chapters, and reviews on psychoanalytic process and technique, intersubjectivity, the treatment of primitive personality disorders, and the consequences and treatment of early trauma and childhood sexual abuse. He is the editor of *Adult Analysis and Childhood Sexual Abuse* (Analytic Press, 1990), co-editor of *Growth and Turbulence in the Container/Contained* (Routledge, 2013), *Unrepresented States and the Construction of Meaning* (Karnac, 2013), *Responses to Freud's Screen Memories Paper* (Karnac, 2014), and (forthcoming) *The Wilfred Bion Tradition*, and *Bion in Brazil.*

Chris Mawson is a training and supervising analyst of the British Psychoanalytical Society and works in private practice as a psychoanalyst. He is also interested in the study of groups and organizations from a psychoanalytic perspective, particularly that pursued by those of the British Group Relations orientation. He is editor of *The Complete Works of W. R. Bion* (Karnac, 2014), and *Bion Today* (2010) in the New Library of Psychoanalysis series. Other publications include: 'The use of play technique in understanding disturbed behaviour in school' (*Psychoanalytic Psychotherapy*, 1986), 'Containing anxiety in work with damaged children' in *The Unconscious at Work*, ed. A. Obholzer & V. Z. Roberts (1994), and 'Pseudo-free association: the sophisticated analytic patient and "as-if" relating' (*British Journal of Psychotherapy*, 2002).

Claudio Neri is a psychoanalyst and group psychotherapist in private practice. He teaches in the faculty of medicine and psychology at the Sapienza University of Roma and in the faculty of psychology at Turin. He is a training psychoanalyst at the Italian Psychoanalytic Society and has been teaching for some years in France, where he has been visiting professor at the Université Lumiere in Lyon and the Université Descartes in Paris. He also runs supervisory and teaching activities in the Italian national health system with psychiatrists, nursing staff and social workers.

Lee Rather, PhD, is a faculty member at the San Francisco Center for Psychoanalysis and the Psychoanalytic Institute of Northern California where he is also a personal and supervising analyst. In addition to teaching Bion intensively over the last 15 years, he has published and presented on topics including maternal and paternal psychic function, the existential aspects of mourning, the unconscious aspects of creativity, and the psychoanalytic dynamics at work in operas by Verdi, Mozart, and Wagner. Dr Rather is in private practice in San Francisco. Website: www.leerather.com.

Igor Romanov is a psychologist, philosopher, and psychoanalyst; an associate professor of theoretical and practical philosophy in the Karazin Kharkiv National University Philosophical

Faculty; a direct member of the IPA; a member of the Ukrainian Psychoanalytic Society; and president of Kharkiv Psychoanalytic Society. He has a private practice in psychoanalysis and psychotherapy. He is editor of *The Era of Countertransference* (in Russian) and author of many papers and books on theory, history, and philosophy of psychoanalysis.

Leandro Stitzman works with children and adults. He coordinates study groups on Bion's works in Argentina, Chile, Brazil and Colombia. He has published many papers in the journals of Latin America and Europe. He has translated Bion and other authors for the publications of Hormé, APdeBA, APPOLA and other editorials. He is creator, developer and organiser of the Bionian Games, and a founder member of the *Memoirs of the Future* web, with contributions by analysts from Argentina, Brazil, Chile, Colombia, Uruguay, Italy and Spain. He is webmaster for the Bion website on FEPAL: www.wrbion.net. In 2011 he published the book *Entrelazamiento: un Ensayo Psicoanalítico* (Promolibro).

Meg Harris Williams lectures widely in the UK and other countries. Her writings discussing Bion's ideas include: '"Underlying pattern" in Bion's *Memoir of the Future*' (*IJP,* 1983), 'Bion's *The Long Weekend*' (*J. of Child Psychotherapy,* 1983), 'The Tiger and O' (*Free Associations,* 1985), *A Strange Way of Killing* (1987), 'A man of achievement: Sophocles' *Oedipus* plays' (*BJP,* 1994), 'The three vertices: science, art and religion' (*BJP,* 2005), *The Vale of Soulmaking* (2005), *The Aesthetic Development* (2010), *Bion's Dream* (2010), a chapter in *Bion Today,* ed. C. Mawson (2010), 'The infant and the infinite: on psychoanalytic faith' (*Psychodynamic Practice,* 2015), and a play and filmscript based on Bion's *Memoir.*

Meg Harris Williams

'What *are* you when you *cease* to be a student of psychoanalysis?'
(Bion, see below, p. 203)

The purpose of this book is not to summarise or interpret Bion's thinking in a comprehensive way, and it is
not an introduction to Bion. As far as Bion goes, the
reader will find nothing new here. Instead, the aim is to picture
the experience of those who have been teaching Bion's ideas in
seminars, talks and supervisions for many years, and who have
evolved their own modes for conveying their personal experience of those ideas. The hope is that this may be useful for
others who are teaching not just Bion but psychoanalysis in
both clinical and applied fields.

As Donald Meltzer said, in his discussion of Bion's *Memoir of
the Future:*

> I am sure, from many personal contacts with Bion, that he never
> wished to implant his thought in other people's heads. His
> vision of the air, like Prospero's island's air, being full of thoughts
> seeking thinkers places the artist-scientist (for they were never
> separated in his mind) in a position of using his special recep-

tiveness and gifts for making public his experiences as an inter-
mediary for others to catch the thoughts that are in the wind at
the moment. (Meltzer, 1994, p. 523)

Or as Bion himself jokes in the *Memoir* itself, in the voice of
one dinosaur speaking to another: 'Ow! What's that? You've
shoved your thoughts into me, you vile creature' (Bion, 1991,
p. 84). Teaching, as the authors of this book are well aware, is
not a matter of manic projective identification – pushing one's
thoughts into others' heads – still less of pretending to push in
the thoughts of somebody else. Rather, teaching is just another
form of learning from experience with the aid of students
who reflect struggles, difficulties and moments of illumina-
tion which are brought into view through the special teaching
relationship, which is perhaps as much a matter of transference and countertransference as psychoanalysis itself. Teaching
demonstrates modes of identification with the author, and is
accompanied by evidence of the internalisation of other past
teachers. Style, cultural context, personal bias and interests
are all important in making the teaching situation a live and
authentic one from which all the participants can select what
speaks to them.

This is not to say that knowledge is not important; 'knowing
about' is always the basis for 'knowing', and 'without memory
and desire' doesn't mean one is let off doing one's homework.
As some authors have observed, one of the problems with the
current Bion bandwagon is the belief that his ideas sprang
from nowhere, in terms of psychoanalytic thinking (never
mind philosophical thinking in general): as if his contact with
Kleinian thinking were purely theoretical, rather than an actual
life-experience of personal analysis with Mrs Klein which was
continuously redigested in the context of the prevailing 'winds'
of circumstance and research, his own and others'. Scholarship
and due awareness of the context of psychoanalytic history
are the background from which a teaching style then emerges,
through selecting what appear to be the essentials. Students
learn from this selective attention, not from disembodied ideas.
Correspondingly, what they learn is personal to themselves.

The teacher is not a barrier between the student and the author but rather an 'intercessor' to use Bion's term, or a 'midwife' to use Socrates'.

The book begins with 'Wilfred Bion: clinical thinker' by Chris Mawson (UK), who sets Bion in the context of some his colleagues in the British society of that era, as well as that of Freud and Klein, and of Keats' wellknown principle of negative capability. Introductory seminars are founded on *Learning from Experience* with reference back to Freud, in particular his 'Recommendations to physicians', and forward to later Kleinans. He explains his choice of texts and the reasons for focusing in detail on specific passages, with a view to tracing the evolution of key concepts such as container–contained, the oscillation $Ps \rightleftharpoons D$, alpha-function, the links of LHK and their negatives.

In the next chapter, Claudo Neri (Rome) formulates the teacher's role as that of a 'Go-between' whose aim is to put the student in touch with Bion's thinking. In this he offers four principles: the idea that the most 'difficult' formulation of an idea is probably the best or closest to whatever Bion was trying to formulate; advice to read the text closely not just to cite the slogans that are so often extracted; a warning against joining the mythical group of 'Bionians' which tempts against the loneliness of individual thinking and self-discovery; and the further warning to avoid what Bion has called 'arrogance', to be differentiated from the legitimate self-respect which also entails respect for others.

In 'Identifying with existential unease', Antonello Correale (Rome) considers in depth the definition of teaching as how we put things inside us, as distinct from simply transmitting knowledge, even though this will always remain the nucleus of the teacher's work. The parallel is drawn between studying Bion and conducting psychoanalysis, both of which demand a loyalty to this existential unease in the face of Bion's giving epistemological matters the primary place. There is conflict both in our relation to Bion and in our own search for truth, as appears in the processes of learning from experience, alpha function, and 'becoming O', Bion's way of describing the process of introjecting the object.

Luiz Carlos Junqueira, Jnr. (São Paulo), in 'Teaching Bion, living life', begins with the way he presents to students the story of Bion's development as a psychoanalytic thinker, using as a basic structure the comparison of Bion's early works and his subsequent *Second Thoughts*. He then summarises his own encounter with Bion's thinking, followed by a list of the courses he has devised and adapted over the years, with some detailed examples of 'significant landscapes' and the texts chosen to illustrate them. 'Teaching' is thus an ever-changing procedure which, like life, is always searching for new links to elaborate.

Lee Rather (California), in 'Building a Bion container', focuses on Bion's emphasis on psychoanalysis as a probe or process of inquiry more than a body of knowledge, and discusses the advantages of critical pluralism: that is, the usefulness of Bion's 'unsaturated' concepts in helping people to discover their own subjective experience, whether teacher or student, so that teaching can be a genuine learning or 'becoming' activity. A 'culturally unsaturated' model also has advantages when teaching in very different societies and in forging links with other disciplines.

Charles W. Dithrich (California) in 'Maintaining a relation to O' discusses the teacher's role in moderating the group atmosphere such that a sense of humility and toleration of uncertainty can prevail and enable shared discovery. He takes Bion's clinical seminars as favourite introductory texts, since they show students Bion's spontaneous and humorous aspects; then proceeds to select passages from the major books, organised on a conceptual basis. A limited amount of reading is given per session so that students are not overwhelmed or persecuted by unfamiliar ideas but find the group a containing setting for the emotions aroused.

Angel Costantino (Buenos Aires) in 'Group learning' considers his primary function as study group leader is the selection of topics for discussion, without any specific goal other than that of facilitating its progress, which entails acknowledging both regressive and progressive moments in its evolution. The inclusion of their own clinical material strengthens both the group and its idea of Bion. Over the course of time, an anchorage was discovered in the concrete description of patient X, who (whether a real or generic character) emerges recognisably in a series of Bion's texts, and offers a model for Bion's way of interpreting that puts his more abstract formulations in a human context.

Michael Eigen (New York) gives a substantial number of student responses in 'Tiger stripes and student voices'. He narrates the story of his first encounters with Bion, in books and in person, and his own movement from 'K–Bion to F–Bion' with the publication of *Attention and Interpretation*, explaining Bion's influence on his own life and writings: 'When I teach Bion, Bion teaches me.' He uses two teaching approaches: the formal setting for students who need a historical overview, and the intimate seminar, which is organised by focusing on the evocative properties of selected words or phrases and the student responses they invite.

Howard B. Levine (Massachusetts) describes the method he uses for 'Dreaming the patient into being', a method which in his personal experience harks back to practising jazz improvisation with the saxophone part left out, so that each student could interpolate their own voice into the existing basic musical structure. An analogous approach to students in a psychoanalytic seminar can enable free associations and the sharing of 'wild thoughts' by way of rehearsal for the 'analytic mind-set' recommended by Bion which focusses more on process than on content.

Leandro Stitzman (Buenos Aires) offers a 'Model kit' of tools he has found useful in recommending a Bionian spirit of proximity to emotional or psychoanalytic 'facts', including awareness of animal origins, wild ideas, and an effort to search for accurate modes of notation. The kit comprises such items as evenly-suspended attention and tolerance of uncertainty; appreciating the difference between theoretical and abstract in Bion's notations; the use of Grid and the 'selected fact' as tools for observation; the value of Bion's recorded seminars as a way to introduce students without jargon; and the value of a shared sense of humour in indicating valuable work is being achieved.

R. D. Hinshelwood (UK), in 'Teaching Bion's teachings', warns of the dangers of fashionably idealising Bion, which often result in glossing over any problems that may arise from Bion's own teaching methods. He suggests there is a lack of continuity in Bion's own ideas and methods which, together with the fact that Bion's own wide-ranging sources are not readily familiar in their totality to most interpreters, makes it especially difficult for teachers to convey his thinking as a unified whole. Copying Bion's own method with groups can arouse anxiety rather than responsibility in the members, so it is a challenge for the leader to find alternative ways.

Robert Harris (UK), in 'Teaching Bion in Russia', is in a position to make interesting comparisons between the different learning climates of Russia and the UK, whilst at the same time picking up certain deep linguistic, humorous and aphoristic ties between the two cultures that are highlighted in the process of 'translating' Bion, in particular his views on group behaviour. He finds that the excellent educational practice endemic in Russia is employed here in the service of a thirst to understand social trauma, and *Experiences in Groups* in particular has a deep resonance.

Igor Romanov (Ukraine) tells of 'Bion's adventures in a country without psychoanalysis', though some would say students are very well informed both in the university setting and from the Kleinian clinical point of view. A long-distance learning approach, he suggests, devolves responsibility onto making links within as wide a context as possible, when forging a professional identity in a pluralistic context. He concludes that Bion's works contribute to communication though not necessarily to consensus between analysts, and that despite their complexity, they provide a good introduction to psychoanalysis.

Dawn Farber (California), in 'On conveying the style of living analysis', compares and contrasts teaching in California and South Africa. The nature of teaching depends on the felt relevance to individuals not only *per se* but as they are in the context of their society and culture. In San Francisco the focus is on 'waking dreaming', yet ideas may be stymied by the American dream of egocentric 'happiness'; while in South Africa Bion's ideas on the tyranny of group basic assumptions are found most valuable, since they offer hope of understanding and therefore escaping from the corruption and violence incurred.

Dorothy Hamilton (UK) describes her experience of 'Teaching Bion through clinical example', using vignettes of several patients to illustrate the motifs of the K link, containment, moral judgement and minus K, catastrophic change from K to O, and Bion's idea of 'suffering'. She says that any potential distortion that might occur in teaching theory primarily via clinical work is amply compensated by the vividness of the interaction between real people, including the relationship between patient and therapist.

Gertraud Diem-Wille (Austria), in 'Teaching theory in the context of child analysis', similarly demonstrates the teaching value of presenting ideas through clinical work, this time focussing on a single case study of the analysis of a three-year-old child, and on the emotional responses aroused in the therapist. She shows how Bion's extension of Kleinian concepts, such as the dynamic link of $Ps \rightleftharpoons D$ and the move from beta-elements to alpha-function, enriches clinical understanding and supports the analyst's capacity to tolerate projections.

Meg Harris Williams (UK), in 'The living mind – Bion's vision', describes two scenarios in which she teaches Bion: in groups and through writing. In the academic setting, she concentrates on Bion's model of the mind and its post-Kleinian context, rather than on his theoretical formulations, which are brought in secondarily; this encompasses the question of what is a psychoanalyst, the way the mind grows by digesting thoughts, and the hindrances to this growth. She then discusses her experience of writing about Bion's autobiographies, in particular that of co-writing a filmscript based on Bion's *Memoir of the Future*.

Finally a paper of Martha Harris (who worked closely with Bion) is reprinted here from 1978: 'The individual in the group: on learning to work with the psychoanalytical method'. In the context of the foundational principles of the teaching method at the Tavistock Clinic, she describes how Bion's insights into group behaviour can be used to modulate the tension between the individual and the group, making it container rather than constrictor. Through a correlation of vertices, the individual can be enabled to learn through 'transformations in O' despite the establishment group's pressure to reinforce basic assumptions.

CHAPTER ONE

Wilfred Bion: clinical thinker

Chris Mawson

The difficulty of reading Bion I address using the following two quotations, the first from a letter to his daugher Nicola:

How difficult it is to realise that with certain books one does not 'read' them – one has to have an emotional experience of reading them. This seems so slow compared with the easy slick reading, especially if you feel you have exams to pass, that it is very difficult to give one's self the time and other conditions necessary for it – especially the time. (Bion, 1985, p. 178)

The second is from the introduction to *Learning from Experience*:

Some obscurities are due to the impossibility of writing without pre-supposing familiarity with some aspect of a problem that is only worked on later. If the reader will read straight through, these points will become clearer as he proceeds. Unfortunately obscurities also exist because of my inability to make them clearer. The reader may find the effort to clarify these for himself is rewarding and not simply work that has been forced on him because I have not done it myself. (Bion, 1961a, p. viii)

We discuss the issue – reminding ourselves that getting to grips with the writing of Freud and Klein too is hardly an easy matter in spite of the beautiful clarity of the former. Bion's own suggestion to readers about their approach to the task has similarities to the optimal mental attitude required to be receptive to the communications arising within the analytic relationship itself. His work needs to be digested as well as possible by the reader, as an emotional experience of reading, and then subsequently allowed to rest in the background, where, in time, it may be integrated through learning from experience in the clinical situation, and (again, in time) augment and enrich the practitioner's clinical thinking. I encourage students to bring into the discussion anything from their clinical work which comes to mind in the course of our reading. Also, at certain places in his work, Bion's mode of writing recreates uncannily in the reader's thought processes the very phenomena being discussed in the text, as André Green (1998) has described. I provide some examples from *Cogitations* in order to illustrate this, and we have also had the chance to study recently discovered cogitations not included in the original book.

I then begin a series of seminars, beginning with a brief talk reminding us that Bion had both horizontal and vertical roots. The purpose of this is to counter the erroneous belief that Bion and his work exist, somehow, 'out on their own'. In doing so I emphasise that Bion's contributions were rooted vertically in Freud and Klein, and were supported also by a significant degree of fraternal support from, and collaboration with, Hanna Segal, Herbert Rosenfeld, and Melanie Klein, in the late 1950s and 1960s; it is not always possible to distinguish their exact individual contributions to the developing theory of splitting, projective identification, unconscious phantasy and the use of countertransference. I clarify also that it makes absolutely no sense whatsoever to speak of 'Bionians', or of a 'Bionian' method. In my teaching I emphasise that Bion had no desire to found another 'school' of psychoanalysis; neither does his work support a modification of the fundamental Freudian and Kleinian method of working in the transference within the traditional analytic setting. As he wrote in his first chapter of *Transformations*, he aimed to 'suggest a method of critical approach to psychoanalytic practice and not new psychoanalytical theories' (1965, p. 6). I show by considering Bion's seminars when we get to them, that in his clinical work and supervision Bion worked as a recognisably Kleinian analyst towards an insightful appreciation of psychic reality through a disciplined, intuitive sensibility to indications of the transference, and the corresponding and eventually uncovered countertransference. In other words, in Bion's work the setting and the method – however much his terminology might occasionally suggest otherwise – remains rigorously psychoanalytic.

In terms of psychoanalysis I begin, as did Bion, with Freud and with Klein, and here I take as read some familiarity with Freud's method, particularly his emphasis on the specific nature of psychoanalytic attention, and the centrality of transference, and the clinical value of countertransference. This I explain as crucial groundwork before even beginning to read Bion, and I find it useful to direct students to the following quotation from a letter to Jung in 1909 that refers to Jung's enactment of the transference–countertransference with his patient 'Sp' (Spielrein):

> Such experiences, though painful, are necessary and hard to avoid. Without them we cannot really know life and what we are dealing with. I myself have never been taken in quite so badly, but I have come very close to it a number of times and had a narrow escape … But no lasting harm is done. They help us to develop the thick skin we need and to dominate 'countertransference', which is after all a permanent problem for us; they teach us to displace our own affects to best advantage. They are a 'blessing in disguise'. (McGuire, 1974, pp. 230–32)

Receptivity to the unconscious, as it emerges in the transference neurosis, is preferred in this method to attempts to use elements of suggestion, education or reassurance to produce change. In order to offset any prior reading the students may have done which suggests that Bion's method is a new and improved one which dispenses with the foundation of Freudian psychoanalysis, I make frequent links between Bion, Freud and Klein. Meltzer's writing on this subject (1978, 1986) is of great help.

Optimising the capacity for receptivity to the unconscious was as essential for Bion as it was for Freud. The latter wrote of evenly-suspended attention, and Bion drew not only on Freud's 'Recommendations' (1912) but also on various sources, including Tibetan and Indian texts and the writings of St John of the Cross to formulate his own often-quoted recommendation of 'without memory, desire, or understanding'. Bion's version has been more frequently misunderstood and misapplied than Freud's. In his expanded version of his 1966 paper 'Catastrophic change', which appears as chapter 12 of *Attention and Interpretation* (1970), Bion states the essence of his 'memory and desire' recommendation, to which he gives centrality as 'the most important mechanism employed by the practising psychoanalyst'. I give special emphasis in my teaching on Bion to this passage:

> The discussion of the configuration of container and contained has occupied a considerable space in this book. It may, therefore, seem surprising if, at this stage and in relatively few sentences, I describe what is perhaps the most important mechanism employed by the practising psychoanalyst. It requires less description and is relatively more easily grasped. It is for these reasons only that it occupies what may appear to be an insignificant place in this book. It is derived from Melanie Klein's descriptions of the paranoid—schizoid and depressive positions, and to these the reader should refer. Here, briefly, is my formulation of this matter as it concerns the practising analyst:
>
> In every session the psychoanalyst should be able, if he has followed what I have said in this book, particularly with regard to memory and desire, to be aware of the aspects of the material that, however familiar they may seem to be, relate to what is unknown both to him and to the analysand. Any attempt to cling to what he knows must be resisted for the sake of achieving a state of mind analogous to the paranoid—schizoid position. For this state I have coined the term 'patience' to distinguish it from 'paranoid—schizoid position', which should be left to describe the pathological state for which Melanie Klein used it. I mean the term to retain its association with suffering and tolerance of frustration.

'Patience' should be retained without 'irritable reaching after fact and reason' until a pattern 'evolves'. This state is the analogue to what Melanie Klein has called the depressive position. For this state I use the term 'security'. This I mean to leave with its association of safety and diminished anxiety. I consider that no analyst is entitled to believe that he has done the work required to give an interpretation unless he has passed through both phases – 'patience' and 'security'. The passage from the one to the other may be very short, as in the terminal stages of analysis, or it may be long. Few, if any, psychoanalysts should believe that they are likely to escape the feelings of persecution and depression commonly associated with the pathological states known as the para-noid–schizoid and depressive positions. In short, a sense of achievement of a correct interpretation will be commonly found to be followed almost immediately by a sense of depression. I consider the experience of oscillation between 'patience' and 'security' to be an indication that valuable work is being achieved. (Bion, 1970, pp. 123–124)

It is sometimes forgotten that Bion meant his comments about the importance of divesting oneself of past knowledge of the patient and of one's desires for his 'betterment' to be under-stood, not only in the context of Freud's recommendations, but also with the apophatic principle described by John Keats as 'Negative Capability':

> Several things dovetailed in my mind, and at once it struck me what quality went to form a Man of Achievement especially in Literature & which Shakespeare possessed so enormously – I mean Negative Capability, that is when a man is capable of being in uncertainties, Mysteries, doubts, without any irritable reaching after fact & reason (Gittings, 1970, p. 43)

When we get to this issue in teaching seminars I demon-strate the similarities between Freud's and Bion's intentions in using these concepts. The specific teaching points from Freud required as a foundation for my subsequent seminars on Bion's writings concern psychoanalytic attention and the use of the transference. I pay special attention to the following passages from Freud's 'Recommendations to physicians' (1912b) – the first on 'evenly-suspended attention':

> The technique, however, is a very simple one. As we shall see, it rejects the use of any special expedient (even that of taking notes). It consists simply in not directing one's notice to anything in particular and in maintaining the same 'evenly-suspended attention' (as I have called it) in the face of all that one hears. (Freud, 1912b, p. 111)

The second piece of advice points out the problems inherent in selecting material:

> In making the selection, if he follows his expectations he is in danger of never finding anything but what he already knows; and if he follows his inclinations he will certainly falsify what he may perceive. It must not be forgotten that the things one hears are for the most part things whose meaning is only recognised later on. (Freud, 1912b, p. 112)

The attempt therefore to 'give equal notice to everything' is, he says, a 'fundamental rule of psychoanalysis'. The third of Freud's 'rules' concerns the need to rely on unconscious memory:

> The rule for the doctor may be expressed: 'He should withhold all conscious influences from his capacity to attend, and give himself over completely to his 'unconscious memory'.' Or, to put it purely in terms of technique: 'He should simply listen, and not bother about whether he is keeping anything in mind.' What is achieved in this manner will be sufficient for all requirements during the treatment. (Freud, 1912b, p. 112)

The fourth uses a metaphor to describe the contact between the unconscious of the analyst and that of the patient:

> To put it in a formula: he must turn his own unconscious like a receptive organ towards the transmitting unconscious of the patient. He must adjust himself to the patient as a telephone receiver is adjusted to the transmitting microphone. Just as the receiver converts back into sound waves the elec-

tric oscillations in the telephone line which were set up by sound waves, so the doctor's unconscious is able, from the derivatives of the unconscious which are communicated to him, to reconstruct that unconscious, which has determined the patient's free associations (Freud, 1912b, p. 116)

In addition to this, on the current course of teaching, the three required Freud readings are: 'The dynamics of transference' (1912a), 'Remembering, repeating and working-through' (1914), and 'Formulations on the two principles of mental functioning' (1911), a paper central to Bion's ideas throughout his life as a thinker and as an analyst. The latter has a direct bearing on the distinction prominent in Bion's work between measures intended to evade reality and measures designed to modify it.

The other piece of pre-reading is Klein's 1946 paper, 'Notes on some schizoid mechanisms', in which she introduced the term projective identification, a concept already in clinical use by Herbert Rosenfeld, Hanna Segal and Wilfred Bion in their pioneering analytic work with patients in psychotic states, later expanded by Bion into a normally-occurring communicative process between mother and infant in his container–contained model.

After the preparatory groundwork I begin by locating Bion in an historical context, with key biographical aspects (including being an eighteen year old in tank warfare) which contributed to the development of his ideas. As I said earlier, I also emphasise that however seemingly 'out on his own' his ideas may seem, he was a member of an unusually creative small group of clinicians applying and expanding Klein's ideas from the late 1950s until his departure for Los Angeles in January 1968. Members of the seminar are each allocated different biographical pieces, and in the seminar are asked to speak – preferably without notes – for ten minutes or so about anything from their reading which has interested them.

In addition to autobiographical writings I ask the seminar to read Francesca Bion's (1995) paper 'The Days of our Years', which she gave as an address in Toronto in 1994. Also included is Edna O'Shaughnessy's (2005) concise paper 'Whose Bion?', to remind us that his ideas and place in psychoanalysis can vary according to the perspective and uses which writers wish to make of them. She also states her view that Bion's significance is as a leading contributor in a triumvirate, as it were, alongside Segal and Rosenfeld as part of the Freud–Klein development, and that studies of enactment, for example, and psychic retreats (Steiner) are further developments of this.

In terms of an introduction to Bion's clinical ideas and theory of thinking, I organise the teaching so the seminar can study how Bion expanded Klein's original concept of projective identification and introduced the related concepts of containment and the oscillation between mental states organised around Klein's two positions – the paranoid-schizoid position and the depressive position. Some understanding of Klein's concepts of projective identification, splitting, unconscious phantasy and the internal world is assumed. Extensive use is made of *Experiences in Groups* (1961) to show how many of the later ideas are foreshadowed in his earlier work with group mentality, especially how Bion used his experiences derived from groups which had their own mental functioning as their focus of study in order to understand how projective identification underpins countertransference. In passing we consider how his ideas on this differed from those of Klein, who did not accept this use of countertransference.

From Bion's expansion of the concept of projective identification the introductory seminars trace how he developed other psychoanalytic conceptual tools in order to investigate a wide variety of phenomena, including the ego functions of attention, discrimination, and particularly thinking. We study how for Bion this was not only a cognitive set of processes but one in which emotion is central. This entails an understanding of the importance for him of Freud's 'Two principles' (1911) and of his 'Recommendations' to the analyst (1912b) and the links Bion saw between these and Keats' negative capability. In this context we look at the related concept of the selected fact (introduced by Poincaré in 1913).

In looking at *Learning from Experience* I draw out with the seminar the conceptual connections between the following notions: the container–contained model of thinking emotional thoughts ($♀♂$); the oscillation between states of mind organised along Klein's two positions ($Ps \rightleftharpoons D$); alpha-function; beta-elements; primitive dread and fear of extinction; L, H and K links, and the 'minus' varieties of these; the idea of transformation; and the ego-destructive superego. The latter idea was developed largely from detailed discussions between Bion and Rosenfeld, and also Segal, all of whom worked with borderline and psychotic patients.

On the subject of what is perhaps Bion's best-known concept, his model of container–contained, I first of all highlight a clinical description of Bion's – to be found in his 1958 paper on hallucination, which has Bion's first use of the term 'container' in relation to Klein's concept of projective identification.

Concerning the patient's fear of his impulses harming or killing his analyst, Bion wrote:

> I was able to show him that he was splitting off painful feelings, mostly envy and revenge, of which he hoped to rid himself by forcing them into me. There the session ended. Melanie Klein has described how this mechanism produces problems for the patient by engendering fear of the analyst who now is a container of a bad part of himself. (Bion, 1958a, p. 68)

In 1961, while he was engaged in writing *Learning from Experience,* Bion wrote a paper called 'The conception of man', for a book of that name which was not published. In the teaching seminars I include his unpublished paper, in which Bion stated his future intention to make an expanded use of Melanie Klein's concept of projective identification, as an essential and normal factor in the inception of communication and mental development in the infant, aided by the essential and irreplaceable helper, the mother. Explaining his expansion of Klein's concept of projective identification he wrote:

> The theory of projective identification and those derived from it explain more than what their propounder intended; they satisfy the criterion that requires the theory to show itself capable of coherent and uncontradictory development when used in scientific investigation. I shall use the theory of

projective identification as a model for early development of the processes that have later come to be known as thinking. The model supposes the existence of a couple; I use it to represent an internal apparatus in the individual. What originally represented a relationship between mother and infant, or breast and mouth, now represents these objects internalised. The representation of these internalised objects is used as a model for the mental mechanisms involved in thinking. The signs ♀ and ♂ can be used to represent the internal apparatus by the sign ♀♂. (Bion, 1961b, unpublished)

In making this step, Bion was following Freud's early, pre-psychoanalytic thinking about the infant's first experiences of pleasure, pain and satisfaction.

After discussing the 1958 paper insofar as it introduces the notion of the container, we turn to an important section in his 1959 paper 'Attacks on linking'. The passage is headed 'Denial of normal degrees of projective identification'. Studying this passage we look at how Bion had made a crucial clinical observation about the impact on a patient of the analyst's (Bion's) failure adequately to take in the patient's communications. This enabled Bion to consider the consequences in analysis, and earlier, in infancy, of the denial by the primary object of normal and necessary degrees of projective identification. This really was the beginning of Bion's use of what we now know as his container–contained (♀♂) model. It is worth reproducing here because of its central importance in my teaching seminars and in showing the clinical foundation for Bion's clinical work. It is the basis for the ideas featured in *Learning from Experience* and represents the clearest and most concise version of his catastrophic change and container–contained model:

> When the patient strove to rid himself of fears of death which were felt to be too powerful for his personality to contain he split off his fears and put them into me, the idea apparently being that if they were allowed to repose there long enough they would undergo modification by my psyche and could then be safely reintrojected. On the occasion I have in mind the patient had felt, probably for reasons similar to those I give in my fifth illustration, the probabil-

ity clouds, that I evacuated them so quickly that the feelings were not modified, but had become more painful.

Associations from a period in the analysis earlier than that from which these illustrations have been drawn showed an increasing intensity of emotions in the patient. This originated in what he felt was my refusal to accept parts of his personality. Consequently he strove to force them into me with increased desperation and violence. His behaviour, isolated from the context of the analysis, might have appeared to be an expression of primary aggression. The more violent his phantasies of projective identification, the more frightened he became of me. There were sessions in which such behaviour expressed unprovoked aggression, but I quote this series because it shows the patient in a different light, his violence a reaction to what he felt was my hostile defensiveness. The analytic situation built up in my mind a sense of witnessing an extremely early scene. I felt that the patient had experienced in infancy a mother who dutifully responded to the infant's emotional displays. The dutiful response had in it an element of impatient, 'I don't know what's the matter with the child'. My deduction was that in order to understand what the child wanted the mother should have treated the infant's cry as more than a demand for her presence. From the infant's point of view she should have taken into her, and thus experienced, the fear that the child was dying. It was this fear that the child could not contain. He strove to split it off together with the part of the personality in which it lay and project it into the mother. An understanding mother is able to experience the feeling of dread, that this baby was striving to deal with by projective identification, and yet retain a balanced outlook. This patient had had to deal with a mother who could not tolerate experiencing such feelings and reacted either by denying them ingress, or alternatively by becoming a prey to the anxiety which resulted from introjection of the infant's feelings. (Bion, 1959, p. 312).

Bion's discussion in the 1959 paper, and in *Second Thoughts*, of the dire consequences for mental development of the infant's experience of an object felt to refuse entry to its projected distress, stands as one of the most important discoveries in psychoanalysis. It is one of the factors which may be instrumental in the formation of a primary bad object. Reaching back to Freud's earliest writings, Bion allows us to consider how such an object is liable to be experienced as wishing unalleviated distress upon the infant, which at some level can be felt as a desire of an authoritarian internal object for the infant to suffer, or even to die.

In the introductory seminars on Bion I draw out the clinical implications of an experience of denial by the analyst, standing for the patient's primary object, of normal and necessary degrees of projective identification – how we can make use of this work in trying to trace the consequences for the patient of our failures to really take in the impact of what they are saying and doing to us, and to be willing to explore with them what they feel we are intending when we speak, or do not.

In the seminars I make repeated links back to Klein, making clear, for example, that in his work on the conjoined concepts of catastrophic change and container–contained, Bion was referring to a complex, dynamic notion, envisaging ♀ ♂ as a mental condition influencing, and being influenced by, the operation of oscillation between Klein's two positions, denoted as $Ps \rightleftharpoons D$. As Bion's eldest daughter, Parthenope (a psychoanalyst), stated:

> It may be considered as representing approximately (a) the reaction between what Melanie Klein described as the paranoid-schizoid and depressive positions – which has been called oscillation – and (b) the reaction precipitated by what Poincaré (1946) described as the discovery of the selected fact. This selected fact is one which the thinking individual recognises as unexpectedly harmonising all the other scattered facts – it is one of them, but it allows the thinker to 'see' the meaning which had previously not been visible. (Talamo, 1981, p. 626).

She added that Bion felt that the accompanying emotions of $Ps \rightleftharpoons D$ are sensations of persecution and frustration, followed by a moment of comprehension and a 'coagulation of depression', with the discomfort of the latter becoming, in turn, an element of the next problem. For Bion, this sort of oscillation permeated with emotions, requiring a containing object, lies at the bedrock of human thought.

Towards the end of the introductory series I provide reading to bring out the clinical importance of the receptive state Bion described as the optimal attention required for the operation of these processes, pointing to it by use of the word 'reverie'; he suggested that this relatively calm and open-minded state represents the mother's willingness and capacity to use her mind to contain and to suffer, in the service of understanding and relieving, the infant's specific mental pain; success in this is a necessary condition for the establishment of communication and mental growth. It parallels Freud's description in the *Project for a Scientific Psychology* of the conditions necessary for the formation of a mental system in the infant, in terms of the relevant or specific action of the mother in alleviating the pain accumulating inside her baby.

Bion also described how the establishment and maintenance of a functioning boundary between conscious and unconscious systems depended on container–contained and a capacity, initially in the mother alone, for alpha-function, based on emotional linkages and the toleration of mental pain; and how such a membrane becomes eroded and destroyed by methods developed to evade thinking – resulting in concreteness, hallucination, psychosomatic illness, these being a product of stripped and degraded elements, referred to as beta-elements.

The seminar group studies *Learning from Experience*, in which Bion extended this model further, developing a conceptual apparatus that is both descriptively powerful and analytically useful, and which has remained alive and relevant today amongst those clinicians who have incorporated the ideas into their basic technique. A sign of life in the ideas is the fact they can be developed further and not remain static, or stagnate into 'received wisdom'. Britton (2001, 2010), for example, has taken the operation of $Ps \rightleftharpoons D$ further, in his idea of the post-depressive Ps position that he denominates 'Ps $(n+1)$':

> In order to hold fast to any sense of security whilst in the position I have called Ps $(n+1)$ a belief in probability is necessary: you could call it faith. Faith in what you might ask? I

think it is faith that an answer exists that will sooner or later be found. In physics it is a belief in science; in psychoanalysis it is a belief in psychoanalysis; fundamentally it is a belief that continued inquiry leads towards it and that things ultimately make sense though that sense is unknown. (Britton, 2001, p. 79)

The introductory series of seminars on Bion concludes with a study some of the ways that Bion's basic clinical concepts have been taken further by Kleinian analysts, and some of the possible implications for the way we work. For example, Britton's expansion of Bion's Ps $\rightleftharpoons$ D opens up a valuable area of exploration into the tolerance of probability in mental life. Another example of the concepts from *Learning from Experience* being taken further in recent years is Britton's and Steiner's work on distinguishing between selected facts and over-valued ideas. This is an important contribution because it alerts us to the way in which the latter may resemble and substitute for the former, because there is a similarity between the emergence of an underlying pattern from a selected fact and the 'crystallisation of delusional certainty from an overvalued idea'. Britton and Steiner described the serious risks to the patient of imposing on them an overvalued idea hardened into an interpretation.

Edna O'Shaughnessy in her paper 'Relating to the super-ego' (1999) – a recommended reading – has described how the consequences of such an imposition can lead to the analysis deteriorating into a relationship between two mad superegos, or one in which the analyst may actually give way to looking down or crushing the patient's ego. One important development of Bion's use of the selected fact concept, and of Britton and Steiner's application of it to the formation of interpretations, is the attention which nowadays is given to following up – in the moment-by-moment progression of the analytic session – the subtle consequences of the analyst's interventions. This is strongly represented in the work of Betty Joseph (1985, 1989).

In making a bridge to the next series of seminars, with the title 'Further Bion', I describe how it was the integrity of this internalised model which gave Bion the courage to abandon the security of his model – with its emphasis on clinical observation; the K link; the Grid; scientific deductive systems; axiomatic thinking – in order to find a approach from a new direction (he called it a vertex) to investigate psychoanalytic attention itself, with his concepts of selected fact, faith, and his controversial ideas of memory and desire and 'O'. In my view this was possible because Bion was prepared to enter and to utilise what Britton called the post-depressive paranoid-schizoid position, or Ps (n+1).

By the end of the introductory series, members of the seminar can appreciate that the modern version of projective identification informing the clinical thinking of many analysts in the UK is Bion's expanded one – which brings it closer to his earlier explanation for countertransference and Klein's emphasis on the transference of total situations (Klein, 1952).

At the end of the introductory seminar series I encourage those who are interested to take their reading further to find out how different forms of projective identification are being identified in the clinical situation, categorised for example according to whether the principle aim appears to be communicative, acquisitive, evacuative and so on, and whether it appears to have been carried out with the potential for reversibility (Steiner, 1993). I suggest students look into Steiner's concept of psychic retreats, and also into Rosenfeld's discussions of complex pathological organisations of mind and the organised patterns of defence that maintain such structures.

In particular I recommend readings which build on the observations of Klein, Bion, Segal, Rosenfeld and others (including Joseph, Feldman and O'Shaughnessy) in describing the destructive and formative operation in the internal world of a terrifying superego, described by Bion in terms of an object enshrining a minus version of $\mathcal{Q}\mathcal{S}$: an unbearably hypocritical superior object asserting its superiority by finding fault with everything – as he put it, in *Learning from Experience,* 'an envious assertion of moral superiority without any morals' (Bion, 1962b, p. 97).

I hope that by the end of the initial seminar series the members of the group have a sense not only of the concepts covered in the readings and teaching, but also have a grasp of

Bion's distinctive conception of what psychoanalysis is and the core values underpinning it. Without such a foundation, and some clinical experience of the transference situation of analysis, I doubt that students will be able to begin to comprehend Bion's later work, which moves into the area of psychoanalytic attention, intuition and the limits of representability.

CHAPTER TWO

The Go-between

Claudio Neri

Rather than 'teaching Bion' I prefer to say that what I aim to do is to put students 'in touch' with Bion's thinking. His thinking is modern, futuristic, also frank and strong: aware of both the rights and duties of the individual; serious and at the same time full or irony and humour.

Students therefore benefit from being brought in touch with something that is actually present already in themselves spontaneously, namely to become inspired and pursue a path that is not already mapped out for them. They perceive that Bion supports them in this courageous objective, whilst at the same time offering a discipline and realistic sense of the need to take responsibility for their own pathway, which is something that may be lacking in younger people however enthusiastic.

I consider in my role as go-between, I can offer four instruments to help them in this task: 1) the idea that the most difficult is the best; 2) reading the text not just the slogan; 3) why we are not Bionians; and 4) avoiding arrogance. I will discuss these tools below.

The most difficult reading is the best

Many years ago, when I studied ancient Greek, I was taught that when there are varies copies of a fragment and the original is lost, it is best to choose the copy whose meaning appears more difficult and abstruse. This is most likely to be the correct one because while copyist A, finding it difficult to understand, will have corrected it in the direction of making it simpler and more comprehensible, copyist B will have transcribed the original text verbatim even if he did not understand it. So copyist B's version is more likely to correspond to the author's original thought, whereas copyist A will have adapted it to suit whatever is already understood.

I decided this rule was also useful for reading Bion. When his writings appear to be different ways of expressing the same idea, in principle all versions are acceptable; but if I had to choose one above the others I would prefer the more difficult version. Bion's texts are to be read literally, that is, I take it he was trying to say and write exactly what he meant, even though this might seem foolish or confused. Therefore it should not be corrected, still less should one flatten the readings to make them simpler or more consistent.

Read the text not the slogan

The density of writing and assertiveness with which Bion presents his ideas means that they can be implemented as slogans: slogans that are easy to repeat without making the effort to think about what you really mean by using those words. Indeed the conciseness of Bion's claims can have the effect of blocking rather than promoting the activity of thinking. The reader can take them as a truth rather than as a tool for seeking the truth.

So, after first presenting literally Bion's text and commenting on it in a straightforward way, I always dedicate a portion of the lesson to the illustration of ideas, assumptions, objections and fantasies that this text has triggered in me personally. This approach usually elicits a corresponding movement of imaginative and speculative association in the listeners. In turn, they feel invited and encouraged to propose their own hypotheses and thoughts, born from contact with the ideas in the text.

It is important, however, to learn to keep their own ideas separate from those that Bion had probably wanted to express. A good rule of journalism is to separate the statement of facts from the opinions of the writer. In discussing Bion, we should behave similarly and bear this distinction in mind.

Why we are not Bionians

Bion did not want to give rise to a school or an organised current of thought such as the one that was formed around Melanie Klein, or that which belongs to Relational Psychoanalysis. His fundamental point was that we cannot be 'Kleinian' or 'Bionian' but only ourselves. From this derives the necessity for responsibility in the session with the patient. In the session there is only a place for what we think ourselves, not for what Melanie Klein or Wilfred Bion may have thought.

I try to emphasise this fact when I speak of Bion with clinical trainees. Therapeutic work with patients requires taking responsibility, and this can only be experienced by feeling one's loneliness during the session. The idea of trying to be 'Bionian' pollutes this essential loneliness and makes us fantasise about being part of a movement or group. It diminishes our sense of responsibility, making us liable to suppose that what is important for the patient is what Bion wrote, and not what we think and can communicate at that moment.

Avoid arrogance like the plague

Bion in his article 'On arrogance' (1958b) says that the tree of pride produces two fruits different in nature and taste: the sweet and nutritious fruit of self-respect (which includes respect for others) and the bitter and poisonous fruit of arrogance.

Whoever embarks on a quest for the 'truth', aiming to become a more authentic and self-aware person, runs the risk of arrogance and megalomania. Putting students in touch with Bion's ideas means pointing out the possibilities and dangers of this quest. After that, everyone will pursue it in their own way and format.

It is not useful however to warn excessively against the risk of arrogance: to over-emphasise heavily the risks of being over-curious, stupid or violent whilst believing one is pursuing truth. Teiresias tried repeatedly to reason with Oedipus but to no avail. Rather than issuing warnings, I believe that the remedy may be found in an honest attempt to answer all students' questions with respect, even those which may seem at first to be trivial or unnecessary. I try to understand them thoroughly, and to encourage participation and interest.

Conclusion

And for myself – what did I learn?

I learned to be very happy – and I would say, enthusiastic – on seeing how much the students enjoyed what they were studying. I learned that they could be very different from me and also from how I had imagined they would be or I might want them to be, but that equally– I would say even more so – I could recognise them as my students. I learned that reciprocity between different generations and between people who hold different roles is essential to the teaching and learning experience.

CHAPTER THREE

Identifying with existential unease

Antonello Correale

Before discussing how we may go about teaching Bion's ideas, I think it is essential to make a few introductory remarks. If I were to try to summarise in a single concept the inspiration, the motivation, even the mission or the task that Bion felt he should carry out in his lifetime, as a scholar and a psychoanalyst, I think I would identify this concept as the ethical function of seeking truth. Of course truth is too philosophically complex to be reduced to something simple and flat. I believe we can say that Bion sees the 'truth' in terms of the courage to have our own thoughts, where 'thoughts' are the products of our mind, as bizarre, unusual, or unwelcome they may be.

This idea of having the courage to think our own thoughts includes at least two further concepts. The first is about specificity. Bion strongly believes in the individual as the receiver of thoughts, and in not deferring to pre-constructed ideas or to the widespread, pacifying assumptions of common sense. Bion's invitation to the truth is an invitation to have the courage to be ourselves, where to be ourselves means, mostly, not to retreat from what appears in our mind. The products of the mind are always the outcome of a meeting between the individual and that which is external to him – which can never be completely defined, but always leaves room for elements of surprise, of the unknown, of doubt.

As well as specificity, but also linked to the unique and non-replicable nature of the individual, Bion seems to give value to the weird, the bizarre, the peripheral, the unusual features of a thought. Bion values what comes from the mind, so a thought that seems lacking, airy, not belonging to anyone, without land or home, might be intercepted by the individual mind at some stage with fear and surprise, sometimes with terror and sometimes with enthusiasm. They are wandering thoughts or 'thoughts without a thinker'. With these poetic images, Bion wants to talk about those thoughts that seem not to belong to us, that are in conflict with the rest of our personality and that in groups seem almost to make us wander us from one mind to the other without a filter. They are waiting to be placed within a wider thinking apparatus, that can contain and contextualise them.

This is the famous distinction between thoughts and the apparatus for thinking thoughts. The thoughts are images, representations, emotions, born from the encounter with the object and from the emotion that this encounter triggers. The apparatus for thinking thoughts is the language in its syntactic form, the reasoning ability, the connective function of the mind.

Part of Bion's preoccupation is with how the apparatus for thinking thoughts can welcome them and place them within a shared and recognisable web. Essentially it is alpha-function that places the thoughts in an apparatus able to 'think them', therefore to recognise them as our own and to make them able to be transmitted to others around us.

What is teaching?

Bion himself, at this point, would have probably said, most likely in an ironic and Anglo-Saxon way, that first we need to understand what 'teaching' means, then what 'teaching psychoanalysis' means, and lastly what it means to 'teach psychoanalysis according to Bion'. The ethical need that we have identified at the beginning helps us answer this question.

First of all, what does it mean to teach? It is well known from centuries of pedagogy and the history of education that 'to teach' does not mean just to transmit knowledge, even if this stays the essential indestructible nucleus of a teacher's work. To teach means to put something inside ourselves, something that stays and transforms itself inside of us. Teaching is not just knowledge, it is helping the student to see the world with new eyes. The knowledge I transmit must be first of all be a way to observe things, that allows ever wider connections, unexpected links, openings and contrasts, that can in turn produce new syntheses.

In this sense, I think that Bion, who never got tired of presenting this understanding of teaching, follows in the tradition of ancient philosophy as a spiritual exercise. Hadot, the French scholar who analysed this point thoroughly, defines 'spiritual exercise' as an exercise of wisdom, and understands wisdom as the ability to put every idea, thought and representation against the widest, most universal, background possible. It is not a matter of valuing the particular over the universal or the universal over the particular, but of endlessly connecting one with the other, in a continuous cycle of connections and cross-references.

Ancient Greek philosophers thought that philosophising meant to learn to live life with the deepest participation and the strongest detachment at the same time. I believe Bion would have agreed with this vision of the world. After all, to put ourselves in front of the object, of the reality, of the world like something that is always unsaturated, never fully known, means to have faith in a sort of direct link with the object, in relations that are unfiltered and without following ideas put forward by others; but at the same time it means to converse with the ideas and thoughts of others in the language that we have inherited from the people who have accompanied us from birth.

It is this ongoing synthesis, often an unresolved and lacerating conflict, that characterises Bion's thought and that enters emphatically into the theme of teaching. To put something inside us, to acquire wisdom – it's an endless process, where contrast and conflict are dominant but also pull the process forwards. Bion seems to think that without conflict there is no psychic life and only the conflict is real: we might even say that the truth is our own thought measuring itself and interacting with the thoughts of others. We can maybe say that only from this dialectic between our own and the other's can the idea of truth be born. Otherwise, as Hegel would probably say, we have certainty but not truth: certainty being a strong personal conviction, and truth being that same strong personal conviction put through the test of the strong personal convictions of others.

I believe Bion thought that to practise psychoanalysis, or teach it, or in any way 'know' it, always involves discovering the other that is in us, the intrinsically extraneous dimension of the personality. He quotes Freud's famous dictum that we are not masters in our own home. Inside ourselves, there is always something that we do not know, ready to scare and surprise us, to make us feel confused and disoriented. From the acceptance and the development of this confusion the thought can be born and our self-knowledge can develop; without conflict between the known and the unknown, the growth of knowledge is impossible. This explains, I think, two important aspects of Bion's thinking that affect the way we teach: discourse and mathematics.

Discourse and mathematics

Bion had a profound intolerance for purely intellectualistic psychoanalytical discourse, that he thought was detached from the direct experience of the object and of ourselves. He did not find justifiable the tendency to intellectualise, to get lost in details, to defend a theory only because it is beautiful or because we are attached to it or because we heard it from a loved teacher. There was a sort of austere severity in him, a strict ethic of truth, a continuous tendency to remove the masks, to strip bare. Thus: what do you mean by this word? What emotion, in relation to the object, are you referring to? Is it you talking or is it someone else, when you articulate these words?

In this intolerance for complacent and repetitive discourse there is something rigorous and inflexible that can lead, with some justification, to consider Bion as having a quality that seems cold or unwelcoming, unempathic. Sometimes, his attitude seems to lead us into a certain depersonalisation, estrangement, disorientation. Is it me who is talking or it is someone else? Which part of me are you talking to?

The famous invitation to 'renounce memory and desire', abused and often repeated in the most non-Bionian way, is used in T. S. Eliot's *The Waste Land* to limit the already known, to focus on what is hidden, what is distant, what is peripheral, but is now more essential than what is obvious. There is a severity, beautiful and important, in this attitude and it is important that the person who teaches Bion understands all its aspects, conflicting, progressive, distressing, with the element of discovery.

This is why we should beware of an a-critical idealisation of Bion. To learn from Bion means to accept all the fatigue and unpleasantness of the search for the truth, in the sense of that continuous dialogue between ourselves and the other.

The second point that affects the way we teach concerns Bion's 'mathematisation' of psychoanalysis. It's because he was looking for the essential and wanted to bring psychoanalysis back to its basic principles, the ones that he calls the 'elements of psychoanalysis', that Bion tried to cut a way through the wood of theories that grew around it, to bring it back to its core principles, as a clinical practice and as a means to knowledge.

To 'mathematise' for Bion means to study how our mind produces and organises thoughts, and how they are contextualised – how they are made visible to others and to ourselves. This is why he studies thinking more than other aspects of psychoanalysis. He does not reject drive theory but makes it secondary to the pursuit of knowledge, considering how the drive facilitates or hinders the creation of thoughts or the function of the apparatus for thinking them, or the process of connecting them with each other and with the thoughts of others.

With these general points in mind I would now like to refer more specifically to some of Bion's central concepts. Teaching means not just transmitting knowledge but also selecting and extracting the points that the teacher finds most inspiring. I find the most useful concepts when teaching are: learning from experience, alpha-function, and finally 'O' to denote the origin, end and substance of any psychoanalytical work.

Learning from experience

Learning from experience involves opening ourselves to that which is outside us, including those aspects of the object which we do not want to assimilate, which our mind can never completely contain, and which are never absolute and unchangeable data. In my view (by contrast with some interpreters) Bion thinks that the perception of the experience – the direct contact with the object, with the other – is just the beginning of the experience. His philosophy does not stop at what is immediate, the original perceived data. What then makes meaningful this original perception are two factors: emotion and interconnection.

Bion seems to insist that the pure cognitive data are subject to misunderstanding and lies, because the influence of others' thoughts or assumptions is so prevalent that at the end of the day, a large part of psychic life is a battle for freedom. Emotion, however, cannot lie, since it derives from the body with its personal specificity: it belongs to that person and not to any other. Emotion is thus our first and most basic link with the outside world, even though the process of thinking is required for it to become knowledge.

The second important factor in learning from experience could be defined as the interconnecting of the cognitive data. The initial event is repeated, divided, travelled over in our mind. Only through this type of remembering can we move from the almost illusional to the cognitive, which is almost a rediscovery of the thought. We could say that for Bion all the work of getting-to-know consists in dealing with something disturbing, sticking with it rather than expelling it too quickly; the emotion of the impact, and the return to the emotion. In the process of symbolisation the initial almost 'auroral' moment permeates all these other linkages and places them in a containing network.

Once again we might see Bion as strict and demanding, little open to empathy and the comforts of imagination or illusion, driving always in the direction of observed facts. He prioritises the function of attention, which includes implicitly the idea of respect for the object, of taking time beside it. We want to take in the details, the shadows, the nuances, the periphery of the frame, to understand the totality of it. 'Attention' means to hold on to all details, to understand the relationship between object and background, to value the shadows, the nuances. And we must always bear in mind the origins of the cognitive impact, not just the 'transformations', which recent scholars emphasise perhaps excessively.

Alpha-function

Alpha function is central to Bion's idea of the actual process of thinking, that follows the initial impact of reality and must always remain tied to it. He includes in this all the processes of integration and symbolisation of the cognitive experience into figurative or verbal language.

Bion's man is a knowledge man, as much as Freud's is a drive man. It is not by accident that Bion moves the model of knowledge from Freud's reflex arc to the digestive system. In Freud's reflex arc, the thought is always born through delaying the action, as an experiment, and drive is paramount. The Freudian man is always moved by instinct, by desire, and the struggle to satisfy these. This gives an electrical charge to the delaying power of thought. Bion however, in a wellknown metaphor, envisages a digestive apparatus, in which the person is moved not just by his own desires but by the impact of reality, which can never be incorporated without pain. This incorporation or digestion turns the impact of facts and their truth from alien to thinkable. I think the metaphor of digesting thoughts has both strengths and weaknesses; it can run the risk of annihilating the various functions that it wants to aggregate. The crucial point is to do with splitting and repression. If an experience is too painful, it gets split off and expelled to a distance through excessive projective identification. The mind is therefore filled with images that are almost hallucinatory in nature, sensorial and perception-based fragments that have a shape but not a meaning, emotions that are suspended and distanced. Bion calls these unplaced mental elements 'beta-elements'.

If the mind is successful in the type of repression or at least in a partial non-destructive negation, these mental elements can find a place within a linguistic or figurative web. This sort of repression has a light and shadow effect, a chiaroscuro of gradual and sustainable separation of some elements in the cone of light; the splitting is fractional, not violent. There is detachment without expulsion; we feel that something obtrudes on us less, but doesn't get eliminated from the field of knowledge.

This nuanced ability that we use on mental elements instead of violently splitting them away, is called by Bion reverie, the ability to dream. Dreaming is the ability to put things in an order which is emotional rather than logical or rational. There is a momentary forgetting of the rational. Dreaming has its own priorities, anticipations and delays, lights and shadows. If we can dream, we can build a web, and the expelled hallucinatory image can come back to the field of consciousness, from where it can be shared with others.

All Bion's thinking focuses on this crucial point: how can we transform the hallucinatory image, or psychotic accumulation of beta-elements, into dream? How can we diminish the delusional and paralysing effect of emotional trauma into a shared ability to dream, or reverie? If the container is the mind of the analyst, Bion doesn't answer this question; he leaves it open as a task for us, who come after him, to study and follow.

During seminars and training courses with students, the distinction between wandering or 'wild' thoughts and thoughts caught within a meaningful network has proven particularly useful.

The wandering or wild thoughts are thoughts that are very close to perception, and have not yet found representations. They come from the individual and they are his or her truth, that of course must be compared with and modified by the encounter with the truth of the other, but that are nonetheless a guarantee of authenticity and subjectivity.

Students also deeply appreciate the attempt to deepen the concept of the thing-in-itself that, if left alone, has an aura that is too wide and difficult to define. The thing-in-itself is the object before it becomes represented in a collective linguistic network; although it maintains a very strong presence it stays poorly defined and mysterious.

The search for this quality in thoughts is the subject of the mystic orientation, that sees it as transcendent; but it is also the goal of psychoanalysis, for which an attraction to the thing-in-itself (*das Ding* in Freud, O in Bion) is a deep human drive and desire.

Becoming O

The theme of 'O' recurs in Bion, with many philosophical, poetic, and emotional nuances. It is perhaps contrary to Bion's intentions to attempt an exact definition of it, because this would eliminate the halo of indetermination that Bion has always cherished; but from the teaching perspective we can cite his allusions to O as the thing-in-itself, the Kantian noumenon, that constantly hovers on the fringes of our consciousness. Kant's idea of the moral law as something that exists inside us, as much as the starry sky exists outside, applies also to O which is not only outside us, but also inside. In Bion there is no immutable moral law, but he seems to think that the emotion that is sparked off by contact between the subject and the object is innate to human nature. The truth of the object is given by the emotion that it stirs in us. This sets off the thinking process, alpha-function, and the endless striving for knowledge which forms the matrix of mental health.

Bion is not so naïve as to think we can have a pure thought, fully detached from already existing thoughts. The problem is, how to create within ourselves a possible opening that does not negate the little knowledge we have already acquired, but allows for a temporary separation, a sense of loss of direction, a bearable estrangement. Bion seems to think that there is no specific and personal thought without a certain element of depersonalisation, in the sense of the momentary separation from the familiarity of what is known and therefore also from the internal objects that help and support us in life.

If the sense of loss is excessive – Bion often talks about frustration – the absence becomes a negative presence and the person feels persecuted and incapable of thinking. The role of the analyst is therefore to help his patient to access this bearable sorrow, so that the loss of the familiar object is not turned into an internal persecutory object. Bion called it an absence that becomes a no-thing, a cruel and intolerant superego figure. If the sorrow is made bearable through an internal dialogue, the absence becomes a productive opening, a possibility of discovery.

Bion speaks in a suggestive rather than an exact way when he says we must become O even though we cannot know the thing-in-itself. Some schools of religion and mysticism hold that we cannot know God but we can feel him inside ourselves, like a universal presence that animates everything. In this sense, God is a sensation, a state of mind, an intuition. In terms closer to object relations, we can say that is not a matter of fusing or becoming one with with the object. On the contrary, few ideas of experience are as different from Bion's world picture as those of fusion with the object, of blind immersion in the whole.

By 'becoming O', Bion probably means the process of intro-jecting the object, living with its presence as something that reopens and reactivates our personal conflicts. We say the bell always tolls for me; it is me that history is about. The object resounds within us as something which is ours in so far as we allow it to re-engage with our present interior conflict.

At the end of the day, it is the word that changes everything and that places the emotion within the appropriate linguistic web; but the language must be warm and full, to be able to offer the emotion a vessel that is meaningful not sterile.

Conclusion

To teach is to interpret the thought of an author, staying as loyal as possible to his perceived intentions and his existential unease, and to make public as far as is possible what was born as exclu-sively and unspeakably private and personal.

I have tried to give a synthesis of what seem to me the essen-tial or so to speak the matrix-ideas of Bion, in the conviction that to teach means essentially to identify how the author saw his mission or task, like Fichte's intellectual, and the questions he formulated as a duty towards his contemporaries and himself. I have left out many important Bionian ideas, for instance the ones about groups and about institutions and all his later work, that James Joyce would have loved. But I believe that all these aspects become 'teachable' if we can grasp the basic inspiration that I have tried to delineate.

CHAPTER FOUR

Teaching Bion, living life

Luiz Carlos Uchôa Junqueira, Jnr.

The past presented

This is the title Bion chose for volume 2 of *A Memoir of the Future* (1991 [1977]). Meg Harris Williams has suggested it was drawn from Milton's *Samson Agonistes*:

> … restless thoughts, that like a deadly swarm
> Of hornets armed, no sooner found alone,
> But rush upon me thronging, and present
> Times past, what once I was, and what am now.
> (cited in Williams, 1983a, p. 75)

'What once I was' around 1984 when I began teaching Bion, could perhaps be described as an enthusiastic 'talmudic guide', highly concerned with remaining faithful to the essence of his texts. I was fairly conscious of being lucky in having been analysed by someone who in his turn, had been analysed first by Melanie Klein and afterwards by Bion himself. In fact, having such a person amongst us helped a lot in the diffusion of Bion's work in São Paulo, and was decisive in his subsequent visits to Brazil.

In that period I wrote a paper entitled 'The pre-conceived work of "Bion"' (Junqueira, 1985), in which I tried not only to make a summary of his writings, but also to follow the changes in his writing style. The inverted commas around Bion's name in the title of the paper are intended to stress the subordinate role he himself attributed to the thinker concerning his very own thoughts. I began by discussing his autobiographical narratives, starting with *The Long Weekend* in which the experienced psychoanalyst tells us how the child born in India managed to survive emotionally in an English public school and, afterwards, was drowned in the horrors of First World War, from which he emerged as a war hero. I believe these caesuras, intermingled with the subtle observation of psychic experience lived inside and outside the analytical situation, spawned a consistent matrix of pre-conceptions for his psychoanalytical formulations. I shall briefly go over my view of Bion's development as a psychoanalytic thinker, as I present it to students.

The following paragraphs summarise my own encounter with Bion's thinking, and after that I describe how I have endeavoured to communicate this journey to students.

Second Thoughts

As we know, Bion's qualifying paper for the British Psychoanalytical Society, 'The imaginary twin' (1950), was given at age 53, a time in which he was deeply involved in the investigation of group dynamics, the differentiation of the psychotic and non-psychotic parts of the personality, and also in developing a theory of thinking. The articles of this period, later republished in *Second Thoughts*, are highly suffused with his Kleinian background; he uses pieces of clinical material interspersed with theoretical reflection, whence he works out in detail concepts directly involved in thought disorders, such as bizarre objects, hallucinosis, attacks on linking, and mindlessness. At the end of this book, in the Commentary, Bion makes a creative exercise of re-thinking his past formulations as 'second thoughts'; in other words, he demonstrates in practice the new world that confronts us when we change our vertices. In teaching Bion our reading becomes richer if we make use of these cross-connections.

Between those early works and his 'second thoughts' about them, three very important books poured out of Bion within a very short time: *Learning from Experience* (1962), *Elements of Psychoanalysis* (1963), and *Transformations* (1965). In the first book he tackles the subject of emotional experiences as related to theories of knowledge and to clinical psychoanalysis, and the matter of understanding our understanding. In *Elements* he seeks a way of expressing the various combinations of 'elements' that underlie 'all the theories essential to the working psychoanalyst'. In his experience these psychoanalytical objects have three dimensions: extension in the domain of sense, extension in the domain of myth, and extension in the domain of passion.

In *Transformations*, Bion constructs a critical approach to clinical experience and not, as many students think, a new psychoanalytical theory. The analyst's transformations should be immune to the distortions from love and hate, but the patient's transformations suffer these distortions; these are clarified by means of the analyst's move from observation to interpretation, in line with the O (the ultimate reality) of the transformation. In the language of transformations, the psychoanalytic domain can be described as extended between the point at which a personality receives sensory impressions, and the point at which it can express the transformations incurred.

Transformations creates pedagogic problems owing to Bion's attempt to define emotional experience using the model of projective geometry, such as the point that represents the empty breast and the line that represents the penis. Nevertheless, the book helps us enormously in understanding the clinical implications of catastrophic change, perhaps the most aesthetic of Bion's concepts. Analysing retrospectively the methodology of these three books, we can see Bion seeking to find abstract formulations that could cover all types of interpretive statement. The loss in comprehensibility is complemented by finding models that have a kinship with dreams and myths.

To return now to the Commentary in *Second Thoughts*. In the light of his efforts in these last three books we can now see these points more clearly:

1. The value of a notational record does not reside in its capacity to preserve the conscience of the past, but in its power to evoke expectations of the future.

2. Psychoanalytical models should always include a notion of 'direction' to enable a better past or future representation of a psychoanalytical fact.

3. The reason psychoanalytical interpretations are difficult to formulate is because of the non-sensuous quality of emotional facts, but the sensuous background of the words available to describe them.

4. Clinical psychoanalysis suffers consequences from the fact that mental and spiritual lives are suffused with ideas of cure, founded on the pleasure principle and sensuous experiences.

We can also appreciate the practical exercise in the changing of vertices, something very useful in clinical psychoanalysis, that was introduced in *Transformations,* then expanded in Chapter 8 of *Attention and Interpretation*, and spread throughout the trilogy *A Memoir of the Future.*

Emotional communication

The question of the nature of emotional communication, and the problems of describing it, lie at the heart of how we teach Bion's ideas.

Bion frequently expressed his conviction of the political nature of human beings: that is, he was interested in the cross-connections between the phenomena that arise in intimate individual situations, and those that arise in the environment in relation to other people. It may be this was one factor that drew him towards the realms of psychoanalysis after his studies in classical antiquity, modern history, and medicine, and after having also acquired a sound experience in group dynamics.

Understanding that everyday human experience depends on the integration of the 'narciss-istic' and 'social-istic' trends in each single individual, he wrote a paper in 1952 that demarcated group behaviour in terms of a resonance of emotional reactions as psychoanalytically described by Freud and Melanie Klein.

Throughout *Attention and Interpretation* (1970) he investigates minutely the nature of insight and the factors that interfere in emotional communication within the personality, between a pair of individuals, and between individuals in a group. He pays particular attention to 'the lie', stressing that this psychoanalytic object is intrinsic to human personality.

The efficacy of the analyst's communication depends, nevertheless, on methods that support the counterpart of the physician's role in durability and extension but in a domain in which there is neither space nor time as in the world of senses; he named this method the 'language of achievement'. As he sharply warns us, the gift of speech 'has been elaborated as much for the purpose of concealing thought by dissimulation and lying as for the purpose of elucidating or communicating thought' (1970, p. 3).

From now on, Bion's own language crosses a watershed, leaving behind his more dense and conceptual formulations in favour of using a 'presentational form' (in Susanne Langer's terminology), or in his own words: 'The illustrations are C category elements used as preparation for theoretical formulations that can stand by themselves: the reader should regard the illustrations as psychological aids to understanding the theories proper' (1970, p. 19). That is why in my present seminars on Bion I always include the discussion of dream images, under the heading of 'plastic representations of emotional experiences'. For instance, in my current course (over five months) I selected one image from Fellini's *Book of Dreams,* and some images from the sketchbooks of Lourenço Mutarelli (a famous Brazilian cartoonist).

The liberation from 'scientificity'

As López Corvo (2006, p. 22) so well stresses, we psychoanalysts should never be constrained by the elusive need to claim scientific rigour, owing to the simple fact that our object of study, the human mind, is 'built' from ignorance, self-deception, conflicts, defects, and paradoxes.

Nevertheless, at the beginning of his career, Bion like Freud felt the need to use definitions forged in areas such as mathematics, projective geometry, logic, philosophy of language, and so on. But, after having 'proved' that psychoanalysis is open to use models originating in any field of human knowledge, he finally felt himself free to write *A Memoir of the Future* in which, through Socratic dialogues and 'science fictions', he approached mental experience by means of C category and aesthetic elements. In this trilogy he used a dramatised language intended to dissolve the heaviness of theoretical statements, orienting them toward the vividness of clinical experiences.

The voice we hear now is of a Bion sometimes evangelist, sometimes sceptic, sometimes provocateur, spreading himself in a series of polyphonic utterances, representing at bottom all the voices of his previous life: personal, intellectual and professional. In the elaboration of his constructions Bion resorts now to strategic expressive resources like reversed perspective, binocular vision and the creation of neologisms, skills frequently used by vanguard artists and philosophers like Joyce, Wittgenstein and Beckett. In all of them we can recognise a modernist gestalt of form and content prone to ludic experiments, to the violation of limits and the testing of formulations.

Let us take as example the neologism 'without-ness' that Bion associates with the condition of an emptied self that arises when a –K link prevails. A wonderful image to represent this condition would be Gustave Doré's engraving showing the provençal troubadour Bertran de Born who, in Canto XXVIII of Dante's *Inferno*, is depicted as holding his severed head in his right hand, hanging from the hair. This is a tremendous punishment for a sinner accused of arousing dissension between father and son. If we look to the hanging head we almost can 'see' the leakage of blood and the oozing away of his own self, while he himself is hindered from doing so provided he is now without eyes, or insight. Here, as in the ideogram evoked by Bion as a consequence of alpha-function, an abstract concept can be expressively represented by an image.

Another good example of the visual language of the *Memoir* is Bion's question regarding the catastrophic change intrinsic to mental growth: 'Is it a break-up, a break-down, a break-in, a break-out or a break-through?' he asks. This multi-faceted language tries to describe a complex process rooted in the unconscious: starting with a central nucleus, the verb 'to break', with its connotations of fracture, rupture, interruption, storage, waste, bankruptcy, penetration and so on; some aspects denote direction (upwards and downwards), others describe inwardness and outwardness and even a searching penetration (through).

Starting thematic seminars

When I felt myself secure in my own apprehension of some of Bion's basic epistemological concepts, I found myself (perhaps mirroring Bion, or so I felt) turning towards offering themed seminars to our students. The spirit behind this move was mainly to prevent the boredom, and even the somnolence, aroused during the canonical readings that prevailed in my first seminars, but also to venture into the exploration of specific areas of mental functioning, in the company of other participants.

Consulting my files, I was surprised to see that the first course I held, in 1984, was named 'Introductory studies of some of Bion's works', in which, over the course of 23 seminars, we explored six major fields of interest in Bion's work: Bion's (pre-)conceived work; human groups and mental life; learning with the psychotic part of the personality; apprehension of the psychoanalytical object: the Grid and a theory of thinking; psychoanalytical practice; and statements that look to future developments.

In the first series, we discussed my article on 'The pre-conceived work of "Bion"' (1985). In the second we read chapters 6 and 15 of *The Long Weekend* and the paper on group dynamics. In the third we read Bion's notes on schizophrenia (1954), the paper 'On hallucination' (1958), and 'Attacks on linking' (1959). In the fourth series we read chapters from *Learning from Experience* and *Elements of Psychoanalysis*, the paper on the Grid (1963, 1977a), 'A theory of thinking' (1962a) and 'Lies and the thinker', chapter 11 of *Attention and Interpretation*. In the fifth series we read chapters from *Transformations* and chapters 3, 4, 7 and 12 of *Attention and Interpretation*; and the paper on the caesura (1977b). In the sixth we read parts of *A Memoir of the Future*: chapter 17 of Book I, *The Dream*; chapters 1–3 of Book 2, *The Past Presented*; chapter 1 of Book 3, *The Dawn of Oblivion*.

As far as I remember, in this first course I wrote no introductory text and neither did I ask, at the end, that the students should write a monograph on it. I modified the course slightly a couple of years later, making the bibliography more general, including *Second Thoughts, Elements of Psychoanalysis, Transformations, Attention and Interpretation*, and *Two Papers: The Grid and Caesura*, but without singling out specific chapters since the underlying idea was to study the main issues in an unruffled way, without feeling obliged to exhaustively extract all the meaning from the prescribed chapters.

Subsequent courses developed and altered as follows:

1987: Bion's contribution to the observation of psychic reality.
1988: Psychic growth.
1991: Bion's contribution to becoming a psychoanalyst.
1992: The Grid: theory and practice.
1994: Bion and the observation of emotional experience.
1995: From intuitive experience to the formulation of psychoanalytical concepts.
2001: Bion: observation, intuition, public-ation.
2002: The genesis of a theory of thinking in Bion.
2003: Elements of psychoanalysis.
2005: Bion: the clinical work of construction.
2012: Bion' selected texts on thinking and lying.
2013: Bion: the man, his thinking, and his clinical work.

Until the middle of the above period, I always asked students to write a monograph about any topic from the course, and invited the author to discuss their work personally. Although for reasons of time I no longer do this, I still believe it is a very useful practice and students have welcomed this opportunity. Meanwhile I spent more time in preparing introductory texts to delineate our areas of study and clarify the concepts of Bion under discussion.

By way of example I have transcribed below two of these short teaching texts.

Significant landscapes

For a course held in 2011, entitled 'Significant landscapes in Bion's work', I wrote the following text:

> Every meeting inevitably becomes dated. These seminars are no different: in agreeing to attend them, you will encounter my current view of Bion's work, and present interests. In the Houaiss Dictionary there is an interesting definition of the word 'landscape': 'The limits of the region that the eye can take in at one glance.'
>
> So I would like to share with all of you my current views of the main landscapes described by Bion in the wide and dense field of mental life. Although I have had plenty of experience discussing Bion's works in seminars, the items I have chosen here will be offered in a personal fashion in the hope of being absorbed in a useful manner. These extracts will appear with gaps in between, which I hope we will be able to fill in our discussions. In his introduction to *Learning from Experience*, Bion warns us that: 'The book is designed to be read straight through once without checking at parts that might be obscure at first. Some obscurities are due to the impossibility of writing without pre-supposing familiarity with some aspect of a problem that is only worked on later. If the reader will read straight through, these points will become clearer as he proceeds. Unfortunately obscurities also exist because of my inability to make them clearer. The reader may find the effort to clarify these for himself is rewarding and not simply work that is forced on him because I have not done it myself' (Bion, 1962b, p. viii).
>
> Given our time limitations, I have arranged the seminars such that each one gives a glimpse of a certain dimension of the territory scrutinised by Bion, as well a chance to test in yourselves the range of his vision. We will not have the chance to 'read straight through once', besides

other disadvantages, but on the other hand, I expect this new method of introducing Bion's work could also have its benefits.

In this course I selected twelve 'landscapes': 1) Group mentality: 'narciss-ism'⇌'social-ism'; 2) Links: constitution and dissolution; 3) A theory of thinking; 4) Differentiation of the psychotic from the non-psychotic personalities; 5) Theory of functions: alpha-function; 6) Reverie; 7) The Grid; 8) Reality sensuous and psychic; 9) Opacity of memory and desire; 10) Caesura: states of transience; 11) The theory of transformations; 12) Psychic growth: 'catastrophic change'.

At the end, in line with what Bion did in his article about the caesura, I also offered as stimulus some quotations taken from his books, from Milton's *Paradise Lost* and from Borges' tale *The Thread of the Fable*; the underlying idea being (to paraphrase Bion) to delineate the universe of discourse within which this course is confined.

The elements of psychoanalysis

For a course held in 2005, entitled 'Who cares, after all, about the elements of psychoanalysis?', I gave students the following introductory text:

> If we take this question at face value, we would answer: clinical psychoanalysts, for sure. The clinical setting is an ocean we must navigate whatever happens, be it as passengers, sailors, or even cast adrift. The success of the navigation depends on the one hand on the navigability conditions and on the other, on the experience and technique of the navigator. As we shall see, the elements of psychoanalysis interfere with both ends of the process.
>
> The essential condition for navigation is floating; the essential condition for psychoanalysis is thinking. In order to float we need a balance, so to speak, between the segment of the body inside a given medium, and the segment that remains outside. In order to think we need a balanced inter-

action between the segments of psychic 'body' inside and outside the medium of consciousness.

We must bear in mind that the main dynamic in both processes is one that enables us to imagine an inside in which to lodge an object, and an outside from where this object can be retrieved: this container–contained configuration is viewed by Bion as central to thinking, and we should scrutinise it incessantly in our psychoanalytical practice.

This configuration is founded on a relational paradigm, that the container is always searching for a content and viceversa; to stress this, Bion represents it by the sign ♀♂ on the model of sexual intercourse. However, the constitution of the container and contained is reminiscent of the integration⇌disintegration mechanism, represented by Bion by the sign Ps⇌D, inspired by the oscillation between Melanie Klein's paranoid-schizoid and depressive positions. His formula of ♀♂ was made when he recognised that projective identification, also described by her, is the matrix of every interpsychic communication. Both mechanisms, ♀♂ and Ps⇌D, are primary and interchangeable.

Bion's theory of thinking, the theory of dream-work-alpha, takes for granted the existence of a psyche that projects psychic contents that have no meaning, and the existence of other psyches that can receive these contents and detoxify their catastrophic character, through the attribution of meaning; this 'digester container' is somehow equivalent to Melanie Klein's good breast.

The link between container and contained (and, on a more complex level, between psychoanalytical objects) is of three kinds: loving (L), hating (H), and cognitive (K). Depending on the relative blend between these components, the final result will be benign or malignant.

It is up to the analyst to evaluate the analysand's behaviour or speech, roughly understood as 'associations'; it is up to him alone, too, to decide on his interventions, roughly considered as 'interpretations'. The analyst, besides a microscopic vision turned to elemental categories, must hold a macroscopic vision to keep him in permanent contact with the analysand's 'narrative flow'.

The prominence given to the analyst's loneliness is not fortuitous: it mirrors, complements and in a certain way is associated with the essential loneliness of the analysand, besides emphasising the private ambience in which an analysis must be conducted. The analytical atmosphere is essentially investigative and, therefore, should renounce any attempt to satisfy the analyst's desires, with the exception of course of the desire to analyse and be analysed.

So far, we have listed the main elements of psychoanalysis noted by Bion in his navigational search for the 'ultimate port' of psychoanalytical phenomenology: the configurations $♀♂$ and $Ps \rightleftharpoons D$, the basic links L, H and K, the pair association/interpretation, the narrative flow of the analysand and the lone decision of the analyst.

What remains is to take into account the analyst's clinical experience and his or her technical instruments. The navigation of psychoanalytical experience involves the use of initiative, of one's personal analysis, and a feel for the elements of psychoanalysis, even before they are theoretically recognised. These technical instruments have to be shaped out at sea, when at the mercy of clinical waves or of a paralysing becalmed sea. That, I take it, is how Bion's Grid was born.

By contrast with the circumspection of the typical maiden voyager, the Grid was born as the log of an experienced psychoanalyst registering his exploration of the mysteries of the human mind. As the information accumulated and the structure grew, Bion began to glimpse its use as a simulator of psychic patterns, to descriptively organise thinking outside the session on a strictly personal basis. These ongoing patterns led him to the 'elements' as constituent units of psychoanalytical objects.

Bion has only loaned his Grid to us in a gesture of scientific solidarity towards his colleagues, not without scrupulously warning that each analyst should elaborate a Grid in agreement with his or her own professional biography. This observation is in itself a Grid exercise, in so far as it opposes content (vertical axis) to its use (horizontal axis). And from the chords sounded by this ontogenetic harp, we should derive a polyphony to represent the multiplicity of mythical, religious, social and historical influences that shape our human psychic phylogenesis.

Here we are, in front of a 'psychic simulator' capable of exploiting the gradation between real and imaginary, oneiric and concrete, falsehood and truth, sacred and profane, the formless and the already formed, evacuation and thinking. In spite of its unpretentious origin, the Grid has acquired such a presence that those who study Bion's work carefully will see in a condensation of his chief theories: the theory of psychoanalytical elements and objects, his theory of thinking, and the theory of transformations.

To think is to transform

Today I recognise that, although a certain degree of canonical study is inevitable concerning Bion's work, we surely will be more at one with his spirit if, in the transmission of his ideas, we should continue his incessant search for models in any field of human knowledge, aiming for a better understanding of psychic functioning.

Let us take as example the importance he attributed to *form* in mental functioning. In *Transformations* he alerts that the term 'transformation' may mislead if we think that a function of personality has form: one of the functions of the Grid, he says, is 'to afford a method of escape from the implications of form through resort to signs for abstract categories' (Bion, 1965, p. 12). In other passages, however, the idea of 'form' is explicitly welcome, as for instance when he says that if the final transformation of a patient is a shapeless lump, the term 'deformation' is not likely to mislead (*ibid.*, p.12); or when he cogitates that 'void is the potency of form', or even when Du (a character representing imaginative conjecture) says in *A Memoir of the Future* 'I am the future of the Past: the shape of the thing-to-come' (Bion, 1991, p. 274).

In the wake of Bion, I began thinking recently that form could well be understood as a crucial element in the transition from word to image. As I already mentioned, Bion himself recognised the importance of 'illustrations as psychological aids to understanding the theories proper': here, he probably was following in the footsteps of English nonsense literature as, for instance, the illustrations of John Tenniel or Edward Lear to *Alice in Wonderland*. Tenniel's famous illustrations of the Cheshire Cat (Carroll, 1970, pp. 53, 55) could provide a wonderful topic of discussion in a seminar, considering how images of words can help us to understand something about the complexities of admitting our own madness, the theme of the dialogue between Alice and the Cat.

What I am trying to say is that we, in our role as transmitters of Bion's ideas, should always look for sources that could amplify or complement his concepts and ideas as, for example, Mary Jacobus and Pierre-Henry Castel have done in relation to the influence of Poincaré's formulations. In fact, Jacobus (2005) reminds us of a wonderful passage in Poincaré's *Scientific Method* concerning the importance of deformation in our view of the world and in our perception of ourselves:

> If we look at the world in one of those mirrors of complicated form which deforms objects in an odd way, the mutual relations of the different parts of the world are not altered ... we readily perceive the deformation, but it is because the real world exists beside its deformed image ... But if we imagine our body itself deformed, and in the same way as if it were seen in the mirror, these measuring instruments will fail us in their turn, and deformation will no longer be ascertained. (Poincaré, cited in Jacobus, 2005, p. 236, fn.)

And Castel (2008) proposes reading Bion's epistemology as a psychoanalytical version of intuitionism, the intellectual movement to which Poincaré was a precursor. Exploring his concept of 'invention–intuition', Castel shows how Bion approached the major premise of his system: what 'looks' like a thinkable object has some possibility of being one. Chance, says Poincaré, knows how to mix things but not how to disentangle; so if we see a homogeneous blend it is likely there is a hidden order behind the phenomenon, hence the 'selected fact' appears as chance (Castel, 2008, pp. 70, 92–99).

Teaching Bion, living life

Concluding this paper, I would like to say a few words on how the teaching of Bion has penetrated my life as 'a beam of intense darkness' in several ways, personally, professionally, and socially. From the time I was first invited to teach Bion's work, by Dr Ronaldo Castro in Brasilia in 1987, where I taught for two years, I have been teaching Bion all around Brazil.

This led me also to get to know colleagues from all over the world, be it those who could visit us in São Paulo (some of them invited by myself), or those I met at the various Bion conferences that I attended abroad. I have no doubt that Bion's theoretical framework is the one that prevails in my clinical practice, although I feel myself also highly indebted to Freud, Klein, Meltzer, and Meg Harris Williams.

But perhaps the greater repercussions of the teaching–learning experience may be found in my relationships with patients and students. What continues to give me pleasure is to share with students my findings, doubts, and hopes, that are attached to this treasure that by chance crossed my life: the work of Bion.

CHAPTER FIVE

Building a 'Bion container'

Lee Rather

Pro captu lectoris habent sua fata libelli (the fate of the book depends on the grasp of the reader)

Terantianus Maurus

My passion for the work of Bion has grown steadily over the last thirty years. My earliest meaningful encounter came in studying *Experiences in Groups* while training as a psychologist and conducting group therapy in a hospital setting. In conjunction with this, a three day Tavistock Group immersed me in a deep personal experience of Bion's discovery of the basic assumption groups. In the early 1980s, the San Francisco psychoanalytic landscape was grounded in the American ego psychology tradition, and the contributions of the British schools were still on the horizon. However, by the time I entered institute training in 1992, a rapidly expanding interest in Klein, Winnicott, and Bion had occurred, and Albert Mason, James Gooch, and James Grotstein were members of our visiting faculty. Mason had been encouraged by Bion to move from England to Los Angeles in the 1970s, and Grotstein and Gooch had been profoundly influenced by their analyses with Bion. Personal contact with these teachers who had known Bion encouraged me to sail further into his mysterious waters, to begin to find my bearings, and to plunge into the profound depths of his psychoanalytic vision. After certification as an analyst in 1998, my interest deepened in dialogue with several respected colleagues, culminating in the formation of a Bion Study Group led by Dr Grotstein. Immersing ourselves in the relaxed setting of my home for a full Saturday, Dr Grotstein guided us in close readings of Bion's texts that we then integrated with case material. I am deeply indebted to Dr Grotstein for his thoughtful elaborations of Bion's concepts and sensibility. His knowledge is encyclopaedic, his comprehension profound, his writing mind-expanding (e.g., 2000, 2007, 2009a, 2009b), and his ability to convey Bion with wisdom, humility, and humour has been of lasting inspiration to me in my own teaching.

During the last twenty years I have introduced therapists to Bion in graduate schools, private study groups, outpatient clinics, and inpatient programmes. At a more advanced level, I have taught Bion seminars for four years at the Psychoanalytic Institute of Northern California, and I am presently engaged in a three year tenure as the Bion instructor for the San Francisco Center for Psychoanalysis. I have developed my ever-evolving sense of Bion in writing (e.g., Rather, 2001) and as part of numerous scientific meetings of local institutes and organisation. In the last few years, my most rewarding endeavour has been finding my own 'Bion voice' in the creation of larger group daylong workshop presentations (2010a, 2013a, b, c, d).

Texts and core concepts

Seminars in our part of the world are usually six to eight weeks long, a brief period that makes it important to focus on the most essential concepts proffered by Bion. I have gradually arrived at a sense of which concepts tend to be 'user-friendly' (the theory of thinking, attacks on linking, alpha-function, container–contained), which are more intermediate in difficulty (O, dream-work-alpha, contact-barrier, reversible perspective), and which are best approached with a more advanced group (e.g., the Grid, transformations in hallucinosis, the mystic and the group, beta-screen). In any case, I proceed from the ground up to see where the group's fulcrum point of learning pivots. My primary texts are three papers: 'Differentiation of the psychotic from the non-psychotic personalities' (1957), 'Attacks on linking' (1959), and 'A theory of thinking' (1962a), and three books: *Learning from Experience* (1962b), *Elements of Psychoanalysis* (1963), and *Attention and Interpretation* (1970). I do inform students of the full scope of Bion's writing, and include selections from the international seminars for examples of Bion's thought-provoking comments to those who came to learn from him. I also provide a bibliography of secondary texts (e.g., Grinberg et al., 1971; Bléandonu, 1994; Symington & Symington, 1996; Grotstein, 2007). I use the same core readings regardless of the group's level, since the 'O' of Bion, when encountered repeatedly, inevitably evokes further evolution of alpha-function and learning from experience in all of us as we allow his writing to work on us.

Building a 'Bion container'

Since students are often baffled, mystified, and disturbed by Bion's style of exposition, I consider it my first task to begin developing a 'Bion learning container' to manage the emotional and intellectual turbulence that naturally arises within the group. I start by presenting a biographical and historical background within which to contextualise Bion's project and to differentiate it from that of Freud and Klein. Most importantly, I try to help students understand, that unlike Freud, Klein, and other theorists who are at pains to clarify exactly what they mean, Bion has quite a different approach. Consistent with his theoretical sensibility, Bion rejected the premature certainties of analytic 'psychobabble' observing that these foreclosed curiosity and deeper contact with the O of the clinical process. Instead he attempted a 'language of achievement', a language that would avoid the pitfalls of certainty. This language is more indexical than iconic, that is, like poetry, it points towards and evokes more expansive thought rather than attempting to nail things down as we are accustomed to with other theorists. With this in mind, I encourage an immersion process wherein they read without the need for too much certainty and to stay engaged even if they feel they do not 'understand' (Ogden, 2004a). Very much in line with Bion's idea of bi-directional oscillation between Ps⇌D, and with the evolution of alpha-function, one has to allow what already seems known to be disassembled before it can re-combined into a new entity.

Points of emphasis

As has been noted, Bion's writing is rich, evocative, and unsaturated and there are many 'Bions' that could be emphasised in teaching (Tabak de Bianchedi, 2005). In discussion with other Bion instructors, it becomes clear that, in addition to teaching the core concepts and canon, each of us approaching the O of Bion will develop subjectified personal points of emphasis. What follows are a few of my own:

1. *Bion is unique as a theorist*

Bion was unique among analytic theorists because he concerned himself not only with the evolution of mental growth in the analysand, but also with issues of mental growth that apply to psychoanalysts as we attempt to grasp the O of the clinical process and generate models of what is happening. Thus Bion offers not only a psychoanalytic theory of the mind, but also a theory of psychoanalysts trying to arrive at such theories.

2. *Bion and critical pluralism*

Creatively extending Klein's concepts (e.g., projective identification and Ps⇌D), Bion's work tends to be associated with the Kleinian school. However, the implications of the conceptual scaffolding he developed go well beyond Klein, and the level of epistemological certainty in Klein's work is foreign to Bion's sensibility. Where Freud and Klein were concerned with the drives, anxieties, defences, and unconscious phantasies that need to become 'known', Bion's focus was on the process of 'knowing' itself. Mental growth is conceived of as a process of continual transformation of O at ever-evolving levels of abstraction while simultaneously maintaining deep emotional contact. At the same time there exists the rather tragic human reality that we are fated to search for truth with inadequate equipment (Meltzer, 1978). Bion emphasised that psychoanalytic theories are better recognised as useful models rather than as scientific truths. I say to students that the implications of this viewpoint argue against becoming an orthodox follower of any analytic tradition, and that anyone taking Bion's work seriously would want to consider all psychoanalytic theories as potentially useful models and favour selective integration over orthodoxy. Selective integration of theory and technique requires us to immerse ourselves in different approaches over time, putting them to use in the crucible of clinical work, and engaging in the conceptual work of bringing them together (where possible) in some sort of continually evolving 'personal' model which is essentially a subjectification of the O of clinical work through alpha-function. In any case, I make the point that Bion's work supports the necessity for us to sustain a sense of critical pluralism, the basic assumption of which is that our understanding of the human psyche is inevitable limited, that no theory can capture it all, and the existence of competing theoretical orientations is of great value (Strenger, 1997, p.127).

3. *Psychoanalysis as a probe*

In line with the comments above, psychoanalysis itself must always be in evolution, and Bion even suggests that we think of it as a process of inquiry rather than a body of knowledge about which we are certain: 'It would be a valid observation to say that psychoanalysis cannot "contain" the mental domain because it is not a "container" but a "probe"' (1970, p. 73). To quote Meltzer, Bion's vision 'enabled psychoanalysis to grow from a narrow theory of the neuroses and perversions, marred by overweening ambitions to explain everything, to a scientific method which may prove to be adequate to investigate and describe everything and explain nothing' (1978, p. 118).

This point of view is enlivening for therapists burdened by the pressure to choose the 'correct' theory, and it also potentiates creativity in the cross-cultural introduction to and reception of psychoanalysis. It opens the door to the possibility of new discovery by emphasising that psychoanalysis is first and foremost a setting and a process, and secondarily a set of theoretical conclusions, thereby representing Bion's epistemological perspective and encouraging the likelihood of 'learning from experience'. Chinese therapists, seeking to use the psychoanalytic approach in a very different cultural milieu, were very receptive to Bion's culturally unsaturated model when I presented his ideas in Beijing and Shanghai (Rather, 2010b, 2010c).

4. The existential side of Bion

As Winnicott (1954) noted, Freud discovered and developed a setting that lends itself to uses other than those that he himself could have envisioned. Freud had developed his version of psychoanalysis primarily for analysands who entered the Oedipus phase as whole persons; Klein had made use of the analytic situation to treat analysands who were still in the process of bringing love and hate together and thereby becoming whole persons; Winnicott discovered a way of using the setting with patients who needed to establish a fundamental self before progressing toward the Kleinian and Freudian developmental tasks. I interpret Bion as further envisioning the setting and process as an existential domain in which the patient becomes increasingly able to 'suffer' the 'ultimate concerns' of reality 'O', including meaninglessness, loneliness, vulnerability, and death, themes normally attended to by existential analysts (e.g., Yalom, 1980). These uses of setting and process are not exclusive to different types of analysands, but rather correspond to different strata of psychological development relevant to every analysand at different moments and phases in treatment.

Teaching Bion as a transformative experience

The culmination of my own 'Bion voice' in evolution has been in creating a series of day-long workshops including: 'Playing with Bion: dreaming life into theory and practice'; Understanding psychotic states in ourselves and our patients: a view from Bion';

and 'Playing it by ear: analytic listening as a creative process'. These six-hour workshops are typically attended by 25 to 50 therapists at different levels of experience, all seeking additional vertices from which to deepen their work. In each workshop, I present my own 'take' on the fundamentals of Bion, and, in conjunction with clinical material presented by myself and group members, use these concepts not only to better apprehend the psychic reality of our patients, but also to notice our own issues in attempting to use the 'psychoanalytic function of the personality' (e.g., Bion, 1962a; Rather, 2001). For example, in a recent workshop, 'All the world's a stage: dream-work-alpha and the waking dream', I used Bion's revolutionary re-conception of dreaming to examine the way people apprehend O through conscious and unconscious alpha-function which can create imprisoning narrative dramas which are self-perpetuating and preclude further learning from experience. The idea that O is always unknowable is not an abstract idea, but a rather tremendously practical tool in helping us help our patients to apprehend the psychic reality they have created in response to O, and within which they are fettered.

While much preparation is required for these longer seminars, they always potentiate a spacious and poetic reverie in me during which I feel myself evolving new ways of looking at Bion's work. Much like a kaleidoscope that has finite number of pieces but an infinite number of conjunctions, Bion's unsaturated concepts allow for, and require, an on-going subjectification by each teacher. When I am discussing theorists such as Freud, Abraham, Ferenzci, Klein and Winnicott, I have a sense of teaching content – teaching what I 'know about'. When I am teaching Bion, I often have a sense of 'becoming' what Bion is pointing toward, and bringing students to a place of being and becoming rather than of 'knowing about'. I will end with a comment that, though focused on analytic treatment, is equally relevant to the experience of teaching Bion:

> If, as I believe, the mind grows in proportion to the extent to which one inquires into it, then the relative proportions of what is known and what is unknown will be reversed the

more the mind has evolved. Thus, at the end of a psychoanalytic treatment, we shall know proportionately less of this
extended mind than we knew of it at the beginning. (Tabak
de Bianchedi, 1991, p. 13)

CHAPTER SIX

Maintaining a relation to O

Charles W. Dithrich

I have been teaching Bion for thirty years. For roughly the last twenty I have taught as faculty for the Psychoanalytic Institute of Northern California, as well as for local professional psychoanalytic organisations and private seminars.

In teaching Bion my intention is to promote an atmosphere conducive to achieving and maintaining a state of mind that is in relation to O. In this sense my intention as an instructor is no different from my intention as a psychoanalyst. Orientating to O optimises opportunities for thinking and learning for group members and for myself. I consider O to be both scientific and mystical. Maintaining an ongoing relationship to O, notably Bion's advice to be at one with O, contributes to the experience of unity in the group, and promotes emotional engagement, curiosity, spontaneity, creativity, timelessness, uncanny experience, and respect for emotional truth. As O can never be fully known, keeping O in mind engenders a sense of humility. This appears to temper envy and competition among class members, and supports an attitude of open mindedness, toleration of uncertainty, cooperation, and shared discovery.

I don't consider myself an expert on Bion. I have simply spent more time with his ideas than most of those whom I teach. I respect and depend on the intrinsic wisdom of the class members individually and as a group, and welcome all questions and comments, not knowing when or from whom the next messianic idea (or question) will appear. Often the 'same' question is asked over and over, by class members or myself. While numerous questions concerning the text inevitably arise and may evoke clear, thoughtful answers, in time, if respect for O is sufficiently well tolerated, a more associational process evolves within the class, a thinking-as-dreaming, dreaming-as-thinking. At such moments class members might share personal or clinical experiences, or refer to another psychoanalytic theory, writer, or paper, or a piece of literature, poetry, art, or cinema, or some other cultural experience, or spirituality, or the process within the group. I view such moments as the equivalent of improvisational passages within an evolving piece of music (the evolving O of the class), and will often contribute my own association, at some point eventually situating the idea or ideas within the context of the text at hand.

Studying Bion is unsettling, and for some, disturbing. I am reminded here of Francis Tustin's description of her first meeting with Bion to arrange analytic sessions, of which she said she had never met anyone she disliked quite so much. The sense of disturbance is due to what he asks of us, namely to forgo familiar yet limited ways of making sense and to allow ourselves to be touched, moved, and disturbed by our patients, particularly in response to their primitive aspects seeking containment and transformation. The need for this profound identification opens class members to their own internal lives, including protomental experiences of beauty, terror, and dread. It is partly for this reason that class members benefit from freely voicing their emotional experience of reading Bion, and their personal reactions to whomever they find Bion to be. Such personal reactions can include 'brilliant', 'rigid', 'inspiring', 'cold', 'aloof', 'visionary', 'too intellectual', 'too abstract', 'spiritual', 'traumatised', and 'psychotic'. I do not question members' assumptions of who Bion was. The freedom to express these responses in an atmosphere of curiosity free of morality, judgement, or expectations of homogeneous compliance, supports members' evolving personalisation of their subjective Bion.

The content of a given course I organise in roughly the same way. Each meeting is centered around a short chapter from Bion's clinical seminars and a chapter or chapters from one of his major works. I deliberately limit the amount of reading per meeting so that class members may read and reread the materials for that day's assignment. Bion's writings call forth a wealth of questions, comments, and ideas. Not having sufficient class time to thoughtfully consider the main ideas in a given day's reading can be frustrating and dispiriting. If this occurs week upon week it becomes demoralising.

Each meeting begins with discussion of the clinical seminar, shifting at some point to the major text. Bion's clinical seminars contain some of my favorite psychoanalytic writings, and offer a chance to get a feel for how Bion thought on his feet in a context similar to the one in which class members find themselves. While members reliably find many of Bion's ideas difficult, obtuse, frustrating, and intimidating, they see a more human, witty, humorous, wise, spontaneous, and approachable side to him in the clinical seminars. Bion's engagement with the cases being presented to him situates his abstract ideas in what members find to be a more familiar and interpersonal context.

My basic organisation of concepts contained in major text chapters is as follows. I begin with Bion's ideas concerning splitting and projective identification in the functioning of the psychotic and non-psychotic parts of the personality. This is followed by attacks on linking and a theory of thinking. I then move to select chapters from *Learning from Experience* (1962b), taking up a further examination of reverie, alpha-function, alpha and beta elements, as well as the contact-barrier, container and contained, and the nature of the specific emotional links L, H, and K. (The concepts noted here are limited for the sake of brevity, and are not a complete list of all that I may cover.)

I then move to chapters on O, and on lying, from *Attention and Interpretation* (1970). 'Caesura' (1977b) and one or two of Bion's last papers on prenatal experience are generally included.

The Grid is discussed and studied, yet not exhaustively. I have found that column 2 experiences are perhaps the most intriguing aspect of the Grid for class members, the idea lending itself to compelling discussions of countertransference, dishonesty, and truth. Over the years the content of a given class changes somewhat, reflecting what I find at the time most interesting, relevant, and lively. At times this involves material that I don't understand as fully as I would like, and provides an opportunity for me to immerse myself more deeply through preparation and joining with class members' exploration.

In any given meeting I have a sense of what I want to touch on. I tend not to formally lecture on the clinical seminars but rather to immediately invite questions and comments, thus opening the discussion and involving the group. As the conversation evolves, I make certain that many if not all of what I feel to be the major ideas in that day's clinical seminar are noted. In practice, I have to do this infrequently, as class members seem to spontaneously find their way to most of the salient points. Once there, the conversation usually deepens rather quickly, and it is only with some reluctance that we must eventually move onto the major text of the day as we never approach exhausting the possibilities for exploration of those few pages.

Once I have explicitly shifted the discussion from the clinical seminar to that meeting's major text I will speak briefly as a way to introduce the text, noting what I feel to be the important concepts and ideas, their development in the text, and the evolution from prior readings, and how they may tie into concepts yet to be formally covered. I locate Bion's ideas in relation to other major psychoanalytic theorists, including Winnicott, Klein, Fairbairn, Meltzer, and Freud, and attempt to describe the clinical application of his concepts when possible. Reliably, questions and comments from class members involving their own clinical work arise and offer rich opportunities for exploring applications of Bion's ideas to transference, countertransference, thinking, lying, and so on. In responding to questions from the class I do not limit myself to ideas and concepts contained in the text at hand, but will touch on related concepts and ideas that might be formally taken up several weeks hence. This creates a circular movement, with ideas often repeatedly and unpredictably surfacing in various contexts before being formally studied. While I do not assign readings from secondary texts, I tend to refer freely to those writers whom I believe have creatively and substantially extended Bion's ideas, such as Civitarese, Ferro, Grotstein, Meltzer, Ogden, Tabak de Bianchedi, and Reiner, among others.

The ongoing effort to maintain a state of mind for the group and myself conducive to contact with O appears to widen members emotionally experiencing certain ideas more fully in the here and now of class time. Speaking of the K link as a never ending getting-to-know as opposed to a finite possession knowledge softens the attraction for members to adopt an obsessional approach to learning and supports creative and innovative thought. Discussing the amoral pseudo-morality of the super superego and its opposition to thinking seems to sharpen class members' capacity to think and heightens their sensitivity to arrogance and philistinism. Contemplating the language of achievement and negative capability appears to have a salutary effect on the group's toleration of ambiguity and uncertainty. Considering the notion of thoughts in search of a thinker and the concept of F (faith) seems to promote a feeling of receptivity, trust, generativity and hope.

My expectations of class members are relatively simple. I expect members to read the materials and participate in discussions to the extent to which they feel moved to do so. What they ultimately find useful I leave up to them.

CHAPTER SEVEN

Group learning

Angel Costantino

> It was not only difficult for him to understand that the generic term 'dog' embraced so many specimens of differing sizes and different forms; he was disturbed by the fact that a dog at three-fourteen (seen in profile) should have the same name as the dog at three-fifteen (seen from the front).
>
> (Borges, 1962)

After Benito López's death, I was coordinating study groups on Meltzer until one day I realised that I no longer understood him. The way I chose to overcome this obstacle was to go back to studying Bion. Since then, I have been doing that: I study trying to be at one with him. For this purpose, I gathered together a few people who help me feel committed to learning Bion's work in depth and who over time have given me strong encouragement. Therefore, it would be wiser to say that I am a student rather than a teacher. Perhaps I might accept such a title if we take it that a teacher's role is to select points for observation and discussion. This group came to me with the assumption that I could perform such a task, on no evidential basis other than perhaps my experience in teaching Freud, Klein, and Meltzer. This implies a basic assumption of dependence in the group, highly annoying to bear, since I was not in a position – or willing – to explain our topic, but rather wanting to pay attention to what was lying in the dark. The basic assumption status is not permanent: there are oscillations, a search for alternative leaders within the group, dialogues amongst participants without my involvement, and – almost always stimulating – situations of rivalry.

How rigorously could we follow the advice to read and wait until time reveals the ideas, instead of looking for them? We studied the texts, reading alone and then discussing them in the group. When no light was shed this led to increased uncertainty and distress, and it might take several weeks before somebody, not necessarily me, found a clue. Such a clue would lead us to take a step backwards that would help us integrate scattered paragraphs into a whole that marked out a line of thinking, which in turn was not fixed but movable.

We faced another difficulty: in Latin America: we are not sufficiently acquainted with the writings of Shakespeare, Milton, and Lewis Carroll to recognise a randomly interspersed phrase. Most of us are medical doctors and neither do we have enough philosophical, mathematical, theological, or scientific knowledge, amongst other types, to follow all Bion's references in the texts. Sometimes we turn to knowledgeable people who are not psychoanalysts, for example, my elder son, who demonstrated how to solve the complex conjugate problem using imaginary numbers.

The group

I do not know the difference between my role and the role of the other participants. I guess they have faith in me, and I, with my own faith, bear that burden. Other than when we take a step backwards to review our progress, I have no plan whatsoever.

Some members, such as Mrs G, take notes; I find it amazing that she always has something to note down. Mr S rarely takes any notes, although he used to. He is a more thorough reader than I am. If he does take notes it indicates that I might have said something new. Mr R and Mr S listen and hardly ever make any contribution. Mr A found an analogy that I will quote later. Mrs Z participates a lot; she is not afraid of asking what it seems obvious, which is useful.

Elisabeth Tabak once asked me what, in my opinion, was the 'new idea' embodied by Jesus in relation to the Old Testament. I do have a view on that, but it made me wonder what was the essential idea that set Bion apart from those before him. I said I thought it was the transition from the familial to the social domain. I still believe so, though I can also see the importance of an effective projective identification and of his fine concept of reverie based on the analysis of borderline or psychotic patients. I could have said that he stands out because he makes clear the existence of gods in a human shared reality, but that is merely one aspect of the transition from the familial to the social domain, considering the various facets of God in the different areas.

When I received the invitation to participate in this book, we were reading 'Reverence and awe' in *Cogitations* (Bion, 1967b). If I am to show how I work, with all the repetitions, mistakes, and also good moments, I thought that rather than choosing an extraordinary occasion, I would relate what we are doing today, using of course an artificial mode of recording it.

The theme is Bion's demonstration of the dynamics of Klein's theory of positions through recurring patterns, where some sessions show intense splitting, and others the patient's cooperation. Since Bion use a clinical episode, note-taking will be as much of a problem as it is for me to retell this. Notes and recordings exasperate him, as he is not interested in verbal content. However, even though they exasperate him, we see that in this book his notes on a patient he calls X appear several times. We note his repetition throughout the text of the term 'familiar' to refer to the 'known'. We believe that it is no coincidence: familiar[1] is opposite to group.

There is no history of the patient; Bion describes him as a stream of words dotted with gossip that he believes Bion shares. The patient implies he knows so much nobody will be able to deceive him. We delve into Bion's way of interpreting:

---

1   The author is using the word in the sense of 'family' (Ed.)

1. He interrupts the stream of words, an outpouring of highly split material.

2. He ignores verbal content.

3. The patient is convinced that he has a clear idea about what analysis is, so he cannot be disabused.

4. Instead of talking, Bion does another thing he calls 'associating'. *This is something that we always take into account.*

5. He makes sure that nothing 'unfamiliar' is likely to happen. *We suspect that the gods come into play; he has been insisting for several chapters on the unconscious need for religious beliefs in order to be a social being.*

He seems to have told us many times that we have to talk about that man's way of operating, rather than about 'psychoanalysis', since the facts of the session only fit into column 2 of the Grid. However, then the patient welcomes an interpretation that does not appear to be one, and collaborates by making associations.

The next interpretation is part of a pattern: three sessions are split outpourings of statements, and in the next session the analysand cooperates, using colloquial English. *We think: 'without memory' means to accurately describe the new things that we see, not to interpret as we interpreted before.*

Bion points out the pattern to the patient, and tells him that if he believes he understands his outpourings, then he assumes that he (Bion) is an omniscient God. Then he suggests that the analyst has to experience feelings of persecution and depression before interpreting. If every session is not a crisis, everything goes wrong. *This is a good model because it refers to medicine and, although it acknowledges the medical meaning of crisis, it modifies this meaning to suggest that in fact there is crisis all the time.*

Bion continues with an interpretation that brings in the need for gods. In this case, the patient worships a god who inspires reverence and awe, and hates the analyst because he does not stand up to intellectual scrutiny.

Finally, he states the need to differentiate between two kinds of patients. *We do not quote this part as we have not been able to solve that dilemma yet.*

Beginning

I decided to start with Bion's works on groups, guided by Meltzer in *The Kleinian Development* (1978). With *Experiences in Groups* (1961) we found ourselves looking at a bold experiment, designed to test the hypotheses of Freud's social writings. It was a fundamental piece of research with unforeseeable therapeutic effects, an early piece of writing that exemplified the rules that Bion later believed clinical analysts should observe, such as abandoning memory and desire. Studying this, at the risk of dying in the attempt, turned out for us to be an effort as fruitful as only a few others in this field.

Since it would be impossible to list all Bion's ideas, I will name just a few: 1) the basic assumptions; 2) the association of Love, Hate and Knowledge (LHK), which recurs until the end of his work owing to the importance given to emotional turbulence; and 3) the significance of countertransference, that puts to the test the analyst's determination to continue with this work. Usually we employ the term 'project', referring to the hypothesis of an effective projective identification, which in this book shows that it is the group who chooses the leader and, in psychoanalytic treatment, this means the need for the analyst to recognise reactions that the patient has aroused in him; 4) the new approach to group interaction that sees the members' verbal contributions no longer as formulations of the unconscious but rather as statements conveying no valuable meaning, with a Tower-of-Babel quality; and 5) the types of action and of psychosomatic expression that occur when thinking fails.

Discovering the patient

We read *Second Thoughts* (Bion, 1967c) in two stages. At first we were not ready for the second part, which we studied later; however, the attention that we devoted to the first clinical approach, which was narrated in an original way yet not too far from the usual way of presenting, was essential for us, and Bion takes it up repeatedly even when he does not explicitly say so. We were deeply moved when we discerned the existence of a certain patient, referred to as X in *Cogitations*, who seems to have a had a similar importance to Freud's Wolf Man, and who made clinical continuity with the papers 'The differentiation of the psychotic from the non-psychotic personalities' and 'On hallucination'. It was both exciting and enlightening to observe the hard work that the analyst has to do to stay in contact with the non-psychotic part while testing in the clinical field his version of the Oedipus myth, which highlights the K link and moves L to the background. In X, Bion recognises Oedipus in exile, the one who stabbed his own eyes out in order not to see what it is important to see, the one who only sees furniture – often animate – but does not stumble against it, just like Dick, who looked at Klein as a piece of furniture. Particularly inspiring was to see that, when X recovered his sight, he also recovered his capacity for attention and *saw* something missing, something which is not sensory – the weekend. And then, the confirmation of that work done, when in 'On hallucination' X keeps his movements in time with those of Bion's, whom first he failed to look at but now watches. We will resume the remaining sessions later, when he discusses the concepts of reverie and becoming O, sharing transformations in hallucinosis with X to collaborate with one another. It should be noted that Bion's interpretations in the first session contain the ideas that will be later consolidated into his idea of enforced splitting, especially that of getting rid of the functions that could result in pain (attention and memory.)

This reading gave us confidence to submit a paper (Costantino et al., 2000) about Bion's vision of the Oedipus complex: placing Oedipus (the arrogant) and Tiresias and Oedipus in exile in the self, and the sphinx and the oracle in the superego.

Elements and the Grid

In *Learning from Experience* (1962) Bion astonishes us with the idea that thoughts are looking for someone to think them. In the infant–breast relationship innate pre-conceptions find the mother's alpha-function of reverie, and thus, the infant in turn takes on its own alpha-function and selects facts, learning to evacuate stimuli as proposed by Freud. Bion asserts here (in chapter 6) that in the evolution of the species innate dreams became inserted into the body of the human animal, which was poorly prepared for thinking, thus forcing it to find realisations for them.

The alpha-function shares aspects of both the mathematical and digestive functions. Bion takes the latter as a model for the apparatus for learning to think. He uses models as an intermediate step to go from the current emotional experience to both abstraction and the scientific deductive system and, conversely, from there to concretisation. The model brings back images from the past, and the abstraction used as pre-conception fosters future developments. The essential theme of this book is the search for truth using 'common sense' which, in our work, is as important as food for growth.

Knowing that the life process depends on the interplay between projective identifications and introjections, Bion uses the Grid as a model for the mental apparatus and proposes the concept of transformations to study these exchanges. The Grid is intended to help identify any statement during a session. Rigid motion transformations are those where the importance of the content prevails, and there is a notion of cause and guilt. The term encompasses those collaborations listed in columns C and D for the patient, and D and F for the analyst. These transformations imply an agreement between them on their respective roles. Projective transformations cause a reaction, and are useful for the transition from A to C.

On my hard disc I have the fruits of our exploration of *Elements* (Bion, 1963). Let me evoke the overall impression that made an impact on our memory, making use of Bion's category of C3 (Bion, 1967c, p. 124). The windows are closed; light bothers me. We were walking in the dark with the theoretical elements, far from the occurrence of the phenomenal elements and the uses of the Grid in the book. It was not me, but Dr A, who underlined an analogy between pre-conception and conception, and preconscious and consciousness. I noted that we were reading chapter 7; I rotated the grid 90 degrees, and the schematic 'comb' psychical apparatus of the other chapter 7 slapped us in the face. The grid was split in two parts. From C downwards, there was little to add to Freud and Klein's work. A to C listed Bion's innovations. The picture of static splitting is inspiring.

The horizontal axis helps evaluate the insight or its absence. It consists of six columns that match the functions of the ego, described by Freud in 'Formulations on the two principles of mental functioning' (1911), which provides for an easier understanding of the material from a dynamic point of view. Columns 2 and 4–5 show the conflict in question. If the material applies only to columns 1, 2, and 6, there is no insight or learning from experience. Therefore, upon interpretation, there is a movement from 4 to 1. Column 2 is essential for the analyst. The analyst can only move forward with his investigation if he takes into account his mistakes and repetitions.

The vertical axis helps assess the elaboration. It is applicable to long periods of time. As an example, we describe the value of a dream in each row: in A, the patient fails to distinguish asleep from awake; he sees what he says while he is saying it, as for example when one said: 'I see two probability clouds.' In B, the patient no longer sees what he speaks of; what he says is referential. In C, the patient tells a dream, but has no idea of its value in analysis. In D, the patient tells a dream, but he already knows that dreams have meaning; he expects a transferential experience to relate to the dream. In E, the patient finds some sort of meaning for the dream. In F, the patient learns concepts, such as castration anxiety or incest, based on the analysis of dreams (Costantino et al., 2001).

The actual emotional situation, both unknown and unknowable, Bion terms 'O' and, in practice, it is the analyst's statement for the patient and the patient's statement for the analyst. We can learn about O, approach it through transformations in K. The transformations in O may be either unfortunate or favourable when, through the analysis of disorders of thought, we succeed in helping the patient think with things – transformations in hallucinosis – and we take part in that exchange, until he is capable of finding and storing selected facts which are not things-in-themselves, but instead are representations of things. At that point, we go up the vertical axis of the Grid to create a new opportunity for reverie, so that the patient recovers alpha- function. Staying in contact with the neurosis, and with the mission to describe what is going on there, is 'becoming O'. The progress downwards also transforms who we are, from worshippers and gods to workers in a garage or laboratory. In our group we 'suffered' every chapter of *Elements,* as recorded in our paper 'D4: radar turbulences' (Costantino et al., 2009).

Back to X

Attention and Interpretation required patience while we moved onward through its chapters until we managed to be at one with Bion. I will choose only the transition from row A to C, the analytical work on reverie. There he emphasises that O cannot be known but only 'become': 'In so far as the analyst becomes O he is able to know the events that are *evolutions* of O' and that O is an evolution 'common to analyst and analysand' (1970, p. 27). It was not easy to understand the meaning of these assertions. They became much more consistent once we analysed the notes on clinical experiences that he includes as examples. It was a huge relief to find the real or artificial patient again, whom he refers to as X (perhaps it is a person; perhaps it is a synthesis based on the few psychotic patients that he analysed before taking on analysands who were actively seeking analysis).

Bion describes how the patient seemed to think his words flew over his head and could be detected in the patterns on a cushion, adding that once the patient had smelled coffee in the house where he was working (p. 39). On reading this, we first went back to 'On hallucination' to find the example he used to illustrate transformations in hallucinosis and the becoming of O. There he refers to several sessions. I have already quoted the first one, where it is evident that the patient recovered his sight. Further on he says this session was called by the patient a 'good' session. But these sessions were followed with great consistency by 'bad' sessions (in 1967c, p. 73). In the next session, Bion was unable to take clear notes, but we find a vivid allusion to coffee. And then, he describes the patient's response as moving his head and eyes 'as if my words were visible objects which were passing over his head to become impacted on the opposite wall'

(p. 75). Three years before, this patient had a way of trying to bring objects together so violently that 'fission and fusion were adumbrated in terms of atomic explosions' (p. 68).

Thanks to the compilation of the writings in *Cogitations*, we were able to make a second move back in time to many sessions with X, including this one, which in synthesis shed light on the language of chapter 6 in *Learning from Experience*; in this way we could understand better what he means by things-in-themselves, and how the psychotic X could only dream during the sessions, as this is the only time the movement Ps $\rightleftharpoons$ D occurs, which Bion puts on a level with the selected fact. To return to the last session of 'On hallucination', we see the patient using the matter-of-fact tone that characterised the rare occasions when he spoke rationally and coherently: 'I had a peculiar dream', he said: 'You were in it' (1967c, p. 77).

Two pillars – supervision and analysis

I have already said that the inclusion of clinical material – both my own and that of supervisees – strengthens the group. How can we convey some of Bion's legacy behind the couch? I would draw attention to these five items: his theories of observation; weighing up whether or not disturbance can be contained in the treatment; bearing in mind that analysis is a matter of life or death; using colloquial language; and being free.

In this context, supervisions constitute a privileged moment to observe again what the therapist has already observed. I found a very neat example in material from Mrs G, with whom I had to try hard in order to learn about the analysis of children. Her observations are described in a study in which she distinguishes whether the child who seems to be playing is in fact playing or doing something else. Likewise, I recall two illuminating clinical examples from S: one in which a patient was 'politicising' and the verbal contents were difficult to reproduce given their incoherence, and another one who – every three sentences – said: 'nothing, nothing'.

Always the medical and civil priority is to determine whether or not I have the capacity to act as a container for potentially dangerous actions. As prophesised by Freud in 1912, it is reck-less to avoid the benefits that antipsychotic drugs can offer today. I remember at least three times when I gave up treating patients in whom I saw no progress and too much suffering. On several occasions I refused to treat patients because I thought I would not be able to help them. These cases involved patients suffering from highly deteriorating schizophrenia and simple schizophre-nia, a torturer who aroused too much hate in me, and jobless or uneducated addicts. While Bion asserts that the desire for cure disturbs observation, he also writes of the dangers of suicide and a 'fragmentation so minute that reparation of the ego becomes impossible' (1967c, p. 80), and he makes it very clear that he is not indifferent to the deterioration or improvement of this type of patient.

Within life or death issues, drug addiction has become a topic requiring special attention. There is no clear agreement among group participants on how much it matters that the patient give up hard drugs. It is necessary to describe that world on a case by case basis, as well as the existence of other possible worlds which could appear during the session. The question of life or death looms large in personality disorders and disorders of thought when it is more deceitful but less spectacular. While I have not discovered any new hypothesis, I have faith and patience to deal with situations where I hope life and passion may arise. Between sessions I think – and go on thinking, when I open the door of my office: 'Do my words to this particular human being mean "Life is worthwhile, at least for now"?'

Since my interpretations are custom-made, they would not be useful on some other occasion. I always speak colloquial Spanish. Jargon is toxic; it is like making a movement 4 to 1 in the Grid, which means taking as known what has just been given a sophisticated name. I was able to recognise the importance of both splitting and projective identification in examples of this kind: a patient, who is a lawyer, remained silent at the end of a session where I interpreted to him that the attacks he felt coming from outside were triggered by his conscience, which accused him of being useless, thus helping him dodge responsibilities. I asked him what happened, since 'What do you think?' implies an answer already. He said: 'Many worthless files', and I recognised that those were the remnants of my interpretation. However, the following session – when he is afraid of going insane – results in a deeper understanding of and interaction within his environment. He even dared to cooperate with his brother, toward whom he feels submissive. Soon he recalled new anecdotes in which he described his brother as a pragmatic miserly tyrant, and himself as a compassionate human being. He asked me if I understood the description; I said that I did, but I did not have a personal opinion – and I think, I do not have one because he does not know the value of money when the amount has more than four digits.

Final thoughts

As a candidate, I published a paper explaining that the frequency of four weekly sessions was a mere convention. To automatically follow the rules of the classical framework, according to Bion, would result in a good imitation of analysis instead of an analytic tool. The great masters worked six sessions a week; four were required during my training, though I have been a five–session analyst and patient for a while. However, while today a frequency of three or two is officially accepted, in practice the choice lies between two and one. The number is not essential, but it is essential for us to live true emotional experiences that provide food for thought. Who better than Bion, who dared to treat patients in a group (with not much idea of what he could accomplish) to offer us freedom within non-classical frameworks? Who better than him to give us the chance to be honest?

Let us remember the quote at the head of this chapter which describes Borges' character Funes who, after an accident, lost his ability to abstract and could not help but remember absolutely every sensory impression that he perceived. As a poet, Borges describes some of the alterations in thinking that Bion picked up. This emphasises that artists are keen psychoanalytic researchers, which can be traced back to the classical Greeks who dreamt the Theban saga.

CHAPTER EIGHT

Tiger stripes and student voices

Michael Eigen

I began teaching W. R. Bion in the 1970s and D. W. Winnicott in the 1960s. I met Winnicott in 1968 and Bion in 1977. Both were important not only to my psychoanalytic learning but personal growth.

In the one week I saw Bion in New York, he told me to stop analysis and get married. He said, 'Marriage isn't what you think. It's two people telling the truth to one another, helping to mitigate the severity to yourself.' I was forty-one, in and out of relationships. His remark initiated a series of events that in three years led to my becoming a married father. Something in his mien and manner reached me, enabling what I wanted to do for decades. How did this happen? Other parts of the time we spent together also are bearing fruit, some only now as a senior citizen. Out of the blue, he asked me about the Kabbalah, then after brief discussion paused and remarked, 'I use the Kabbalah as a framework for psychoanalysis.' I met Bion two years before he died. Now I am one year short of his age when we met and recently published two books exploring links between Bion and Kabbalah (Eigen, 2012, 2014).

I started teaching Bion before we met. I knew the groups book and papers on psychotic thinking and used them in my courses. What exerted a greater pull was the series of amazing works that came out in the 1960s, which overlapped with his own sixties and early seventies, particularly, *Learning from Experience, Elements of Psychoanalysis, Transformations* and for me, a climactic life-changing work, *Attention and Interpretation.* I needed to read these works closely and as a way in began teaching *Learning from Experience,* the first of this series. I taught in order to learn. We did a little at a time, relishing themes, phrases, words, or para-graphs. A sense of psychic reality opened before our eyes. Trails taking us through psychotic turns of mind, bursting or trickling off into mystic moments.

Gradually, I moved from K–Bion to F–Bion – not that the two are unrelated. Earlier in my teaching, there was more empha-sis on K and –K, linking and attacks on linking, knowing (K) and attacks on knowing. Having and using one's mind, *vs.* ridding oneself of this disturbing vehicle, through which one often sees and hears and learns things one would rather not know, intoler-able things, intolerable no-things (Eigen, 1996).

In my first book (1986), I included a chapter called 'Mindlessness', in which I discussed difficulties Bion raised with regard to being a mindful creature, difficulties in tolerating tensions that are part of mental life. It touched one of his hall-mark concerns, evacuation of mental processes to avoid psychic pain. To avoid psychic pain one may attempt to destroy capacities that experience it, including the possibility of destroying one's own mind in order to avoid contact with intolerable perceptions, intolerable emotional realities. Instead of facing and modulat-ing – destruction. Or, as fits reality, both. When we spoke, Bion brought up *The Zohar,* a principal book of the Kabbalah, mean-ing splendour or radiance. It is no accident that the book of radi-ance encompasses catastrophic realities.

Throughout his work, Bion often portrays situations with no solution, no way out – situations one must sit with, tolerate, grow through. Bion wrote of most dreams being semi-aborted, since only so much build-up of emotion is tolerable. In *Cogitations* (1994) he suggests that psychic intensity can damage psychic functioning. The psyche can not take itself or can only take so much of itself. We can find ourselves in the predicament of getting damaged by our attempts to process damage (see Eigen, 2007, 2009, 2010–2011, 2011, 2012).

Once I started to teach *Attention and Interpretation* (1970), I could not stop. I taught it many years and one of my students is now teaching it. I wrote about it in *The Psychoanalytic Mystic* (1998) and often since. Faith in and transformations in O are central to the book (I made a little chant of these two notations in *Kabbalah and Psychoanalysis*, 2012). Faith in O is a notation for unknowable emotional reality, and transformations in O, although unknown, may impact us. Does Bion, whose work is so tied to a sense of evolving, reach for the absolute? He writes: 'Psychoanalysis itself is just a stripe on the coat of the tiger. Ultimately it may meet the Tiger – The Thing Itself – O' (Bion, 1991, I: 112). Not just a hand on the elephant but part of the elephant itself, part of the tiger. We will meet what we are part of, the thing itself, the Real, O.

Bion sees faith as the psychoanalytic attitude, a state of being without memory, expectation, understanding or desire, radically open. An ideal, of course, but a path, a way, a practice. He feels it necessary for the repair and growth of intuition. Since one of his special interests is psychotic experiencing and functioning, the O of the moment may be intuited via catastrophic impacts. O as ultimate emotional reality is sometimes characterised as a cata-strophic Origin, in which case a sense of 'catastrophe' cements or binds personality.

I felt I could go on teaching *Attention and Interpretation* forever but at a certain point decided that I also needed to do something else. I wanted to teach *A Memoir of the Future* and felt reading *Cogitations* (1992) would be good preparation. I have been teaching it over fifteen years.

When I pick a section for an institute class, there are often students who feel lost without a historical overview or birdseye summary of Bion's thought. I recommend readings for that. But there also are students who want to dive in, feel liberated by focus-ing on a bit of terrain and letting it build itself. Over the course of a semester I do try to give a bit of overview, usually growing out of problems inherent in the reading. In the end, some leave frustrated. But it is worth teaching this way for those who find it nourishing, who feel doors opening.

This was something I found my way to early in my teaching life, not just with Bion but years before in universities and training programmes. I could only teach what I loved and was happy if lights went on for one or two students. I gravitated to Bion and Winnicott because they did that for me. I taught the way I wanted to be taught, out of the depths of my being, with a living sense of psychic reality. In time, I tried to write that way too, and sometimes was lucky.

My private seminar has been ongoing nearly forty years and is well attended. It takes place every other week, alternating Bion with readings from Lacan, Winnicott, or Eigen. Teaching this seminar has advantages. For one thing, it is self-selective. Those who find it meaningful to work this way stay. Those for whom it is senseless or intolerable leave. I go for the jugular in each class, plunge in, take off. When I teach Bion, Bion teaches me. Or perhaps something happens that is not quite either of us, x, 'it'. I learn as I teach. Things come out I had no idea about moments before. Much of my writing on Bion grew out of living moments in class. I often say about Rilke that he creates realities as he writes. Bion is terrific for this. Immerse yourself in a phrase, a section, a paragraph, and reality opens, you open, some class members open. We are taken to places we did not expect and might not have reached ourselves. Not every writer has this capacity. If you think of the deadening quality of so many psychoanalytic publications, you appreciate all the more the opening of living reality by some.

There are pithy sentences throughout Bion's work. One can not read any of his works without at least one sentence that strikes an alarm, touches a nerve, makes you wince, gives permission to think and feel. His work can intrigue, evoke wonder. Just as you think things couldn't be worse, he takes you further into a mangled aspect of psyche, desolation, demolition. You want to say, things can't be this bad, then realise that in the background of your being you are shaking.

Most people who attend my private seminar are experienced analysts, others are fresh graduates. Some of us have grown old together. We have a wide range of 'schools' and interests, workers from diverse institutes and callings, including a nun, Buddhists, one deep into Lacan, many steeped in Winnicott, several in self psychology, a couple who went to Tavistock, several artists, others. I ask no commitment with regard to attendance, pay only for days you come. I like a free feeling that way. I want the commitment, if that is a 'right' name, to be on another level, something to do with what is real, valuable, helpful – the seminar as a resource for those who find it so. Yet in all periods of its existence, a reliable group has come.

Student voices

I asked my students if anyone would like to write about her or his experience of learning/teaching Bion. Let me dip into some responses.

Student A, an experienced analyst with little exposure to Bion, joined my Bion seminar less than three months ago. She writes:

> Concerning Bion and the tremendous difficulty I was having understanding him: I found it immensely useful not just to re-read your chapter, 'Infinite surfaces, catastrophe, faith' in *The Psychoanalytic Mystic* but also to take notes on it. After I did that, and spent some time trying to explain Bion via Eigen to my husband (who works on Wall Street but can't wait until he retires so he can take philosophy classes again), I had what was actually a quite jarring experience. The next time I opened Bion's *Cogitations* – which was two days later – I read a paragraph that I've read at least five times previously with very little understanding, only this time, I understood so much more that I was really taken aback. I recalled your having said – or written – that understanding Bion is sometimes like gaining vision in a dark cave, when your eyes slowly adjust and gradually, forms come into focus. I've had that experience in the last several weeks but my experience the other day was different. It was much more sudden, like someone unexpectedly raised a window shade on a sunny day. It was so jarring that it was a little weird.

In class we were speaking of wordless music, Bion's 'doodling in sound', Chassidic 'ninguns' (humming/chanting without words, arousing the spirit, traversing a variety of states), Rabbi Nachman's dancing so still he did not seem to move, opening new dimensions of stillness (Eigen, 2012). The same student applied some of this to reading a text like Bion's:

> I know this to be true – that I, too, who cannot carry a tune, who can never remember a song or melody, find myself humming. If I take the writings as metaphor for something about the soul expressing/growing/putting something of one's internal world outside oneself, no matter how tentatively and quietly (though, at times, not quietly at all – Bion's screaming explosiveness), I definitely get that.
>
> I'm reading the chapter you suggested in *The Psychoanalytic Mystic* and want to let you know I've found it incredibly helpful and grounding. I feel that I may be beginning to understand why Bion wrote in his often confusing style. My window into it at this point is that it has to do with him wanting the reader to experience the thing about which she is reading. Point of impact, stripping away intellectualised understanding, staying with experience.
>
> About faith: I'm beginning to think of it like the air we breathe or the ground we walk on. We tend not to notice it until it's not there. And it's really quite difficult to bring it into focus and hold it in focus – like meditating on one's breathing is difficult. Is Bion saying that without faith your aliveness, your emotions become more destructive, that destructive attacks on linking begin to pervade, to the point where one's own being is destroyed?
>
> I have a patient I've seen for fifteen years whom this chapter helped me understand. So much of my challenge has been how to help him re-grow a world and psyche in which linking processes can evolve and in which life is possible. For one thing, this man, who I first saw when he was twenty-one years old, would come in and be unable to talk. Imprisoned in immobility, overwhelmed alternately by the infinite surfaces and then done in by explosiveness. For a 'good girl' like me who was, at that time, on internship and trying to play by

the rules, e.g., let the patient speak first, this man blew that all out of the water! At six, he was unable to clean his room, sitting in front of blocks and the box they went in, unable to lift his arm and make it put the blocks in the box. At 40, he sat in his car for five hours at a time, outside his work, unable to go in, unable to leave, unable to phone me or a friend, immobilised. And then he told me of a memory from four, of screaming hysterically, unable to believe that his parents were not coming, that he could not make them come to him. Now he needs to know constantly whether he affects me, does he have an impact on me, what is it, how can he be sure.

But most of our work has been without words, outside of words. Psychoanalysis as expanding capacity for experiencing – I like that. Expanding capacity for experiencing variety and intensity. Not as explaining, boxing in, closing down. My analyst and I laughed when we realised that after twenty-one years of work together, my favorite thing that she said was 'and then what?'

Student B took a five-class Bion seminar with me through a local institute:

The class required a change of gear. I initially found the readings and discussion frustratingly non-focussed. Over time I became aware that this frustration arose in significant degree in response to my reflexive resistance to the 'exploded container'. I made the connection to my own work with suicidal psychotic patients. It was critically important that I felt comfortable enough to discuss this experience openly in the class. Generally, I have learned not to discuss such things too openly.

I think that the concepts of O and F have been intuitively part of my identity as a clinician since – well, since long before I became a clinician – but that these aspects of myself were something that I was trained to regard as unprofessional or even worse, mystical – training that I have come over the years to increasingly regard as erroneous. Bion offers something more than rebellion – a sense of how to integrate psychoanalysis with the deeper level of human experience.

Student C is a psychoanalyst, teacher, writer, and musician, and has been in my private seminar for sixteen years:

I have been studying Bion in Mike's seminars for sixteen years and never cease to experience a sense of wonder, reverence and awe. I find myself moving into a meditative state and have left the seminar feeling as if I have been immersed in a state of prayer. There is a truth beyond words which gets evoked for me in witnessing and participating in these seminars. We enter deeply into Bion's work, responding to rays of meaning easily overlooked when one reads the text on one's own.

When I started the seminar we read *Transformations* and eventually moved into *Cogitations*. We stay close to the text, reading a phrase, perhaps an entire sentence, opening Bion's words with clinical and personal associations. Week after week, we may return to the same passage, musically repeating a word, a phrase, cross-referencing what we are reading with other texts. The experience is rich, dynamic and moving. The seminar offers an incredibly nourishing experience for those who want to journey into the infinity of emotional reality Bion's work provides.

One of the central issues Bion addresses is the primacy of emotional experience and how emotional experience itself is a problem insofar we have not developed equipment to metabolise, digest, and process our emotional life. Over and over we come back to the challenge each of us is faced with when demands made on us by our emotional life seem more than we can deal with. Echoing the work of Bion, Mike notes ways in which overwhelming emotional experience can deform our psyches or stimulate evolution of equipment needed to partner with the latter. While acknowledging Bion's thoughts on the ubiquity of lying and ways cognition can close as well as open emotional experience, Mike speaks of Bion's notion of faith in the face of catastrophe. Even with our fundamental insufficiency in face of emotional life, 'unknown intimacies' emerge through contacting unknown–unknowing regions of experience.

Mike speaks of psychoanalysis as an evolutionary adventure. We are mixed beings 'aching to evolve'; at the same time mind destroys itself in order not to experience the pain of life on personal, social and political levels. Participating in this seminar has been a transformative and humbling adventure, stimulating my own evolution personally and professionally.

Student D attends my private seminar in partial fulfilment of an institute-independent studies course. One thing she likes is to jot down quotes, bits that have moved her, with her response:

> *Bion*: Then between the lot of us we can find some kind of response.
> *She*: We do this in the class, I love how it happens, how you provide the environment for it to happen.
> *Bion*: When you see your patient tomorrow, will you be able to detect, in the material which is available to you, signs that there is a ghost of a puppet? If you can, you may still be able to breathe some life into that tiny survival.
> *She*: Applicable at the same time to oneself.

She continues:

> I like finding how a single line or word or phrase is so rich for meditating on. I think this is what I appreciate most about these last three months. The breadth of my familiarity with Bion is much wider, so the close reading is even richer. Gaining access to my own experienced experience. This is some of what drew me to the seminar when I began: studying frustration, studying destructiveness, studying omniscience, especially as I need to understand them in relation to my work with patients. I've only scratched the surface. Conscious effort to understand has yielded less than I thought it would.
>
> Regarding the clinical application of Bion's ideas, I have gotten more than I thought I would, but not in the form I expected. It's from Bion's own interactions with people and the way he talks about working with patients. Especially in *The Italian Seminars*, where he keeps bringing it back to 'the patient you are going to see tomorrow in your consulting room.' I love how he busts up all kinds of assumptions (e.g., that there are two personalities in the room) – constantly dissolving omniscient positions. And at the same time he cares so much about the analyst taking responsibility for the treat-

ment. 'Our problem is to be sensitive to the sufferings of people who come to us for assistance, but not be so affected by them as to interfere with our thinking clearly about the work in hand ... If a patient tries to throw you out of your window, it may be difficult to appreciate that he comes to you because he wants help.' And then: 'This same force which may be manifesting itself in a physical struggle with you, is what he has to live with.' Suddenly I feel deeply for this patient.

What I have absorbed, from hanging out with you and Bion and everyone in the seminar, is hard to describe but I feel it evident in my work. It has something to do with experiencing more, breathing experience rather than managing it. This is what I value most.

Student E is a poet, author, and leader of seminars on spirituality:

A liberating experience: the dark self gains legitimacy and validation. Faith is stressed as a disposition that supports life, not without fear, but with persistence. Bion's and Eigen's confessional tone prompts a sense of openings to unexpected realities. Sticking with the insoluble becomes grounds for new possibilities. A sense of mystery is welcome. How refreshing to embrace the unknown, while allowing the unconscious and preconscious to unravel, and slowly see the light of day.

Student F is a psychotherapist who was in my seminar ten years ago for two years. She writes about Bion's war experiences, the mark it left, and passages that link to emotional dangers of the session. How does one maintain 'sanity' and a 'clear head' in the midst of fears and mad realities? She follows lines of destructiveness in our time and moments of possibility. She refers to a point we were discussing in one of Bion's autobiographical works (1985) where Bion describes his immobility when his baby daughter tried to crawl across the yard to reach him:

I hadn't read Bion's autobiography until just recently, but hearing you talk about this incident, I had already been startled that he was willing to share such agony about something that could have made him look bad. I realised that I had already been feeling something for him through your teaching – a deep respect and also something like empathy, not just for him, for everyone including myself. It was a disorienting experience. It made me feel there was a great humility about him, something I feel for you as well. Humility and compassion.

As many students of Bion have said, Bion is not easy. I believe that one way you helped learning about him is by spending a year or so on one sentence. That has become an affectionate joke and it's hard to believe unless one has been there – moving away from the sentence and back again, starting over and trusting your ability seamlessly to introduce literature, poetry, philosophy, mathematics, physics, philosophy, your own clinical experience, making it possible to drift almost unconsciously a little deeper without having to make immediate sense of it. It's been immensely helpful to me in feeling my own catastrophes, my faith and lack of faith, being damaged, damaging others, being loved, loving others, feeling broken, paralysed, and recovering, opening up to bear a little more of what I'm experiencing of what makes me 'me', enjoying both the hard work and moments of grace.

And sometimes it feels like too much to me. Like I've just found 'the truth', a place to rest for awhile and, before I know it, it feels like you're destroying my secure place. It's a little like Leonard Cohen's line 'There is a crack in everything/ That's how the light gets in.' What did you say? What do you mean, 'There's a crack in the light'?

Student G is a psychoanalyst and author:

In Bion, there is a strange formalism, references to scientific deductive systems and the Grid. At first I took it on a kind of psychoanalytic faith that it was worth persevering to get to the core of it. It would be too easy to say that I persevered and finally 'got it'. The truth is more that I found a way of being more comfortable in my oscillations between paranoid-schizoid and depressive positions, between what became after a long time a kind of love for Bion and a persistent discomfort before a writing that often remains opaque and alien. But gradually, I found my way to Bion's own voice, not the poetic jazz-beat improvisational rhythms of Eigen but a different kind of music, an elegantly stark mathematical minimalism. Still, if not for Eigen's classes I would have given up.

I remember one class, Eigen working on a section from *Cogitations*. He starts by reading an excerpt: 'The patient comes to the door and looks away to avoid my eyes. He is dirty and unkempt; he wears gloves but they are not a pair. His face expresses almost physical pain. He holds out his hand limply to allow it to be shaken, but he seems almost to dissociate himself from the act physically as well as mentally. He lies down on the couch. "Well", he says, "I don't seem to have much to say."' (Bion, 1992, p. 218)

Eigen does not rush forward to get to the essence of the case, doesn't grab for psychological landmarks, familiar constructions to bolster our sense of our own analytic sharpness. Eigen goes slow, savouring the essence of what is being described. He repeats phrases: 'He holds out his hand limply to allow it to be shaken.' Now we must pause before this limp hand, we must hold the limp hand, hold the dissociated holding. There is a timelessness about the account as if the patient has always been there, offering his hand, saying very little and Bion has always been there, observing this moment, seeing the pain on the patient's face, feeling the limpness of that hand. Eigen takes in Bion's account with the same slow, precise caution as Bion takes in the patient. There is nowhere to go, the sense of timelessness characteristic of intellectual immersion and fascination mixes with the timelessness of the psychotic state. We have to hold the tension, the wish to hold and the wish to dissociate.

Later in the same passage, Bion writes, 'In short, I cannot have as much confidence in my ability to tell the reader what happened as I have in my ability to do something to the reader that I have had done to me. I have had an emotional experience; I feel confident in my ability to recreate that emotional experience, but not to represent it' (p. 219). Eigen, as a teacher of Bion, is true to this focus. Something that was done to Bion was done to Eigen. The words of this vignette, now read in class, may now again cause something to be done in all of us. I remember a question, a classmate challenging Bion's assumptions, his authoritative role as the analyst confident in his own impressions of the psychotic patient. But Eigen is not swayed to respond or think in these terms. He doesn't say much but tries to stay situated at the moment of impact, to tolerate the seemingly meaningless flow of a session that seems like an excerpt from a Beckett play. For a moment the disembodied disturbance of the patient in the vignette seems present in the class. It is hard to know what is happening. Nobody is writing notes. We try to take in what is happening.

Student H is a recent institute graduate who found Bion through her supervisor and became a Bion reader. She took my institute seminars and joined my private seminar in the past few years, and hopes to teach soon. I have always been impressed by her knowledge of *A Memoir of the Future* and her feel for poetry:

Bion has entered my psyche in bits and pieces. Sometimes the bits are a digestible amount, like an infant's happy feed; sometimes more than I can handle, like shrapnel from a mortar burst. I have learned Bion from the dialectic between sitting in Bion seminars and sitting in analytic sessions, deepening attunement to shock waves.

Learning to read Bion is learning to read slowly, deeply, word for word. Chewing cuds. This translates into deeper listening in sessions. Letting words have impact. Learning the language of impact and catastrophe. Leaving room for the impact of silence too.

The image of Bion emerging from the slaughter of World War I has stayed with me and often crops up in sessions, alerting me to deep trauma, ghosts and murder in the room. A wounded soul emerging amidst a gray fog, a fog I have learned to sit with.

Student J took an institute course on Bion with me a year or two ago and recently joined my private seminar. She had been reading Bion and the Kleinians a long time. A special interest was severe, chronic depression. She writes:

I began reading Bion, the Kleinians and post-Kleinians in the 1990s and found them enormously helpful in making intellectual sense of what I have been up against clinically and personally. Your contribution for me has been to bring feeling into the picture. When you describe the real frailty of the psychic apparatus to do the work that it is supposed to, to manage the emotional floods of intense affect, I can begin to find some space for feeling, compassion, empathy, rather than judgment in the face of my own frustration, rage, anxiety, sadness, and at times hopelessness. This leads to a very different position in relation to the work both with the patient and with myself. What previously was understood as a refusal to suffer can now be understood and responded to as an inability to suffer.

She referred to Bion's idea of developing a capacity to suffer rather than evading suffering, sensing in an earlier intellectual stance the subtle distancing or blame attached to evasion when emphasis was placed on the patient's 'refusal'. Pressure began to lift when she thought more in terms of working with incapacity and, if possible, gradually helping to build capacity, a ground for compassion and care. A subtle but important shift of attitude.

Student K took institute classes with me more than a decade ago and now teaches Bion and other writers at institutes, presents at conferences, and writes papers.

I've experienced group euphoria in a classroom when we read Bion's remark that the psychoanalyst should aim at achieving a state of mind where at every session he feels he has not seen the patient before; if he feels he has, he is treating the wrong patient.
    A typical question:
Student: What do I say to the patient who stormed out of the office, slamming the door when, or if, he comes back next session?
Teacher: How about 'hello'?
Student: Really? I don't have to analyze the meltdown from last session?
Teacher: The patient (personality part) who returned to see

you may not be the same patient (personality part) who could not bear being with you. If the same part returns, he'll let you know he's there and what to say can start to evolve.

Student L is a longtime reader of Bion and of my work, as well as many related writers, such as Grotstein, Ferro, Meltzer. He attended a few of my seminars when I gave events in his city or if he visited mine. He is a psychoanalyst, writer, and teacher:

Teaching Bion is an oxymoron. You can't really teach Bion. I believe you can commit to a process of exploring Bion's work, of getting-to-know the variety of problems he posed for the practicing psychoanalyst. Getting to know Bion is like getting to know any wilderness. You have to return to that place over and over again and begin to live there. Things don't stand still. You start to have many new impressions that arise at levels you never noticed before. At best you can be a guide a little way into the wilderness, but there are no experts.

You can share the emotional impact of states Bion points to and become interested in experiences others have and how they think about them. Getting to know Bion helps ground you as well as crack you, helps you to develop courage.'

Student M is a longtime seminar member. She is a psychotherapist, a Buddhist, and incorporates body work. She tries to express what a Bion seminar hour feels like for her.

I walk in, heart settles, breath slows, my edges expand, another world emerges. The human constructs of time and space blend/bleed, warmth flows as I relax. There is no separation between teacher, subject and student, all is possible. Intuition ignites, mind wanders through dreams and associations. Willingness to be present grows word by word. Reading, speaking, we tumble out loud. We find vectors that reach, threads that get tangled or unbound, secret joy of the endless. There is a daring sense of freedom to explore the darkest, unspeakable corners, playing in the sometimes graspable innermost thinking, feeling being of Bion. The hour is over, I leave elated, exhausted, full. Gratitude pours through me as I walk back to my office.

Student N sent me a piece that is too long to quote but I wish to mention her as her history is different from others here. She began with Bion's group work in the 1970s, doing Bion-derived groups in a university setting, helping to train businessmen. Since then she used a Bion-based group model for problems that arise in her own university classrooms. She applied Bion to individual and group work with addicts, who may, in part, use drugs in lieu of missing or diminished psychic functions. She began reading my work in the 1980s which added emphasis on the work of faith, catastrophic processes, and wounded capacities to sustain and process experience. Since we live very far from each other, she has not been in my seminars, except for one meeting when she came to New York, yet our paths crossed psychically through shared interests.

Student O is a psychoanalyst and teacher. He studied Bion with me for fourteen years and has strong interest in the interface of Bion, Wittgenstein, and Buddhism:

> I think of the passage in *Cogitations* in which Bion distinguishes between two kinds of problems, those where 'an emotional experience ... is secondary to a problem that awaits solution' and those in which 'the emotional experience itself is the problem' (1992, pp. 234–235). Of the first, 'it is possible to regard the problem as one of unrelated objects requiring synthesis.' However, with regard to the second, 'there is probably no way of regarding the problem "as" anything at all.' I recall several meetings of our Bion group that were spent in the vicinity of this powerful remark.
>
> What seems striking centres around the use of 'no' here. No way of regarding the problem as anything at all. No way. Here something is different. In the one instance, there is a way; here there is none. We are left, as it were, looking into space. We come up against our desire to see something, to proceed one way, but that way vanishes before us. Now we are someplace different. To find our way about here is to bear this 'no way'. When we think of the centrality for Bion of bearing emptiness, bearing the 'no-thing', of the way in which this 'patience' (Ps $\rightleftharpoons$ D) with the no-thing is a condi-

tion for thought, we are struck that *we* have been brought *in this moment* to such a place, brought to feel it from the inside.

Conclusion

Rather than elaborate on the above student–teacher sketches related to learning, teaching or using Bion, I will let them speak for themselves. Some notes I received, but omitted here because of space considerations, wrote of class-work as dream-work and of Bion writing of sessions as dream-work. I think of a remark he made about a patient: 'I am his other self and it is called a dream' (1992, p. 186). Much work goes on at a level that might be described as dream to dream.

One thread I want to emphasise is how uplifting it can be to be released to go to the darkest or unknown places. To be able to sit in emotional darkness and find patience, endurance, care and love even in frustration, hate, impatience and hopelessness stimulates possible growth of a new kind of capacity, partly involving creative waiting, intuitive sensing, letting psyche speak or grunt or weep or rip. Hidden ecstasy runs through psychic life, as does catastrophic destructiveness (Eigen, 2001). Too often the two are fused and indistinguishable. It is, perhaps, in the domain of indistinguishable unknowns that Bion's dogged perseverance in the face of everything is most striking and encouraging.

CHAPTER NINE

Dreaming the patient into being: a methodology for clinical seminars

Howard B. Levine

This methodology has evolved over the past twenty-five years and has been used with colleagues at all levels of experience, ranging from candidates in analytic training to graduate analysts, in analytic societies and institutes, and at seminars, conferences and congresses in Boston and throughout all three regions of the IPA.

'Teaching Bion', like doing analysis, is a highly subjective enterprise. In my experience, it has been less about content than it is about facilitating the development of a certain analytic attitude. Consequently, I have come to prefer not to teach content-specific seminars or lecture courses, but instead try to recreate the experience of the analytic session in clinical workshops through an exercise that I call 'dreaming the patient into being'. As raw material for this exercise, I ask someone to present detailed process from two or three consecutive sessions, accompanied by only the barest minimum of context and history.

I begin the session by announcing that the work task of the group will be for each participant to try to place him or herself in the imagined role of the analyst as the presentation unfolds. In order to help them to do so, I describe the system for practising jazz improvisation that I encountered many years ago as an aspiring tenor saxophone student. There was a series of recordings of jazz arrangements for saxophone quartet of classic songs called *Music Minus One*, which included only piano, bass and drums. The saxophone part was left out, so that each student could play along and provide his or her own improvisation. Although each student was presented with the same song and was responding to the same basic rhythm, melody and chord changes, we had the freedom – indeed the requirement – to interpret and interpolate the sax line in our own personal way. The analogy to the seminar as 'rehearsal' is clear.

I next remind the group that each presenting analyst will unconsciously carry more of the turbulence of the treatment than he or she can possibly know of, and that we can expect that something of or related to the not yet metabolised elements of this turbulence will be unwittingly projected into the group by the words and affective currents unconsciously and silently embedded in the presentation. This sets up the idea of a parallel process that exists between presenter and group, and patient and analyst, and encourages participants to free associate to the material that they will be hearing and to 'make room for wild thoughts'. The rationale is that if we pay attention to what strikes each of us and share our observations and feelings, we stand a better chance of 'unpacking' more of the enigmatic and unspoken dimensions of the analytic encounter that we are hearing about.

I then caution that we can expect that hearing a presentation of process material without a great deal of accompanying history or context will usually generate a number of questions in the listening audience. However, I suggest that the impulse to ask questions, especially historical factual questions, is often an expression, at least in part, of a reaction to an emotional disturbance set off in the listener (that is, 'irritable reaching after fact'). And so I ask participants to resist that impulse, keep open the internal space for not knowing ('negative capability') and reflect upon and perhaps share their thoughts on why they might want to ask that question at that moment, so that we might learn something about the disturbance that has been induced.

This request also underlines the analyst's role as guardian of the process, a role which I then try to model whenever possible, especially at the start of the case discussion, by encouraging and prioritising hearing the responses of the members of the group to the material presented, rather than offering my own.

What I am aiming for is the creation of a setting in the classroom that allows participants to practice establishing an analytic mind-set and exercising an analytic function, so that they can have a first hand analytic-like experience in the group. This goal is consistent with the view drawn from Bion that, rather than being a decoder of the patient's unconscious or an arbiter of some 'truth', the analyst 'functions as catalyst and guardian of an emergent, inexhaustible process that expands the bounds of the patient's psyche – the very realm that analysis seeks to explore' (Levine, 2012b, p. 19).

Just as in the clinical setting, where the analyst's ultimate aim is not to inform the patient or transmit knowledge, but rather to help patients develop the tools for thinking, dreaming and creating meaning in their lives, so it is in the classroom. Assisting the students in the discovery and strengthening of their own capacities to think, inquire, and bear not knowing, takes precedence over the transmission of 'facts.'

The exercise that I am describing helps train and reinforce the development of the analyst's capacities to listen, free associate, 'dream while awake', dwell in uncertainty and keep open an internal psychic space in which to engage in a receptive and free-ranging reverie. These are the means through which the analyst in the consulting room attempts to make room within himself to observe the emergence of the unbidden and the unexpected – i.e., 'wild thoughts', fantasies, dreams and inclinations to action – that appear in reaction to and in concert with similar phenomena in the patient. Allowing this process to spontaneously occur is particularly important, because it is a mind-set through which analysts can help patients transform what was ineffable and unthinkable into articulable feelings and thoughts. In this way the patient's own capacity to think and feel is developed.

What I am trying to convey is that my approach to teaching Bion is far more about experience, listening stance, the deepening of one's capacity for reverie and enhancing the receptivity of one's mind than it is about specific dynamics, complexes or factual knowledge. To be sure, there is a language and notation that must be learned in order to gain facility in reading Bion – alpha and beta-elements, container–contained, emotional turbulence, catastrophic change, making room for wild thoughts, different transformations, even the Grid, etc. – but more than familiarising students with a strange and new technical vocabulary it is about how to use Bion to prepare analysts' minds for their encounters with their patients – and with themselves.

Put another way, teaching Bion is more O than K; 'becoming' rather than 'knowing about'. In that sense, Bion offers us a meta-theory that transcends any particular psychoanalytic school or tradition. Some of his work, especially his early writing, is rooted in Kleinian theory, but increasingly, he moved away from the limits of a particular school to general principles and attitudes related to how minds work, individually and in groups, and perhaps most importantly, how two minds may work together unconsciously and intersubjectively in concert.

Bion was fond of telling his audiences, 'The way that *I* do analysis is of no importance to anybody except myself, but it may give you some idea of how you do analysis, and that *is* important' (Bion, 1987, p. 206). He was not interested in creating disciples, acolytes or clones. But what does 'learning something about how one does analysis' imply or require? For Bion, the truest form of learning is 'learning from experience.' All else is 'hearsay evidence'. And in order for that learning to take place, one must 'suffer' (face and tolerate) the truth of one's own existence, even – or especially – when that truth is painful, difficult or unpleasant. If we examine this statement further, we will uncover some of the central tenets of what I have come to rely upon and use as the core of Bion's teachings.

The first thing to notice is that Bion is doubly tentative about knowing. He will *try* to tell you how he *understands* how he 'does analysis'. This leaves open the possibility that he may try and fail or be limited and that his understanding, which is a belief rather than a certainty and therefore subject to all of the many pitfalls that can bedevil human thought and opinion, may be partial or incorrect. His epistemic humility is consistent with his emphasis on negative capability – the importance of the analyst's being able to tolerate ignorance and uncertainty, to wait and allow the organisation or relations that may exist between the various elements of the session to begin to coalesce and emerge around a selected fact.

In contrast to those authors whose theories might endorse or imply a 'knowing' analyst, Bion reminds us that we can only 'know' what we believe to be so, rather than what with certainty *is*. For example, in *Cogitations* he wrote: 'It is very important that the analyst knows not what *is* happening but that he *thinks* it is happening. That is the only certitude to which he lays claim' (Bion, 1992, p. 70). So, whatever 'doing analysis' means, Bion views it as a highly subjective and individualistic endeavour. One cannot teach anyone to do analysis like Bion, but one may perhaps help them to do analysis even more deeply or courageously within the limits and opportunities of their own subjectivity and personal idiom. I am reminded of a parable retold by Martin Buber about Rabbi Zusya, who told his students: 'When I die and appear before the throne of the Almighty in heaven, He will not ask me why I was not in my life more like our forefather Moses. He will ask me why I was not more like Zusya!' (Buber, 1994, p. 17).

The analogous lesson that I would draw from Bion's work is that each analyst must continue to learn to understand and develop his or her own subjectivity (become even more him or her self) so that it may be used in the service of their doing analysis in their own unique and individual way. This lesson was humorously underlined for me in a clinical case conference many years ago by Jim Grotstein, that unparalleled analysand, explicator, student and teacher of Bion. After Grotstein eloquently described what he would say to the patient in a certain difficult situation, he cautioned that he didn't think the presenter should say it. When we asked him why, he responded, 'Because you don't have the courage of my convictions!'

Grotstein was emphasising the point that each analyst had to do analysis in their own subjective, unique and individual way, a point that is also rooted in Bion's assumptions about raw existential experience (O) being only partially knowable, because the elements that make up psychic reality are dependent upon the recognition and exploration of a kind of experience that is not of the senses and therefore does not lend itself to empirical observation. It follows that the ways in which we come to know things related to psychic reality are usually partial and approximate, rather than certain and incontrovertible, and therefore often highly subjective. This subjectivity is reflected in the many different responses to the process material expressed by the group, almost none of which are 'wrong'. Experiencing this as it emerges in the group also begins to help participants to experientially understand Bion's (1970) metaphor of the analyst as 'genius' or 'mystic' and his valorisation of the analyst's intuition in the analytic process.

In *Attention and Interpretation* Bion argued that unlike a physician, who may observe (see) a patient's jaundice, feel (touch) their irregular pulse, or recoil at the stench (smell) of an infected wound, 'the realisations with which a psychoanalyst deals cannot be seen or touched; anxiety has no shape or colour, smell or sound' (Bion, 1970, p. 7). Of course, anxiety may produce physiological changes that are observable, such as rapid pulse or respirations, sweating, etc. However, Bion considered these to be secondary to the thing-in-itself, the psychic state. While these changes may lead one to infer its presence, that inference or indication is not assumed to be the same as observing the psychic state. Thus, there is a sense in which Bion's comments disqualify – or at least limit – the value of empirical observation as a fundamental tool for psychoanalysis. As an alternative, he says he proposes 'to use the term "intuit" as a parallel in the psychoanalyst's domain to the physician's use of "see", "touch", "smell", and "hear"' (*ibid.*).

In my own initial exposure to Bion, as a young psychiatric resident learning how to lead 'Bion groups' with psychiatric in-patients on a hospital ward, I was often asked by my supervisor, Harold Boris, who first introduced me to Bion, not what did the patients say or do, but how did it feel to me? Or what did it feel like? A breast? A penis? While initially, these questions confused and disturbed me, they ultimately planted the seed of an idea that took me beyond the realm of the medical/empirical to the intuitive and the realisation that my feelings, impulses and fantasies were an intrinsic part of the group dynamic process and, since they were uniquely mine, I was potentially lending myself in a 'mystical' or 'oracular' way to giving form to something that was previously unformed or ineffable. Analytic data too are not objective but are to some extent determined by the subjectivity and theories of the observer(s). This is another feature of Bion's teaching that the plurality of responses to the clinical material within the group can illustrate.

In elevating the analyst's intuition to a place analogous to the physician's empirical observation, Bion laid the groundwork for a theory of unconscious, intersubjective co-construction of narrative forms, founded on the concept of unconscious communication through projective identification and the processes of the container–contained relationship.

I take the view that elements of psychic reality are unsaturated and may have no fixed form until named; this is consistent both with Freud's theory of representation in general and his (1915) description of how unconscious drive elements ('thing presentations') reach consciousness as ideational representations only after they are linked with 'word presentations' (see Levine, Reed & Scarfone [eds.], 2013). It is also consistent with Bion's (1963) valorisation of mythmaking as an important dimension of the analyst's interpretation. This as I have described elsewhere (Levine, 2011) reflects a movement from a predominantly de-coding or uncovering view of psychoanalysis to one that emphasises transformation and creation of mind. Thus, another important goal of my attempts to teach Bion is to emphasise that the aims of psychoanalysis are transformational rather than informational.

Put in terms of technique, the interpretation of the here-and-now is not a 'destination', does not exhaust meanings, but is instead a point of departure for new meanings and places not yet known: 'Psychoanalysis is not a symbolic system charged with "deciphering meaning", but "a system for generating new thoughts"'(Ferro and Basile, 2009, p. 92). What this requires of both analyst and patient is the creation and maintenance of a potential or unsaturated space, in which new thoughts may emerge. I have found all of this to be amply illustrated in the unfolding process of the clinical groups that I have been describing. My ultimate goal is that participants will take what they have learned and developed through experience in these groups back to their analytic settings, increasing their capacity for reverie, receptivity and response.

CHAPTER TEN

W. R. Bion: a model kit

Leandro Stitzman

> There is a scarcity of time; a scarcity of knowledge; scarcity of ability. Therefore choice becomes of fundamental importance: choice of time, theories, and facts observed.
>
> (Bion, *Cogitations*)

Teaching Bion is teaching psychoanalysis; learning Bion is learning to psychoanalyse. These premises are the alpha and the omega of why it is a very difficult task for coordinators and participants of study and reading groups to both teach and learn Bion.

Teaching Bion requires that the student learn from experience because what is being transmitted is not a shelf-full of information, but the Bionian spirit of proximity to the 'facts' and to the intimate knowledge of these facts. This means there is no encyclopaedic or scholastic way of communicating a set of ready-to-go items of knowledge but rather, to use a term from Julio Cortázar, a 'model kit'.

I recommend the following advice by way of mental preparation: 'Leave, novitiate reader, your shields and weapons at the entrance. Bring with you enough strength to tolerate the unknown: fields infested by non-Mendelian inheritance, thoughts without thinkers, wild ideas seeking to be tamed, accurate methods of notation, the debris of our primitive animal origins, experiences transmitted through time and space.'

What follows is a selection of approaches that I have used for those who are grounded in the classical psychoanalytic tradition, beginning with introductory thoughts on Bion's tools for observation. I work with small groups of practising analysts (up to nine or ten people), including non-IPA members and training analysts. We use two main systems: on-site (that is, all together in the same room), and with a system of video-conferencing when working with analysts from different countries (Argentina, Colombia, Brazil, Chile, Uruguay, Mexico, etc.). Each group has a designated work to focus on, such as *Seven Servants*, *A Memoir of the Future* or *Cogitations*. I also work with some analysts using thematic searches through the course of Bion's works, such as: pain, turbulence, growth, alpha-dreaming, beta-elements, etc.

Tools for observation

Bion is a restless thinker who requires from the reader plenty of mental and temporal generosity. Mental because he demands we get emotionally involved in reading, as active thinkers stirring up the ideas that are lying there like spores waiting to fertilise a willing mind. Tender, fresh, new ideas are waiting to be unveiled by the adventurous thinker. Temporal, because he demands a real chronological time investment, besides the emotional, for reading and re-reading: time to read beyond the syntax and the semantics presented in his writings. He is an author who can be read straight through or in jumps, in chronological or conceptual order. What is impossible to do is to read him in a rush or seeking specific definitions regarding such-and-such a topic.

Bion has a vast and varied production that can be harmonised through the theory of observation more than that of theory of psychoanalysis. His major publications are *Experiences in Groups, Second Thoughts, Learning from Experience, Elements of Psychoanalysis, Transformations, Attention and Interpretation* (the last four collected in *Seven Servants*), *A Memoir of the Future* (*The Dream, The Past Presented, The Dawn of Oblivion,* and a 'Key'). Many of these topics, along with others, are also explored in papers such as 'The Grid', 'Caesura', 'Emotional turbulence', 'Evidence', 'Making the best of a bad job', 'Catastrophic change', and in posthumous publications such as *Taming Wild Thoughts, Cogitations*, and transcripts of several seminar series given around the world (Rome, Sao Paulo, Rio, New York, the Tavistock).

Bion's main interest is developing a theory of observation and adequate tools for it: for example the theories of functions and factors, transformations, the Grid, and other basic clinical operations. The idea is to build a series of tools useful to any psychoanalytic theory to which the analyst subscribes. And this is no secondary factor: Bion writes for the practising analyst. He introduces a series of properly sharpened tools for the observation of patients and for defining the vertex from which the problem is seen. The phenomenon of practical psychoanalysis is the driving force behind all his works.

Maybe the quintessential example of what is psychoanalytic writing is, as distinct from writing about psychoanalysis, is the outstanding *A Memoir of the Future*. I consider this less a 'semi-autobiographical psychoanalytic novel' (as described by Harry Karnac, 2008) and more as a work dedicated to three great clinical functions that interested Bion during his last years. In addition to Bion's 'thoughts without thinkers' I would add 'actions without agents', as represented by the character Tom, and 'relations without related objects', represented by the characters Alice and Rosemary (see Stitzman, 2011).

I highly recommend reading the *Memoir* straight through, as in Bion's advice in the introduction to *Learning from Experience* (1962b, p. viii). Bion has to be read in the same way we listen to our patients: with evenly-suspended attention – the emotional state he called F or (after Keats) negative capability. The same kind of negative capability is required of readers who are interested in studying Bion. The reader has to be a kind of dowser. We need to ask what it is about the clinical fact that is attracting our attention, without anxiously seeking for a prematurely saturated meaning (such as, 'that's what Freud, Klein, or Lacan also said') or false analogy. He demands generosity of his readers: generosity towards non-saturated ideas, uncertainty, and submergence in the peculiar emotional experience of engaging with new and truthful ideas.

Abstract vs. theoretical

Nobody is surprised to hear analysts recite Bionian syllogisms as if they were analytical mantras. One of the most popular is 'without memory or desire', omitting the eloquent 'without understanding, without sensorial experience'. Or quoting a passage from the *Memoir* without indicating which character has spoken it and therefore ignoring the vertex of meaning from which it derives. Reading Bion requires a certain audacity and when this is lacking his writing is sometimes reduced to the banal.

It is remarkable that in many cases people familiar with algebraic or formulaic thinking have a greater capacity to understand his writing. Nevertheless this is not a necessary condition for reading and comprehension of the spirit of his ideas.

Many times I have heard these kinds of statements: 1) Bion is very theoretical – his theories cannot be put into practice; 2) I don't know anything about mathematics – I'm interested in psychoanalysis not in all these mathematical formulae; 3) The Grid doesn't work for treating patients; it's too cold, too crude.

These are just a few of the most noteworthy comments that I commonly hear from those whose background is classical psychoanalysis. I will briefly focus on the explanations with which I try to deal with these problems.

Firstly, Bion is not theoretical, he is abstract. Theoretical and descriptive thinking, like Freudian or Lacanian, is confused with abstract and instrumental thinking such as the Bionian. What is introduced are tools built with traditional psychoanalytic theories – few, by the way, meant to interpret transformations of the personality.

Secondly, it is not necessary to know anything about maths to comprehend Bion. This is like saying that in order to read Freud one should know classical mechanics and neurology. Bion's aim was not to apply maths to psychoanalysis, but to create a psychoanalytic maths from scratch. For this purpose he proposes emotional 'numbers' such as 'some', 'many', 'few', 'too much'; and a no less interesting algebra, for example, if the sign '+' is sexualized, $1+1=3$.

Then, the so-called Bion 'formulae' are not mathematical formulae but algebraic syllogisms meant to create and name deeply penetrating clinical functions. Some examples are the pre-conception D: Ψ (ξ) and the conception E: Ψ (Ψ) formulae, or the formula for envy introduced in *Transformations* ($- \leftarrow \uparrow$), the result of 'non-existent existence-greedy objects' (1965, p. 123).

Instead of objects there are psychoanalytical 'elements'; instead of positions, there are functions and factors, with unconscious meanings like palimpsests.

Games and practice

It is impossible to be a 'Bionian'. Or rather, the only way to be Bionian is in spirit and not through merely replicating his idiosyncratic jargon. In this we need to stop imitating Bion and to dare to be ourselves; we need to orient ourselves toward a love of the unexpected, an attitude that leads towards the practical realisation of what we call 'psychoanalysis'.

If someone wants to achieve some level of success in transmitting this spirit of enjoyment, they need to offer participants the conditions for learning from the unexpected. I am so convinced by this notion that in the Bionian Games (*Juegos Bionianos*) that we organised in 2013, participants were given the chance to experience the concept of change of vertex through a practical joke: while all the participants were having supper in the main dinning room of the hotel, the staff turned the beds and bedside tables by 90 degrees. We did not have to wait long for the participants' responses: dozens of people screaming, laughing and complaining – always depending on their personal analysis – in the hotel halls in the middle of night.

Discussing the importance of tolerance of the unexpected, and turbulence caused by a change of vertex, is not the same as experiencing them in the flesh. Reciting and knowing topics from Bion's work is not the same as practising and experiencing those topics. As he would say, knowing about Bion is not the same as knowing wisely.

Two tools

The first study groups that I led on Bion had a huge impact on me. I found that in using the traditional scholastic methods of communication I was not able to transmit what seemed to me his spirit. I found I was using lots of jargon but was unable to achieve the proper emotional tone. I wanted to transmit, to transfer those ideas without using a language of substitution, but rather, a language of achievement outside an analytic context, even though sometimes the atmosphere in the group was danger-ously like the sort that arises during an analytic session.

How to do it? One possibility was to use two Bionian tools of observation: the Grid and the 'selected fact'. I found fertile results could be achieved by asking participants of study groups to search for selected facts in each chapter, paper or seminar. Once they have found the selected facts, they need to locate the vertex from which that selected fact was perceived by them, in order to locate its position in the Grid. The aim of this exercise is to find a specific transformation pattern for their own way of thinking.

The selected fact as chosen from a certain vertex and duly located in the Grid then becomes the title of the selected read-ing. The important thing to understand is that there are no right or wrong titles, just the conjunction of selected facts, vertices and categorisation; this is what harmonises and gives whatever meaning may be found. The idea is that this exercise serves as a personal indicator for that particular moment of the statements within that text. For this reason, I also recommend writing down the date on which the selected fact was chosen, in order to make comparisons between this and later readings. The most adven-turous students find it a source of richness and entertainment to catalogue the transformations that the selected facts have gone through over time, in the context of their implications in their own lives. This method becomes a sort of private journal of our own psychoanalytic thinking.

An unsaturated approach

Another approach I found especially useful when working in groups unfamiliar with Bion's ideas was to begin by reading a minor text, 'Brasilia, a new experience' (Bion, 1975b); this is the transcript of a lecture Bion gave in Brasilia to a general audience of architects, engineers, politicians, artists, etc., on the occasion of an anniversary of the founding of the city. In it, the ideas of a naïve view, of thoughts without a thinker, actions without agents and relations without related objects (as I describe them), setting, interpretation, catastrophic change, transference, intolerance of frustration, functions and factors, the end of analysis, groups, institutions, etc., are illustrated and discussable.

The advantage I find in this particular text is that the ideas are introduced in an unsaturated way, and he is constantly using Brasilia, its foundation and history as a model of thinking about the personality and the practice of psychoanalysis. I consider it worthwhile to take some time to read each paragraph over several meetings, and to unravel the implications of the statements for current psychoanalytic practice and technique. For example: 'When an idea is transformed into action it is as if the action commits the people who think like that to an irreversible course' (p. 121), and a little bit later:

> That is a fate of which most people are frightened; it is subscribing to saying either 'yes' or 'no' to the invitation to participate or cooperate in a creative activity. What creative activity? Nobody tells us; nobody knows what the response will be to that invitation. I would say that it looks like an invitation to greatness. What a nasty prospect that is! One feels like saying, 'What, me? What, us? *We* have to be great?' It is so much simpler to say that we have a previous engagement and choose not to accept the invitation. (Bion, 1975b, p. 128)

Here we have the invitation of a rebellious, revolutionary, anarchist spirit to face and contain ideas and, in the best possible scenario, to let some new, fresh ideas bloom in the spring of our minds, a 'small flicker of civilisation' to illuminate the darkness (p. 123).

Algebraic calculus

As we have been discussing, to teach Bion is not to teach a psychoanalytic theory, but psychoanalysis itself: it is not teaching rigid concepts with accurate definitions, but communicating the relations underlying the ideas, that is, how to think and observe psychoanalytically. Maybe there is no idea more opposed to Bionian thinking than the development of a homonymous dictionary or glossary exhibited as a display of wisdom.

In an interview by Anthony G. Banet in Los Angeles during the summer of 1976, Bion said in the context of whether a book such as *Learning from Experience* could ever be considered a 'final view', that he hoped 'certain things' in were worth retaining, but that 'to allow "Bion's Theory" to operate in a rigid way such as print would be ridiculous because that puts a restraint on the growth of the individual and the individuals who make a group' (Bion, 2005a, p. 114).

Reading Bion's published seminars is a deeply profitable activity since he never uses technical terms, and does not gives direct answers questions – probably because of his great respect for them. The answers to students' inquiries have to be oriented towards developing a field of ignorance rather than satisfying their voracious hunger for reassuring knowledge.

It is important to take this into account as a guideline when we face the transmission of Bionian thinking. Just as I began this article with a piece of advice for those wishing to read Bion's works for the first time, I want to wrap it up with an analogous one, but on this occasion, for those who are willing to join in the exciting project of accompanying inspired thinkers in their way of thinking: 'Do not answer questions. Do not communicate ideas you already know. Dare to admit the scope of your ignorance. Take any beam of light and make it darker. Undress yourself. Stop looking backward and take things as they come. Enjoy yourself and respect the facts. Teach observation by observing. Laugh with your group: laughter is a sign that valuable work may be taking place. Be disciplined. Trust in your students as much as you trust in yourself. Use your naivety as a guide. And use the Grid.'

Let's all look together at the new dawn of oblivion.

CHAPTER ELEVEN

Teaching Bion's teachings

R. D. Hinshelwood

There is an apocryphal story about Bion that at one of the many international lectures he gave toward the end of his life, the Chair introduced him with the usual emphasis on his achievements and affiliations; so when Bion eventually got started he said, 'Well, after an introduction like that, I can't wait to hear what I have to say.' This is Bion at his most ironic, a consistency of style from early on. For instance, he held a staff group in January 1946, when back at the Tavistock after the war. This included professionals and lay staff (clerks as he called them), about thirty in all, which no doubt followed from his Northfield experience. He described it in a letter the next day (2 January 1946) to John Rickman, his collaborator at Northfield and his analyst from 1938 to 1939.

According to his own account he began, he says, by asking who would like to form a 'guinea pig group', when they would meet, and what fee should be paid the Clinic. He then paused and noted everyone seemed a bit 'sheepish'. He was asked how groups generally behaved, and replied, 'Just like this.' There followed another awkward pause, and further questions which received a response of 'non-committal grunts', after which, he says:

> The group hunted round a bit and then Dr Stein took the floor to explain, since I wouldn't, what he thought Dr Bion wanted. The group fell on this with gratitude and Dr Stein took over the group. Then they petered out again. Then the topic of Dr Bion cropped up, but without much assistance from Dr Bion. (Bion, cited in Vonofakos & Hinshelwood, 2012, p. 89).

At this point, he humorously observes, 'a certain amount of heat began to be generated'; and he begins to interpret the angry atmosphere:

> I then intervened to point out that they were angry with me because it was becoming clear that when I had said 'group therapy' I meant 'group' therapy and not therapy by Dr Bion. I said that when I hadn't taken the lead they had first fallen back on themselves and had then squeezed Dr Stein into the job since I wouldn't. (*ibid.*, p. 89)

From then on, he says, 'marked hostility and anxiety' became manifest, stirred by another member who seemed selected by the group to represent 'a spy from the enemy's camp'.

Bion's ironic descriptions are characteristic. They raise the issue of how Bion tried to get people to learn; and in consequence how we might get people to learn Bion. The two processes are interestingly intermingled.

Topics and tensions

The group 'hunted around a bit', he says, as if they are as helpless as animals. And indeed he thought that human beings are as helpless as animals – he later refers to people as group animals in his papers on groups (Bion, 1961a). In fact he says 'The human individual is a group animal at war, both with the group and with those aspects of his personality that constitute his "groupishness" ' (Bion, 1952, p. 238). He was very alert to the way human performance falls off in groups – the reality principle is corrupted so that time and thought recede, and become replaced by the blind attitudes of the 'basic assumptions'. The capacity for learning is very restricted in groups, and Bion had a wealth of experience from the reaction of groups of men under the tension of war or invalided home. It is therefore of interest that he thought people should make decisions as groups – i.e. group decisions. For instance, one of his recommendations for officer selection in which he worked for some of the Second World War, was that men in a unit should put forward their selection of who should be considered for officer rank. It was a recommendation the army was not ready for.

So we see Bion in his group at the Tavistock proceeding in a particular way. He introduced a topic and left it to the group to discuss and make some decision – a response the group declined. Instead, faced with the demand on them as a group, the tension increased, and the people became 'sheepish' with an eventual response aimed at reducing the tension rather than addressing the topic. Moreover he drew the group members' attention to it, by indicating, when asked, that groups behave just like this. Whilst there is a wry, almost Pinteresque, quality about such an interaction, there is also a core of meaning that is important. He is saying something like: 'If you want an answer, look to yourselves.' This is clear, I think, from the sequence I extracted above, when he began to deal with leadership and the demands on him to provide it. People as group members lose there capacity to have their own authority, and they fall on anyone who might show authority instead of themselves – the poor Dr Stein in that case.

Group thinking

His teaching style did not get any better over the years. In fact perhaps he refined his 'non-committal grunting'. In one of his Brazilian lectures of 1973–1974, he started by picking up his coffee cup and saying:

> What is the interpretation of this cup that I am holding in my hand? My interpretation could be classified on the Grid as E1, that is to say, an interpretation in sophisticated form.

I could call it an element in a sentential calculus. There are, I am sure, many other interpretations which would probably be better placed in some other Grid category (Bion, 1975a, Vol. 1, p. 57).

He then waited for responses and questions. If this introduction is more than a grunt, it is hardly less non-committal. His 'lectures' by this time were turning into question and answer sessions. Many of his answers were as gnomic and opaque as the quote just given. It is a startling technique and bears traces of the same group method back in 1946. What is Bion hoping to achieve?

Teachers as listeners

What his aphoristic style has always suggested to me is that he sought to get the reader or audience to do their own work, to fill in the missing steps in Bion's arguments; indeed to fill in the conclusions that tantalisingly he seems to leave unexplicated. On the face of it this is not a bad technique. It may even be Socratic, in the sense that it gets the audience to supply the answers. It would therefore be a time-honoured method of teaching; however, it has always struck me that Bion's method was self-defeating because of the work he tried to make it do. In a group, learning is particularly difficult, and this is not helped by racking up the tension. One can in fact rely on the fact that by retreating from being the reassuring and knowledgeable leader of a group, you make the group more anxious and less competent at retrieving its thinking capacities. In other words, the more he wanted his audience to think and learn the more anxious they got and the greater the risk of degenerating into the basic assumption mentality. As I tried to convey when I reviewed the *Brazilian Lectures* (Bion, 1975a), Bion's intentions may not have been realised:

One can only feel for his discomfort. Viewed from this vertex (I suppose the vertex is the one of group dynamics) these lectures are not very successful. The two vertices within the group – Bion holding a scientific humility towards discovering communicable and objectifiable truth, his audience approaching from a religious vertex – were not properly displayed. He may have felt he did not have licence to be explicit about these dynamics within the lectures. (Hinshelwood, 1992, p. 125).

What I am proposing here is that Bion was trying to establish in his audience an attitude of measured enquiry. His uncompromising refusal to be explicatory, and his somewhat tangential allusive style – as with the coffee-cup – may have had the opposite effect from the one intended. Instead of being obscure himself in order to get people to think for themselves, he may have raised the tension so much that his audience became sheepish and entered that sheep-like follow-my-leader mode of the basic assumptions, which put Bion onto his guru-like pedestal. In other words, the more he invited people to think and enquire, the more he set himself up as a sort of guru who embodied all the knowledge.

This of course is a speculative hypothesis on my part, and is not offered with a quality of certainty, though I might say that in response to the published review, I received a personal letter of appreciation from Brazil, from an analyst who had been present at the lectures. However, this is not the important point. The important observation is that intended or not, Bion has achieved a status at the forefront of psychoanalytic innovators. Even beyond.

Fashion and substance

There is a Bion bandwagon booming in America and the publishing world right now. Unfortunately this urge to promote Bion's ideas threatens to inflate them out of proportion. Or, another apocryphal tale, Bion is credited with saying that an idea can achieve such wide currency that it becomes a coin worn so thin it no longer has value. It is important that this should not occur, and yet, can one stop it?

How Bion is appropriated by us, and by the next generation of trainees and analysts, and beyond, is a matter of how to teach Bion's ideas. I was, at one point some time ago, asked to teach Bion to a group of trainees in group therapy. I decided an authentic approach would be to adopt a policy of non-committal grunting, as it were. The group were trainees with some considerable experience by then of the work they had chosen, and they had had the opportunity to read texts for my seminars. So they were knowledgeable themselves, and the question I had to face was to what extent was I able to contribute to their greater knowledge. It was the choice I happen to think that Bion tried to work through. The more a seminar leader plays the game of knowledgeable leader, the more he takes from the mentality of the group members. Of course not playing that game, as we have seen, has its consequences too. One was to raise the level of tension. The tension I found myself most occupied with was my own – arising I believe from my refusing to play the game expected. I don't know how Bion coped with his own tension in this respect, but I found it difficult, and lapsed from time to time. Part of my tension was to be uncertain about whether I had the licence to interpret the need for a leader who would supply knowledge. Indeed it would entail interpreting a group projection into me as the source of all relevant knowledge. Or if I did not have a licence to interpret in a teaching seminar, then what should I do with their pushing me up onto my own pedestal? I don't think I have the answer to that.

From the foregoing it is worth recognising that there are two approaches to understanding Bion and teaching his ideas – approaches that are based on two alternative attitudes: either (a) Bion is the greatest thing since sliced bread, or (b) Bion made a major contribution to certain issues current in his period of mid-twentieth century psychoanalysis which can be critiqued from the vantage point of hindsight. Clearly, the latter, the critiquing option is one that this writer supports. There is nothing disrespectful about critiquing ideas, setting them in their context, and subjecting them to the rough-and-tumble of clinical usage and debate. The only problem with critiquing is that it leaves us with uncertainty. And when faced with patients in intolerable conflicts, in states of shattered identity, the one thing we need is to feel we have something absolutely certain to offer in the face of suffering. So there is no problem in seeing the attraction of having a guru – i.e. choice (a).

Teaching Bion is therefore a conflicted activity. But it is no more difficult than teaching any other set of ideas in a tension-fraught profession. Or, is it really the same as other sets of ideas?

Teaching intuition

There may be something about Bion's message that is especially difficult to teach. Bion, perhaps like no-one else is insistent on relinquishing our secure dependence on having ideas which we comfortably accept as certainly true. If Bion insists on uncertainty, and on the importance of enquiry instead, he insists we adopt not just an enquiry, but something else. He adopted a view that we should only rely on some sort of alternative – an evolving intuition. This became apparent in 1967 with his brief paper on memory and desire (Bion, 1967a), and his extended seminars (Aguayo & Malin, 2013).

In effect we teach not just K (a relationship of knowledge) but we are supposed to teach a non-knowing, called variously 'negative capability', 'reverie', 'abandoning memory and desire', 'intuition', etc. – some sort of inspirational direct knowledge of the object of study. Learning from a teacher is inherently different from allowing oneself to become a parent to evolving intuitions. These are two different things, and in Bion's own teaching they appear to be not just different but actually in opposition to each other. Consider this from one of his seminal texts, that makes an explicit distinction

> ... between two different phenomena which are both usually and indifferently called 'memory'. This I have tried to do by speaking of one as 'evolution', by which I mean the experience where some idea or pictorial impression floats into the mind unbidden and as a whole. From this I wish to distinguish ideas which present themselves in response to a deliberate and conscious attempt at recall; for this last I reserve the term 'memory'. 'Memory' I keep for experience related predominantly to sensuous impressions; 'evolution' I regard as based on experience which has no sensuous background (Bion 1967a, p. 279).

The evidence of Bion's teaching style is that he did indeed think his teaching was a kind of campaign against taught knowledge. Taught knowledge for Bion is already restricted in the Kantian sense by the processes of perception and thought. Bion was after the access that intuition could give to the thing-in-itself – in the case of psychoanalysis, that is a knowledge of the mind of a patient, or the mind of another analyst he is trying to communicate with. In fact any taught knowledge is an actual obstruction to the real knowledge that the psychoanalyst needs.

It appears very likely that Bion was influenced very early on, in fact when at Oxford immediately after the First World War, by reading Henri Bergson, a now neglected philosopher (Torres, 2013). Bergson countered Kantian pessimism about knowing only that which the sense impressions tell us, by stressing a method based on intuition by which we can go through directly to the thing-in-itself. In Bion's mathematics-like notation, Kantian knowledge is 'K', and the direct knowledge of things is 'O'. Whether that philosophical distinction is actually an influence in the background to Bion's own emphasis on intuition late in his life, he never divulged. Even if Bion was purveying a form of direct knowledge, 'O', into the mind of others it is not straightforward. And whatever the need in a difficult stressful practice like psychoanalysis, to have a safety-net of certain knowledge, Bion's 'O' is not easily attained. Though he may seem to offer direct knowledge, it is paradoxically found in eschewing all previous knowledge, and does not offer that in any form. At the same time, whilst requiring us to put aside established knowledge memory and desire, Bion's work seems to be adopted as profound and certain knowledge, handed down from the one who knows. Writing about Bion in that vein is antipathetic to Bion, yet it is sympathetic to clinicians who need a good theory to give them confidence (i.e. most of us probably).

I don't know the answer to Bion's astringent and austere programme of training, or self-training which he delivered in manifesto form in his 1967 paper on memory and desire. I wish to turn to a different concern. It does not dismiss Bion's paradox as unreal or unnecessary, but it attempts to put it in the context of Bion himself.

Catastrophe and knowledge

Bion's message appears to be that we should face uncertainty unflinchingly in our work, and to allow the evolution of mystery and dream, in order to allow to emerge/evolve an intuition from deeply inside him? Or, to put it differently, was Bion in some particular way in touch with the human state of being uncertain? I think we could say that Bion was assaulted by uncertainty, of an extremely intense kind. His First World War experience introduced him to the real uncertainty about life and death.

As Meg Harris Williams starts her review of *The Long Weekend*, his self-contemptuous first step in his late writings: 'Wilfred Bion's *The Long Weekend* is a fascinating account of one man's failure to become an individual, to achieve integrity, to make emotional contact with his internal objects' (Williams, 1983b, p. 69). The book details Bion's character up to the end of the First World War. He faced an uphill climb thereafter to gather himself into some presentable form, as a person. It is fairly clear that he constantly returned to his war experience again and again, just as a sufferer of post-traumatic stress disorder suffers repeated flashbacks of horror. For instance, the description of Sweeting's death is repeated in various texts as Roper (2012) carefully dissected: first in his diary of 1917 dedicated to his parents, and then in three subsequent autobiographical accounts, the *War Memoirs* (Bion, 1997), *The Long Weekend* (Bion, 1982), and *A Memoir of the Future* (1991). Perhaps the question should be whether he did manage to work through some of this experience, and how it influenced the development of his ideas which somehow we have to teach. His erratic and apparently disparate sources of his ideas do not make Bion easy to teach.

I should like to briefly sketch out a response to these questions. Bion's career took off in the early 1940s when his relationship with his previous analyst John Rickman changed, because their war time service put an immediate end to the therapeutic psychoanalysis, so that thereafter their relationship became one of colleagues in the army (Vonofakos & Hinshelwood, 2012). There they discussed and experimented with the social systems of army psychiatry (notably, officer selection, and also life on an in-patient rehabilitation ward). This appears to have been a mentoring relationship which transformed Bion into an original thinker and gifted writer. However, Rickman died aged 60 in 1951. At this point Bion was in good enough order to forge a career. He married in that year, and was about to qualify as a psychoanalyst and finish his second analysis, with Melanie Klein.

Peace after catastrophe?

The twenty years in the doldrums after his tank war was over, and he began his work with schizophrenic patients, in the Kleinian tradition. He was not contented with a conventional career, but was endlessly restless. He moved towards the problem of the endlessly diverging schools of psychoanalysis in the 1950s and 1960s. That problem took him towards a concern with what sort of knowledge is psychoanalysis. This involved a study of the history of science and then mathematics, looking for a way of understanding how knowledge of any kind comes about; and then of how it is disseminated. He explored mathematical notation which had systematised scientific thinking, and then moved to the abstruse mathematics of transformations. He was conceptually nomadic (Hinshelwood, 2013), and eventually gave up on that problem, turning to consider psychoanalysis as a systematic application, not of empirical knowledge leading to discovery, but an inspirational activity based on intuition leading to direct insight, more akin to literary creativity. His move as it is called from 'transformations in K' to 'transformations in O'. This is a sonorous phrase which does not always carry with it the profundity that it appears at first sight to proclaim.

In this journey, there is a disconcerting sequence of newly acquired and relatively quickly discarded sets of ideas. Towards the end of his life his paper 'Caesura' (1977b), following Freud's use of the term, seems to be a sad comment that looks back on his own career punctuated by the series of sparks of hope about making sense of his problems.

It is of course true that many thinkers change and develop their ideas, especially if they go on being creative after the age of 60 or so. Freud for one completed a solid coherent metapsychology by 1916, and wrote out his *Introductory Lectures*. But of course within four years he had also restlessly found too many holes in his conceptual edifice, proceeding during the 1920s to change his fundamental theory of instincts, the mental structure, and anxiety. However Freud locates his readers carefully within the steps of his journey. Bion is not so cautious with his readers and audiences. Bion's transformations from one set of ideas to another tends to be effected as if the processing is self-evident. Or more to the point, it is not just the ideas that change but the method changes – from conscious thought and recall to an intuitive evolving of thought.

It could be said therefore that in consequence there is no continuity to teach. There may be many starts and few completions. The kaleidoscope of ideas is but a wanton inspirational variability. So teaching such a variegated species of approaches has serious problems. It is not easy for teachers to grasp, and often it leads to emphasis being placed on one or other of the conceptual phases according to the proclivities and fascinations of a teacher. There are a number of 'Bions' to be taught, but each is a partial one.

Conclusions

Whilst one can make a link with his catastrophically fragmenting war experience, leading to his own inner problems of getting different aspects of himself to communicate with each other, this is not a helpful explanation for teachers who have to bridge the wide differences between numerous disciplines from where Bion fetched his ideas. It is not possible to follow him through his familiarity with history, holistic medicine, social science, experimental psychoanalytic treatments of psychotics, the epistemology of science, the theory of mathematical notation and transformations, and the 'scientific' application of aesthetic intuition. Bion was a polymath. We who have to teach him are mostly not. Moreover Bion is impenitent, and espoused that inspirational cacophony of voices.

One can easily get the impression that he was never satisfied with the theories he produced. The brilliance of expression he had successfully cultivated, in the end lacked a feeling that he had succeeded in bring all the diverse aspects of psychoanalytic ideas, and diverse schools of psychoanalysis together. If this was an externalisation of his inner trauma which never got completely put right, it seems interesting and significant that the last paper he wrote was called 'Making the best of a bad job' (Bion, 1979). Actually, given the experiences he had suffered he did not do all that bad a job. However as teachers of the ideas of this complex and restless polymath, perhaps we too have to make the best of a bad job as we interpret him.

Unhelpfully, this chapter gives no useful dos and don'ts about how to teach Bion. One can only say, let your class discussions evolve. And in the tension of following that advice, be aware you may be suffering the distant echoes of going into a tank battle in World War 1.

CHAPTER TWELVE

Teaching Bion in Russia

Robert Harris

My first experience of teaching in Russia is on a chilly afternoon in a rather run-down clinic in the industrial suburbs of St Petersburg. I'm giving a lecture on Bion's theories of psychosis for about 30 students who are on a diploma course in group analysis and I focus mainly on the paper 'Differentiation of the psychotic from the non-psychotic personalities' (Bion, 1957).

I'm used to teaching in the UK where I feel lucky if the students have read anything, let alone struggled to understand it, and being unsure of the accessibility of Bion's work in Russia I try to keep things as simple as possible. Katya, the interpreter, follows fluently, never needing to stop to search for a suitable word. We reach the end of my talk, and I ask for questions. The first one is 'Can you please explain to us the construction and intrapsychic function of bizarre objects?'

This Diploma Course in Group Analysis in St Petersburg, Russian Republic, ran for five years of five block weekends a year. Students came to the course from all over Russia, from Siberia in the East to Elista in the South. My work on the course included teaching, clinical supervision of students' 'training' groups' and participating in large and median groups. This experience was followed by a short lecture tour to Kalmykia in southern Russia, and then teaching on a year-long course in clinical supervision for the graduates of the Diploma Course and other professional psychotherapists who were interested in learning how to 'use the group as the medium of supervision'. This course includes three block weekends and weekly Skype 'supervision of supervision' groups. In addition, I run a separate ongoing weekly clinical supervision group on Skype for Russian psychotherapists.

The Russian context

At the end of Diploma Course party, in a beautifully ornate St Petersburg building, a young man who had just been awarded his diploma said to me: 'You know, it is really great to have such a positive feeling about groups again. We haven't had such a good experience with groups in Russia … they get, you could say, a bad press.' It goes almost without saying that Bion's *Experiences in Groups* (1961) has deep resonances with many Russian students. They can quite easily identify dependency, fight–flight, and pairing basic assumption groups, especially the dependency modality. On one occasion when I was in St Petersburg, there had recently been widely internationally circulated pictures of President Putin stripped to the waist on horseback looking like a gay medieval Russian warrior, and this was referred to with amusement by the students as a good example of basic assumption dependency with added fight–flight. This was many months before the conflict with Ukraine broke out, proving unfortunately somewhat prescient.

During the short lecture tour to Kalmykia, I spoke about Hopper's 'fourth basic assumption' of aggregation/massification (Hopper, 2009) and the way in which this tends to follow a massive failure of basic assumption dependency on a societal level. This resonated with the audience, reminding me of Richard Crossman's book *The God that Failed*. The failure and death of Uncle Joe and the communist god. Russian students seem to pick up very quickly on psychoanalytic concepts; some of this is a result of excellent educational practice and an endemic cultural emphasis on education, learning and literature, and partly I think this is due to very recent massive social trauma where overt paranoid madness was very close to the surface and actively enacted. There is a thirst to understand and make sense of these disasters.

In my seminar groups there are students who are related to dispossessed pre-revolution élites, some who have family connections to ethnic groups that were forcibly migrated and others with KGB connections. That we can come together and study mental processes and psychotic states of mind sometimes strikes me as remarkable. I remember one seminar that was about the projection and the projective identification of states of mind and the 'sense of imprisonment that is intensified by the menacing presence of the expelled fragments ... unable to escape from it because he feels he lacks the apparatus of awareness of reality, which is both the key to escape and the freedom itself to which he would escape' (Bion, 1956, p. 39), and feeling what it must have been like to live through the final days of Stalin's life through the paranoia of the days of the 'Doctor's Plot'. What is reality, and who could escape? 'Wisdom or oblivion – take your choice. From that warfare there is no release' (Bion, 1991).

A very pleasant feature of teaching in Russia is the Russian sense of humour. This is very similar in nature to the British – seeing the absurdity of life, rather self-deprecatory and ironic, intelligent and somewhat poetic whilst remaining polite and relatively inoffensive. They love double meanings, proverbs and aphorisms. Nothing gets the notepads out quicker during a seminar than if I use a term like 'It never rains but it pours', or 'The road to Hell is paved with good intentions', or 'He was feeling under the weather' – this was a particular favourite. The students quickly chip in with 'Oh we have a saying like that, we say ...' and then will come up with a Russian version. I think the students appreciate the humour, sometimes well hidden, in Bion's writing – the sense of surprise and absurdities in Bion's clinical observations. During one seminar on the nature and clinical use of projective identification, something that Bion refers to frequently in his writing, a student jumped up and shouted with glee 'Yes, how strange all this is ... it is like magic – it works but you cannot see it!'

The Russian language is wonderfully expressive; intonation, and even volume, is used much more than in is usual in English. This has actually caused problems internationally, in the past – when you say 'niet', for instance, you may say it as if you really mean it. This can give the impression of aggression, or be misinterpreted in other ways.

I spent several happy hours with my translator and friend, Baatr Mandzhiev, finding out stories and figures of speech that would help to illustrate my talk and refining translation so that we had as accurate interpretation as possible. Here is Baatr's account of the experience:

> I refreshed my knowledge of Freud's concepts of superego and the unconscious. There were more names and concepts to mention that I came across with in my preparations: the views of W. R. Bion, especially.
>
> At brief consulting meetings with the lecturer, Bob Harris, I learnt some interesting terms and concepts of psychoanalysis. When we spoke about 'mirroring' we happened to discuss the concept of 'hall of mirrors' and its possible translation into Russian language and idiom.It was interesting to note that in the Russian contextualisation, there could be more than one translation for the phrase. In Russian we have such equivalents as 'room of laughter', 'horror room' or 'fear room'. We used to have fairground attractions with these names back in Soviet times. Some may probably disagree about the correct translation of this concept, but that is another interesting subject for discussion.
>
> We also found similar fairy tales in our different cultures, in which the mirror has a significant role for developing a plot. For example 'Dead Princess and Seven Warriors' by Alexander Pushkin, and 'Snow White and the Seven Dwarfs' by the Grimm brothers both mention a beautiful narcissistic witch with a magic mirror, which she used to convince herself that she was the one and the only most beautiful woman in the world.
>
> To my mind, the cultural similarities should be carefully taken into consideration in the process of accumulating background information for translation and interpretation

purposes. All this led me once again to the conclusion that when translating psychoanalytical concepts from English into Russian, the cultural, ethnic and folklore elements should be taken into account to make a better cultural and understandable contextualisation and to perform a good quality of translation and interpretation.

History, difference, and underlying dynamics

Teaching in Russia, of course, we are aware of their recent history, especially the years of Soviet communism with all the conflicting attitudes to the West that this entails. Also important to remember is that the Soviet Union was composed of many different ethnic groups, many of whom have been incorporated into the modern Russian state but who actually feel quite a different sense of identity from Russians. Baatr, for instance, is Kalmyk; although Kalmykia is now a part of Russia, it has a separate legislature and is the only Buddhist state in Europe. There are quite strong feelings underlying some of these differences, especially as in the fairly recent past there were deportations and real conflict between different ethnic groups. As a rough comparison, it is something like the relationship between England and Scotland; try calling a Scot 'English'.

Intelligent, well educated, very keen to learn; this is my overriding experience of teaching students about Bion in Russia. I have come to feel that culture, and especially expectations and attitudes that arise out of traumatic and complex historical contexts are important to understand and recognise, but actually are thinner and more skin-deep than you might expect. Our mutual fears and paranoias are largely just that – humans are fundamentally very much the same.

Bion developed his thoughts and ideas through his experience of personal and collective trauma in the context of the First World War, and Russians, I think, resonate deeply to this at both conscious and unconscious levels. The ultimate freedom of thought that Bion's thinking offers, including the freedom to dream and let the mind wander – and a certain wildness – is very close to the Russian heart.

CHAPTER THIRTEEN

Bion's adventures in a country without psychoanalysis[1]

Igor Romanov

A t the time of writing this article in Ukraine we have seven IPA analysts and about fifteen candidates. Our society has just started negotiations with the IPA to organise a study group. There is virtually no institutionalised psychoanalysis in our country, and there is an almost boundless theoretical pluralism in the contemporary psychoanalysis that we are just starting to study. Interest in Bion falls between the poles of 'One psychoanalysis or many?' and 'Many psychoanalyses or none?' to adopt Wallerstein's (1988) formulation.

Let me begin by stating that I don't claim to be either an ardent follower of Bion, or even a serious expert on his works, though I have written some articles (possibly the first in Russian) and edited several translations of his works as well as those of some authors who refer to him (Romanov, 2002; 2006; 2009; Hinshelwood, 2007). I can't say that I have a clear grasp of all his ideas, or feel I can unconditionally accept those I understand. But like others I consider Bion to be an outstanding theorist and

---

1 Translated by A. Tiliga

even more, a thinker, who undertook a deep reconsideration of the epistemic foundations of psychoanalytic teaching.

My personal introduction to Bion's ideas was in the late 1990s during a group analytical training. I had already majored in psychology and was writing a thesis on philosophy and starting my practice as a consultant and psychotherapist. In addition to Bion's studies on groups, the concepts of container–contained, alpha-function and beta-elements, and the K-link stirred my attention. Then there was a long and rather peculiar period of psychoanalytic training (a shuttle analysis and rather eclectic theoretical instruction), where Bion's ideas would occasionally emerge in lectures and discussions. Fortunately, a group of my colleagues and I had an opportunity at that time to study contemporary Kleinian theory and technique on a systematic basis, through a series of seminars with British analysts. These were organised with the help of the Melanie Klein Trust and have been running for over ten years; and Bion's ideas were integral in building a bridge between Melanie Klein's works and the fascinating clinical thinking of Betty Joseph, Edna O'Shaughnessy or Ron Britton. I think that Patricia Daniel was keenly aware of our desire to build bridges between classical and contemporary psychoanalysis when she said, 'You feel a lack of solid theoretical background' – and that hit the target. Robert Hinshelwood had the same clear understanding of this need when he came to give a one-week seminar and allowed publication in Russian of his *Dictionary of Kleinian Thought* in 2007, then *Clinical Klein* (in preparation). Other teachers followed, such as Edith Hargreaves, Jane Milton and others (see Garvey, 2010), continuing this 'indicative' welding of theory and practice (Hinshelwood, 1994, pp. 2–3).

Context

As for my own understanding of Bion's fundamental contribution to psychoanalysis, I would like to mention two features that seem directly linked to this issue of finding professional identity in a pluralistic context. These are his descriptions of the 'unthinkable' (which entails a distinction between thoughts and the apparatus for thinking), and of intuition, in psychoanalytic experience.

From his early works on psychoses, through the theory of container–contained and late epistemic essays, Bion focuses on the capacities and even more so on the faults in thought development and destructive attacks on it. Thinking goes beyond Freud's 'consciousness' and its elementary forms cover such phenomena as dreams, phantasies, pre-conceptions – a theme effectively developed by Donald Meltzer in his *Dream Life* (Meltzer, 1983). In locating thinking originally in the communication between baby and mother (and then, between patient and analyst) there is no doubt that Bion follows Klein, who not only introduced and consolidated the object-oriented perspective in psychoanalysis, but also described the capacity of human mind to divide and split itself and to spread itself through projective identification in an interpersonal space. The latter is already described by Klein as a form of communication (Klein, 1946, pp. 7–8). Bion expands on the input of the other party in this – of the mother, analyst, social environment, etc. – through the containment, dreaming, and alpha-function that are essential determinants in the development of one's 'own mind'.

Meanwhile the 'unthinkable' is something more than the Freudian unconscious and, as Robert Caper remarks, should not be confused with the trivial 'oh, it's unthinkable!' (Caper, 1999, pp. 128–129). Rather it refers to interference or destruction of our capacity to think, speak or dream, resulting in delusion, hallucinations, confusion. Bion used the term 'beta-elements' sometimes to refer to the unthinkable, sometimes to the Kantian term 'the-thing-in-itself'. I agree with those who think Bion's usage is rather inaccurate and contradictory, especially from the viewpoint of contemporary philosophy and psychology (Noel-Smith, 2013; Wisdom, 1981; 1987). But both uses of the 'unthinkable' are only hints at experiences which may be completely different according to individual situations. For example one of my patients 'experienced' an unrequited love as a meeting with a sorcerer, physically present in her head ever since; others experience the recurring nightmares of war trauma (as in Freud's description of dream breakdown). The unthinkable is 'deeper' than the unconscious, and only working-through, or thinking, may result in the formation of a contact-barrier between unconscious and conscious, dream and reality. At the same time it relates to sensuously perceptible forms of psychic pain.

This leads to the second feature I would like to highlight: the nature of intuition in psychoanalytic experience. One of the prevailing themes in his works is the issue of 'psychoanalytic objects': how can we understand such a thing as anxiety, or other states of internal reality that have no colour, smell or form? Bion's efforts to investigate intuition – which includes listening without memory or desire, negative capability, etc. – took many forms, from his famous Grid to fiction and some rather provocative seminars in his later years. How can this capacity be developed in psychoanalytical training? How can it be conveyed between one analyst to another, so that there is a dialogue and scientific discourse about something that is felt by everyone?

Digressing a bit, I would like to say that I do not find all Bion's reasoning accurate from a philosophical perspective. Some of his suggestions sound like a repetition of late 19th and early 20th century discussions between Dilthey, the neoKantians and other thinkers regarding the nature of 'human sciences' and the question of whether we depend on *a priori* categories for our spiritual perceptions or on some other cognitive capacities (like 'empathy' in early Dilthey [1983]). From today's point of view we might doubt the statement that anxiety is *really* devoid of colour or smell, as Bion expressed it. I rather share the view expressed by Sartre: 'Tintoretto did not choose this yellow rift in the sky above Golgotha to signify anguish or provoke it. It is anguish and yellow sky at the same time' (Sartre, 1949, p. 9). Similar ideas were expressed by Adrian Stokes in his works about art having its roots in primitive layers of mental life (eg Stokes, 1965). I also doubt the statement that a special capacity to perceive internal reality can be developed owing to a reduction or restriction in our capacity to perceive external reality. It sounds like suggesting we go deaf to hear better. It stimulates a wide spectrum of different readings. For example a number of analysts viewed Bion's famous dictum 'without memory and desire' as a denial of countertransference importance (eg Rosenfeld, 1981, pp. 177–178; Kernberg, 1992, p. 89). Irma Brenman Pick on the other hand sees it as a turning point in rediscovering the importance of countertransference (see the interview in the film *Encounters through Generations*). Others point out the difference between countertransference based on memory and desire, and countertransference based on mental 'evolution'.

Throughout his career Bion was concerned with the dual problem of grasping inner experience and communicating it to others. For a long time he believed abstract or unsaturated terms were the most appropriate for a universal language of psychoanalysis, then he seemed to become disappointed by this approach (Meltzer [1978] expressed his scepticism about it in his review of Bion's *Transformations*). Nonetheless I think that further developments in psychoanalysis have to some extent proven wrong Bion's pessimism about his own efforts. At present-day international conferences we hear Bion's language used in the presentations of Kleinian analysts and intersubjectivists, representatives of the French school, Latin American analysts, etc., and we can say that Bion's conceptions and pre-conceptions are indeed filled with different content. Bion admirably succeeds in focussing on the problem even if we may feel he has not found a final accurate formulation for it. I think that there can be many interpretations, but I hope that I have managed to express my main idea: in today's pluralistic psychoanalytic world Bion's ideas contribute to *communication* about psychic reality, though they are not necessarily a ground for *consensus*.

Teaching settings

Based on this brief account of the topics that are most important for me in Bion's works, I would like now to turn to the problems of studying and teaching Bion. In this, I believe that context is crucial; though this to some extent seems to contradict the great analyst's intent: when reading these texts you have a feeling that the author wanted his ideas to be seen rather like Athena being born from the head of Zeus. In one of the interviews with Hanna Segal she bitterly remarked this peculiar feature of Bion's not to give any references to his predecessors or colleagues

(Quinodoz, 2008, p.45). Bion's attitude in a way resembles the story about Descartes who replied to the question about his manuals by pointing at a dissecting table. Both thinkers suggest relying primarily on 'experience' – though their understanding of experience differs. Nevertheless my method of reading Bion is rather opposite: it is not an intuitive perception of his ideas 'without memory or desire', and not even their systematisation. It is contextualisation.

I use Bion's works in different teaching settings: in our Kleinian seminars, where we try to understand Bion's influence on the contemporary Kleinian tradition, and in courses on psychoanalytic theory for university students in the faculties of Psychology and Philosophy.

In the first setting, we have discussed Bion's texts, as well as works by Money-Kyrle ('Cognitive development', 1968), Segal ('On symbolism', 1978), O'Shaughnessy ('Bion's theory of thinking', 1981), Britton (1992, 1998), etc. I think that all the participants of the seminar will agree if I say that understanding the questions that Bion tried to find answers to in his works about psychosis and thinking, other approaches to solving the same problems, first responses to Bion's ideas by the analysts in his circle, and the revolutionary influence of his ideas on Kleinian thinking, significantly contributed to understanding Bionian theory, as well as to determining his impact on contemporary Kleinian theory and technique.

For example, Bion's idea that the development of a thought is connected with the capacity to cope with the absence of the object (the 'no-thing'), and the ensuing evolutionary model of psychic elements from primitive to abstract forms can be understood better in comparison with Segal's symbolism theory (symbols *vs.* 'symbolic equations') and Money-Kyrle's 'representation' theory. As a matter of fact, Bion's detailed account of this theory completes a long path of trying to understand this topic; though Segal's and Money-Kyrle's simpler and intuitive solutions have their own advantages. So, the above mentioned patient, when she was splitting up with her boyfriend, heard his playful remark, 'you can't just go away,' and she took it literally – as a fact that she had met a sorcerer with control over her mind and body and she really *could not* go away. Should this clinical phenomenon be interpreted as a symbolic equation, that suddenly emerged when she was unable to cope with the separation from the object? Should we think about malfunctions of containment that turn beta-elements into some bizarre objects that destroy the meaning (since then the sorcerer has always been present in her head in the form of some physical presence and prohibited her from speaking about him)? Thinking about the potential direction of working with the patient, is it important to pay particular attention to the development of the idiomatic language of dreams – prior to and in addition to the usual language of common sense (which is Money-Kyrle's particular focus)? I think that this range of questions and solutions considerably extends the possibility of understanding Bion's idea and its application in clinical thinking.

It is also very important to re-establish the context of general Kleinian discussions regarding the theory of projective identification and containment, ego-destructive superego, etc. It always surprises me that there are people who interpret these concepts of Bion without referring to the works of Rosenfeld, Meltzer, Segal, Jaques as well as other authors of this circle.

To turn now to university teaching, in the faculties of Psychology and Philosophy. Unfortunately, there is no opportunity here for a detailed investigation into the history of psychoanalytic thought, and there is no demand for this either. But there is an opportunity to read and discuss Bion's smaller texts in seminars, comparing them with other theories of thinking, communication, development, psychotherapy, etc, that are known to students. And again the context here is of primary importance. I noticed that philosophy students are more interested in the clinical context as this experience is almost unknown to them. The use of theoretical passages from Bion along with his clinical examples or published examples of other authors is very effective (for confidentiality reasons I feel restrained in the use of my own examples in the lecture room). Though philosophy students are free in their reports and course papers to actively investigate the link of Bion with Plato and Kant, or to compare him with Lacan, who is of course more popular in philosophical circles thanks to his rather centrifugal use of psychoanalytic knowledge in human sciences, or Badiou, or to write about Bion and Beckett, etc. The main constraint, in my opinion, is that in our philosophical environment Anglo-Saxon analytical philosophers (Russell, Wittgenstein, Peirce, Quine and others) do not enjoy a wide popularity by comparison with postmodernist French philosophy and the German philosophical tradition from Hegel and Marx to contemporary hermeneutics and social theory. It was a big discovery for me to realise the influence of the abovementioned philosophers on Bion's thinking and style of writing. So this is another context that is to be reconstructed in teaching.

The clinical context is important for psychology students too, as even if they already know the basics of psychotherapy, these are most likely to be some of its humanistic versions. However, and this is not so surprising at all, they often feel a great need to discuss certain theoretical, methodological and philosophical origins of Bion's ideas. So I tell them about Kant, Plato, Dilthey and others. And of course both groups of students are always interested in the biographical context of Bion's works (a book by Blèandonu was a helpful guidebook for me in this respect [Blèandonu, 1994]).

And finally, I do quite a lot of teaching in different psychotherapeutic and psychoanalytic groups in Ukraine, Russia, Belarus. Of course, this is a completely different type of teaching with the main emphasis on technique and clinical practice. But are they possible without theory? Moreover are they possible without what can be called a psychoanalytic way of thinking? And despite the fact that Freud didn't consider psychoanalysis to be a worldview (*Weltanschauung*), he created a comprehensive human science that gave rise to the new way of thinking about human reality, that Bion developed and continued. And this is another context in which I need to use Bion's ideas: their place in the history of psychoanalysis. I found a great help in understanding this in such works as Meltzer's *The Kleinian Development* (1978) and *Studies in Extended Metapsychology* (1986), Segal's 'Changing models of the mind' (2001), some articles by Money-Kyrle, and many of Hinshelwood's works. I think they help with grasping the extent of the revolution in psychoanalytic tradition that Wilfred Bion – I can't say brought about – but most clearly realised and expressed: a simultaneous shift to thinking and communication from the psychology of drives and the egoistic ego.

Bion's language

Thinking about Bion's place in the history of psychoanalysis, I cannot but note a peculiarity that is connected with him and my teaching of psychoanalysis. From the very first lectures and seminars in a new group I spontaneously use some of his gnomic expressions: about the analyst capable of 'thinking under fire'; about listening 'without memory or desire'; about 'the thought as a no-thing'; that the inability to 'suffer pain' results in the inability to 'suffer pleasure'; that the schizophrenic is 'neither asleep nor awake'. Only later do these memorable wordings gain sense within the context of Bion's own theories (when we finally reach them). But I am of the opinion that this peculiar rondo reflects something important in Bion's own influence. As one Bion researcher put it, Bion succeeded in carrying out a fundamental re-theorisation of psychoanalysis. Such wellknown theses as Freud's 'free-floating attention' or 'pleasure principle' sparkled with new colours and acquired new substantiation (rather as the theory of relativity provided new substantiation for classical mechanics). I believe that each such idea is bi-directional: it highlights in a new and different way something that is already wellknown in psychoanalysis, which can then, from its place in Bion's own theory, point to some completely new development of psychoanalytical thought.

There is another important factor related to language that comes into teaching Bion. Unfortunately, the existing Russian translations of Bion's works do not reproduce all the shades of his style. And is it possible to make such a translation in the first place? One of our professional translators noted that unlike Russian, it is more difficult to say something incomprehensible in English, but Bion succeeds in doing just that![2] I think this is

2   I am very grateful to translator Z. Babloyan for our mutual work and numerous discussions of Bion's language and ideas.

a very accurate observation. Bion's sharp, gnomic, intentionally paradoxical wordings especially stand out in the logically strict analytical (in the linguistic sense) English language. It's not surprising that the stylistic device of paradox is widespread in English literature. Russian is a synthetic language where many phrases can be read differently from the offset, so intentional paradoxicality is not so surprising. Another point to mention is Bion's play on the meaning of such words as suffer, contain, publication, achievement, etc., which is virtually impossible to reproduce in translation. It's fascinating to see how the verb 'to contain' is used in its regular meaning to give a more accurate description of a certain phenomenon (in his early papers up to 'On arrogance' and 'Attacks on linking'), until it is gradually transformed into the concrete term 'Learning from experience', but then it is once again polysemantic in Bion's later works. I am yet to see translations that could reconstruct this evolution, and I think it is impossible. In the same way all the existing Russian translations fail to convey the correspondence between the column names in Bion's Grid and Freud's terms from his 'Two principles of mental functioning' (1911) – one of the barriers to that is the problem of translating the term 'notation' (that precedes 'attention'). All these instances require explanation, i.e. another reference to the context, linguistic this time. That's why when students have problems understanding Bion I suggest reading original texts – it may seem strange but even with an intermediate level of English Bion is sometimes better understood without translation.

Another stylistic peculiarity of Bion's texts lies in their capacity to have a certain language impact. The failure to understand it makes Bion's texts much poorer. Speaking of an empty term, Bion creates this empty term. Speaking of no memory or desire, he tries not to have a memory or desires ('Indeed, I would not "desire"anyone to employ this approach' [Bion, 1967a, p. 20]), and thus to provoke the same state in the heads of his readers or audience. I think that this peculiarity of his style is also difficult to reproduce in translation, though this 'language of achievement' must be taken into account.

As an illustration I can refer to a few discussions from student and psychotherapy seminars of Bion's already mentioned brief paper 'Notes on memory and desire' (Bion, 1967a). Many participants note that Bion's fundamental point of listening without memory or desire can be divided into two statements: a trivial and a radical. A trivial or 'weak' (in the logical sense) version of Bion's idea virtually coincides with Freud's recommendation to listen to the patient's material with a free-floating attention which involves reliance on mostly incidental memory (in terms of psychology of memory). With this understanding of the idea, there is no need for postulating any special cognitive capacity such as 'intuition'. As Susan Isaacs wrote:

> Now this becoming aware of the deeper meaning of the patient's material is sometimes described as an intuition. I prefer to avoid this term because of its mystical connotation. It is better described as a perception … Our ability to see it [unconscious meaning] depends, as I have said, on a wealth of processes in ourselves, partly conscious and partly unconscious. But it is an objective perception of what is in the patient, and it is based upon actual data. (Isaacs, 1939, p. 149)

When Bion's statement about memory and desire is interpreted radically, in its 'strong' version (that is already outlined in this article, and is still clearer in his later works – see Aguayo, 2013), it may seem too far from psychoanalysis. A psychoanalyst may find strange the recommendations to 'switch something off' in his or her mind, in particular, when we speak about such mainly unconscious processes as desires or memory. The statement that feelings and emotions are devoid of sensuous qualities is rather arguable. The main idea seems to be a call to attain some meditative state without desires and seems to be an allusion to the *Bhagavad Gita*, that Bion liked. Its purpose may consist in opening something new, connecting with an ultimate reality – anything other than understanding the patient's mental reality and achieving therapeutically relevant results. Many of the participants in these discussions note that in this distinction there is a further divide between ardent followers of 'mystical', 'romantic' Bion, and equally avid critics of what is seen as a digression from clinical reality (O'Shaughnessy, 2005). However, if we take into account the performatory function of Bion's language, and the repeated focus of his thought on the topic of psychoanalytic experience, then the contradiction between the 'mystics' and the 'realists' significantly decreases. His apparently paradoxical statements that draw together belief and reality, mysticism and science, become more understandable.

I have already mentioned that Bion's works contribute to communication between analysts, but do not always result in consensus. It is the same in the teaching process. There will always be those who like Bion for his vagueness, the open space of interpreting him in line with one's own favourite prejudices. In almost all student groups we have those who insist on a deeper study of his texts and word-usage with a view to stressing his idiosyncrasy. But I think that Bion's most grateful readers are those whose own view of psychoanalysis and psychic reality *per se* is changed by his ideas without making them 'Bionians'. It is this very effect that Bion had on Kleinian tradition, and it seems that similar processes are taking place in other analytical schools. It is often the case with regular readers of Bion's works. I think that he would welcome this effect.

In conclusion I may express a paradoxical thought. Despite all their complexity, Bion's ideas are the best introduction to psychoanalysis. At the start of my professional career I studied the psychology of school education, and at that time there was a popular idea of the Russian philosopher Vladimir Bibler that children's questions – about nature, numbers, words – are consonant with the questions asked by the most advanced scientists. And both children and scientists can have a rather productive dialogue. Recently I came across this idea again in Britton's interview (with reference to the physicist Richard Feynman): scientific education must begin not with old knowledge but with the most relevant questions of modern science (*Meeting Ron Britton*, 2012). My experience of teaching Bion is completely in accord with this idea. Simple questions asked by students: 'How can understanding help?', 'Does psychoanalysis make you happy?', 'How can you understand another person?', 'What does a psychoanalyst feel?' – they are all exactly in line with Bion's theoretical questions. There is a productive tension between ignorance and complex theory that motivates and guides our continuing journey over the seas of contemporary psychoanalysis. The results of their meeting can be very different. As of now about 80% of the participants in our Kleinian seminars have started or completed their psychoanalytic training, though this has never been a specific objective. My own seminar with psychotherapists that started many years ago as a 'seminar on Bion' has long become a 'seminar on psychoanalysis'. For university students who do not plan to become analysts, it is the works of Bion that become a bridge connecting their own professional interests with psychoanalytical thought. Psychotherapists of other schools see them as a convincing proof that this thought is alive and developing.

Maybe it was Bion's intention, but it is not surprising that his complex theories in fact contribute to discovering psychoanalysis. What is surprising for us and for Bion as well, is that there are such things as psychoanalysis, the human soul, and our capacity to sometimes understand each other.

CHAPTER FOURTEEN

On communicating the style of living analysis

Dawn Farber

Bion's 'genius' – not only in his own sense, as provocateur to the establishment – is, as is all 'genius' etymologically, the emergent spirit of his place, time and personal history. The imperative to find one's own living style is suggested in the poem by Wallace Stevens:

> The maker's rage to order words of the sea,
> Words of the fragrant portals, dimly-starred,
> And of ourselves and of our origins,
> In ghostlier demarcations, keener sounds.
> ('The idea of order at Key West', 1934)

Far from being a trivial element in thinking, the question of language and style is, for Bion, 'a matter of life or death' (Civitarese, 2013, p.15). And like Stevens' singer in his poem, Bion with his particular personal history, prodigious imagination, intelligence and truth drive (Grotstein, 2004) is the maker of the songs he sings in the contexts in which he has found himself. 'My' Bion would be the first to say: 'If my song inspires you, you must make your own song, where you find yourself.' This always includes each of our unique sensibilities.

Who are the teachers?

Teaching Bion at the turn of the twenty-first century in the San Francisco Bay Area, Northern California; a South African, British-educated cultural anthropologist and literature scholar, without a shred of academic psychology; post-graduate training as an existential psychoanalyst and as a gestalt therapist; and finally a psychoanalyst. All these strands of influence, these presences and absences, my contexts, are inalienably woven into my reading/ teaching of Bion. This is the bad job I must make the best of. As a psychoanalytic psychotherapist, I was raised in the British Middle School, by D. W. Winnicott and Marion Milner, and in the Fairbairnian object relations milieu; and via an immersion in Freud, followed by an immersion in Klein and the British Kleinians in the heyday of their embrace during my analytic training in the mid-1990s, I had my first introduction to Bion. This consisted of twelve hours of discussion of selected individual papers that have become the canon for this course. These include his early very clinical theoretical papers on schizophrenia and hallucinations; on differentiation of psychotic and non-psychotic personality; the theory of thinking, L, H and K, container-contained; memory, desire and understanding; and a brief introduction to 'O' and K–O transformations. I was intrigued, perplexed, and most interestingly, felt a 'catastrophic' sense of existential risk. I engaged Dr Elisabeth Tabak de Bianchedi as a training supervisor. Through her I learned to deeply appreciate Bion's radical meta-psychological evolutions of psychoanalysis, but my clinical 'technique' – a contradiction, in Bion's terms – remained a blend of Middle School and the British Kleinian development, including Meltzer: that is, largely a one-person psychology, though focused on the here-and-now transference process.

Close or creative reading always requires that we surrender to the text on its own terms, to language and ideas that are not our own but 'other' and in so doing, become 'affected' in both senses (influenced by, and emotionally moved/changed) by this other mind. It necessitates our allowing ourselves to become lost and disoriented – the paranoid-schizoid disintegration that we have come to think of as positively disruptive. We must surrender the closures of identity and 'knowing,' of who we believe we are and what we believe we know – the complacencies of the depressive position; and all this in the faith that we will be re-found, refreshed, enlivened by this surrender. Small wonder that Bion, with his 'sense of the Freudian plague ... that element of the sulphurous' (Civitarese, 2008, p.156) – such a far cry from the thread of optimism and self-perfectibility in North American psychology – requires ingenuity on the part of teachers, in conveying him in ways that evoke our students' creativity.

Teaching 'waking dreaming' in the San Francisco Bay Area

I have been teaching Bion here for 16 years. Recently our candidate cohorts are smaller, and at various stages of education and experience in our very vital, multi-perspectival psychoanalytic psychotherapy milieu. While some have had the customary preparation, instituted in North America since non-medically trained candidates won the legal right to psychoanalytic training in 1989, many have not. This includes several years of didactic courses as well as analytic therapy, supervision and case conferences. Also, many of those who would, by these standards, be eligible for analytic training are choosing not to train, as they have excellent opportunities to deepen their work via the affordable didactic programmes and consultation we analysts offer outside of our institutes. Many analytic therapists have graduated from academic psychology programmes in which the emphasis has been on cognitive-behavioural and/or humanistic therapies, and at most, brief dynamic treatments. They come to analytic training as refugees from the frustrations of Managed Care. Post-graduation, some have studied some Freud and American ego psychoanalysis, and perhaps a few chapters of the canon and papers by contemporary Bion-inspired analytic writers. Most have had considerable exposure to the American Relational developments. Generalising very broadly, American Relational analysts write in accessible language, with a minimum of abstract new coinages. In general, their aesthetic is more simply egalitarian and more inclined towards the real than the unconscious transference relationship; and their tone is often more reassuring, less darkly ironic, than that of Bion. No wonder then that for many, Bion, with his Edwardian public school erudition is formidable. Perhaps too, it is deeply ingrained in the American psyche with its famed pragmatism and passion for solutions to problems, that an aesthetic philosophy such as Bion's version of psychoanalysis perplexes many students beyond tolerability. Bion's claim in the introduction to *Seven Servants* (1977) that 'Even psychoanalysis is tainted with ideas of cure that imply a better state' interrogates the widespread lay assumption that psychoanalysis is one among the 'helping professions' which provide cures for socio-psychological problems. His central preoccupations are more existential: he is concerned to respond to the breadth of human representations, and he values personal truth, however painful, more highly than adaptation. I wonder too whether the ingrained North American belief in 'the pursuit of happiness' as a fundamental right also subsumes psychoanalytic therapy in its armament against 'unhappiness'. To this Bion replies: 'I think it is better to know the truth about oneself and the universe in which I exist. But I do not wish to imply that it is nicer or pleasanter.' He continues: 'Whether it is better is a matter of opinion, which each individual has to arrive at for himself: his opinion and only his.' My favourite expression of the analytic position on happiness is that of Judith in Spike Jonze's and Dave Egger's movie of Sendak's *Where the Wild Things Are*. She mutters, in a memorable aside: 'Happiness isn't always the best way to be happy.'

After several years of teaching the canon it seemed to me that while candidates had learned a new vocabulary, they had for the most part not apprehended the heart and soul of Bion's mind, which are not worn on his sleeve in these papers, but are poignantly present in his *Memoir* and in many of his *Clinical Seminars* (1994-2005). I also wondered whether I could assist them in deepening their clinical use of Bion, if we read Ogden's paper about reading Bion (2004a), in which he evokes in his case presentation two unique minds dreaming together. Ogden's minimal use of jargon interrupts the common tendency to degrade terms such as 'beta-elements,' 'alpha-function', 'containment' etc. into sound bites, to trivialise and render them meaningless, or else, sacralise them and render them mystical, rather than very practical (Tabak de Bianchedi, 2005; Grotstein, 2007). I began to experiment with different entrées into Bion.

To begin with, I decided not to teach candidates their single twelve-hour Bion course, in which the concepts need to be conveyed, but instead to teach in a variety of extra-Institute organisations and in my ongoing clinical study groups in which I feel freer to experiment. I created a year-long course for the large umbrella organisation for psychoanalytic psychotherapy in the Bay Area, in 2006–2007, called 'Transforming Bion: the Bionian Development', designed for therapists who had some foundation in Klein and Bion. One hypothesis was that I might help students 'back-up' into reading Bion, by first immersing in the creative syntheses of Bion's work made by contemporary analysts. The course comprised five sections: An introduction to the analyst's dreaming; Bion's theory of clinical transforma-tions; transformations of Bion's thinking in the work of Tustin, Bick and Mitrani; Meltzer's transformations of and by Bion; and Ogden's conversations with Bion. Participants also joined simul-taneous case consultation groups. The course was very success-ful and I subsequently offered variants of it to different groups: 'Ogden Dreams Analysis', a medley of his papers, 1999–2011; and 'A Memoir of the Future of Psychoanalysis', which includes Ferro's and Civitarese's rich hybridisation of field theory with Bion's oneiric model. These have by now been so over-exposed that I recently created an advanced Bion course, for 2014–2015: 'Bion's Quantum Theory: Implications for Clinical Practice'. To date, the classes have been relatively small, though much appreciated by the students. Although my 'backing up' hypoth-esis was disproven – few students actually return to study Bion's writings in greater depth – I finally grasped that Bion might heartily endorse my students' instincts for moving forward, for continual transplantation and creative hybridisation of his work. As he writes: 'The way that I do analysis is of no importance to anybody excepting myself, but it may give you some idea of how you do analysis, and that is important' (1978, p. 206). Grotstein (personal communication) tells a confirmative story:

'I remember when his book *Transformations* came out in the late 1960s. A Los Angeles analyst congratulated him on his book and said he looks forward to reading it. I'll never forget Bion's answer: "I don't know about that, but I certainly look forward to reading yours."' My priority now is to facilitate therapists in finding themselves, not Bion; and in using Bion as an exemplar of scrupulous self-analysis, as he describes his psychic death and ultimate recovery of dream-thinking.

Currently in the Bay Area I teach small, ongoing clinical conferences with intimate working groups, which provide optimal opportunities to develop 'becoming O'. These small groups are the venue in which I feel most able to teach Bion's most radical contribution to the paradigm shift in clinical practice, namely attention to the emergence of unconscious transference–countertransference via reverie in the here-and-now of each clinical hour, 'waking dreaming'. We are, in my lineage of analysis, multi-purpose objects and subjects for our patients: we 'hold' and 'converse' and 'act' interpretively, as well as offer verbal interpretations (Ogden, 2001, 2007). The opportunity for transformation beyond insight afforded by this particular 'non-practice' of reverie is unsurpassable. Reverie cannot be 'practised' *per se*. This is 'becoming' via the specific cues Bion has suggested: the suspension of memory, understanding, desire, which enables very potent presence in the living moment, now. As a lifelong Buddhist this non-judgmental attentional practice comes naturally to me, which in no way guarantees clinical 'success'. Ogden's account of reverie is illuminating: 'I include in the notion of reverie all of the meanderings of the psyche–soma of the analyst, including the most quotidian, unobtrusive thoughts and feelings, ruminations and daydreams, bodily sensations, and so on, which usually feel utterly unrelated to what the patient is saying and doing at the moment. Reveries are not the product of the psyche–soma of the analyst alone, but of the combined unconscious of patient and analyst.' (Ogden, 2004b, p. 862, footnote 5). In my case conferences, we read 'whatever comes to (my) mind' and this often includes poems or passages from fiction and drama; Ogden's papers; Grotstein's ever-growing, imaginative encyclopaedic oeuvre; Ferro and Civitarese. I find it irresistible to include some reading of Winnicott, for the very different aesthetic representation of some profound ideas that resonate with those of Bion, in a different register, and contrapuntally. While I usually choose papers that have most accessible clinical material, I am also aware of the epistemological naivete upon which reading case vignettes is founded: the fiction that this gives us access to 'O'. Bion is centrally concerned with the analyst's imagination and way of observing and intuiting because we cannot know the mind of another, only the way we process the impact of real encounters with another. To this end, I treat process notes as the data of the therapist's dream, and am cautious about reifying them, as though 'the process' could be known via the presentation of (even verbatim) case notes. How can we represent the psychoanalytic encounter, which is essentially an experience of 'O'? For all of us, presenters as well as the group, the best we can do is to share how we are dreaming the presentation, which is a very intimate sharing indeed. Quite often the group can dream the undreamt dreams of the presenting therapist and her patient (Ogden, 2004b).

The loss and recovery of dream-thinking: teaching Bion and Ogden in the Cape

I have also developed a new introductory course on Bion, specifically for introducing him to students in the Cape, South Africa, entitled 'Bion's perspectives on trauma: the loss and recovery of dream-thinking'. After 33 years in exile, I finally returned to South Africa, the country of my birth, first in 2007, and again seven years later, in March 2014. For complex personal reasons, on this recent return, I combined my visit with the few remaining family members and friends with three separate events in which I taught psychoanalysis. I was invited to teach at two universities: Stellenbosch in the wine country, and Rhodes in the Eastern Cape, and to an independent group of self psychologists in Cape Town. The Stellenbosch director had trained in a psychoanalytic clinical psychology programme in Boston USA, and had founded the university's clinical training programme on her return, 30 years ago. Her Rhodes colleague had returned to South Africa six years ago, having spent six years in the psychoanalytically rich environments of Cambridge and London Universities. Both had gradually and of necessity adapted to their environments and though their curricula were quite psychoanalytic, they also blended dynamic thinking with CBT and other modalities.

Teaching Bion in South Africa to graduate students in clinical psychology proved to be both a heartwarming and heartbreaking experience. South African Universities have had a long tradition of teaching psychoanalytic psychotherapy to their clinical candidates. To my dismay, and more importantly to theirs, I was witness to the erosion of that tradition before my very eyes, as the depressingly familiar story of the systematic extinction of analytic talk therapy and its replacement by medication and CBT was being implemented. The clinical directors with whom I worked were at a loss as to how to convey their passion for psychoanalytic thinking to their students, in these circumstances, and they made it clear that I was providing for them a context, however transitory, of thinking and working for which they were ravenous, as well as some containment for their deep sense of loss.

The landscape for the practice and teaching of psychoanalysis, as conceived in our European and American Psychoanalytic Institutes, is sparse. On the initiative of the IPA, Cape Town and Johannesburg have their first study group in development, and a combined twelve-member candidate cohort currently in training, independent of the universities. There are only four analysts serving the country, two of whom are imports. As is true with most twenty-first century psychoanalytic training, and especially with post-colonial psychoanalysis, traditional models are being imaginatively adapted to work within their culture, specifically to meet the needs of community mental health. As readers may imagine, the population that could afford the frequency requirement of a traditional psychoanalysis is negligible, while the exponentially growing multitudes of desperately deprived people render community mental health projects the treatment of choice. I learned of most providers' hunger for short-term psychoanalytic treatments, which offer heart and depth, and notably, relationship to their patients, rather than the pseudo-scientific dispensing of tools, methods, and medications.

I discovered everywhere in South Africa, not just in the institutions of higher learning, an extra-professional culture with surprisingly many people dedicated to serving the community needs of its traumatised people in diverse ways. This is the residue of the Mandela–ANC epoch: there remain pockets of people, robust enough in spirit not to have been so demoralised by the current zeitgeist that they have given up. All of my friends and many family members volunteer significant amounts of time, some through NGAs, others directly in clinics and prisons, offering 'therapy' of one kind or another: teaching 'life skills' to the worst offenders in Pollsmoor Women's Prison, Cape Town; single-handedly founding and organising adoption services for HIV children; teaching theatre to township children and young adults, most of whom have no hope of employment; teaching poetry and art in the schools which are so resourceless that they barely cover basic literacy and arithmetic.

University research, clinical training and practice are oriented to providing community psycho-social interventions; and clinical supervision is correspondingly oriented towards educating students to provide care for (mostly single) mothers and infants; HIV sufferers; women in domestic abuse situations; sexual abuse and rape victims; the homeless etc. There are also many training workshops on the issues of racial and sexual identity, and ongoing racism and discrimination. The best among them insist that psychoanalysis best illuminates the complexities and challenges faced in developing effective community treatment. Their mission descriptions promote psychoanalysis as shedding light on emotional processes in groups, the political determinants of emotional responses, and the emotional dynamics of power. There is a burgeoning literature emerging from South Africa at this time, extremely energised and creative, in which community psychology practices are being conceptualised. It was from this perspective that the Stellenbosch university cohort had, prior to my visit, been given a day-long seminar on Bion, focused on his work with groups.

I chose to teach Bion as I sensed that particular areas of Bion's thinking would be directly relevant and accessible to South African clinicians, working as they do in the cultural context of escalating violence, a class war, as well as ubiquitous relational trauma, trans-generationally transmitted over the past 65 years, under apartheid, with its brutal demolition of families, and dispersal of people to serve white industrial (mining) manufacturing and service needs. Unlike Bion's experience, in which his paradigm-shifting work was written 40 years after his war experiences, the South Africans are all working in dangerous, anarchic times, post-Mandela.

My course on 'Bion's perspectives on trauma' involved reading selections from Bion's memoir, *The Long Weekend* (1982), followed by selected chapters from *Learning from Experience* (chapters 3, 4, 6–10); and Lawrence J. Brown's paper, 'Bion's discovery of alpha-function: thinking under fire in the battlefield and in the consulting room' (2012). My aim was to render Bion much more accessible, bypassing the intimidation and frustration that so many clinicians feel at first, if they are simply exposed to the academic canon. Teaching Bion in this way, I feel something akin to the joy of the archaeologist, who painstakingly researches the provenance of an entire culture, bringing to the surface the precious objects that teach us so much, dusting off the obstacles to their discovery – the earth and rocks of overused complex concepts, and of obscure ones with Greek names.

My students, born into conditions of ongoing violence, so remote from the luxury of having families at all, let alone families in which emotions could be communicated and thought about, found Bion's account of his complex trauma very close to the bone. I also chose to teach Ogden's particular interpretation of Bion. His crystalline prose, and case vignettes in which he shares his unique version of 'reverie', afford an inspiring experience of why studying Bion matters for clinicians working with complex trauma, and the ablation of people's capacity to 'think' or dream. The Ogden works I selected are: 'Reverie and interpretation' (1997), 'This art of psychoanalysis' (2004b), and 'On not being able to dream' (2003). I sent the reader three months in advance, which coincided with their summer break, in the hope that at least some students might read some of the papers before we met.

The Cape Town Self Psychology Group boasts 70 members, and they have established a training programme for a cohort of eight, all but one experienced therapists in various settings, some with private practices. The organisation hires American self psychoanalysts to conduct Skype seminars, and is happy to have visiting analysts teach them, whenever possible. They had insisted on my teaching Shame, rather than Bion, as their curriculum focuses on the self psychology and American relational literatures. These were all well-educated and experienced clinicians, and teaching them was hardly different from teaching their peers in San Francisco, except for the flagrantly violent context in which they work. Ambient violence and beta-speak were the omnipresent backdrop to my visit, and this had material implications for how my teaching of Bion and Ogden 'landed'. The airwaves were dominated by the iteration of violent scandals and technology assured that unedited gore, inciting to violence, was broadcast in shopping malls and other public spaces. The most noteworthy experience during that seminar was that minutes into the seminar, a student had to take an urgent cell phone call and leave the room. A close friend was in the ICU, having been slashed with a knife across his face the previous evening, in his restaurant filled with diners, the cut barely missing a major artery. This was understood as a warning to him from the neighborhood 'security' mafia, that he had to pay protection money to them or he would be killed. This was a commonplace occurrence, not at all newsworthy, and everyone I met was intimately affected by such events. In this context, the texts I had chosen to teach provided an oasis of sanity, safety, true thinking and containment for my students and their faculty. My students all engaged passionately in thinking via Bion's concepts about their political environment, which was a blatant persecuting presence in their personal and professional lives, to an unprecedented degree.

A fellow South African, Duncan Cartwright, has done much of his clinical work with violent men, using Bion's thinking very ably in the analysis of cultures of violence (and of some science fiction too), in which garbled pseudo-thinking or 'beta mentality' masquerades as real thinking. In a recent paper in process, Cartwright describes his work using concepts much more familiar to the 'shameniks' (mostly self psychologists who developed the literature on shame from the 1970s onwards): violence as an unmentalised explosion of rage defending against unbearable shame. This cohort connected with interest, as I introduced the concept of containment, outlining Bion's container–contained model and types of container–contained relationship. They found it useful to consider shame/rage from the perspective of the clinical 'technique' of mentalising the intense motoric-affective explosions, common in diverse 'borderline' phenomena. Discussing the anarchic social fabric which enabled such mafia to flourish, I described the current Zuma government as a perverse container, which led to passionate conversation, the passion justly being as much about their world as about Bion's ideas. They came away with a more complex conceptualisation of what it means to 'contain' a patient, than is offered in models centrally focused on empathy.

Psychoanalysis as a pocket of resistance against inhumanity

In what follows, I will refer mostly to my Rhodes experience which was of longer duration than Stellenbosch. Rhodes is situated in the Eastern Cape. It is a small enclave of thinking, in a vast, mostly unpopulated region, which is one of the most impoverished and resource-poor areas of the country. I had been asked to give a public lecture the evening before the start of the closed seminars, to psychologists in the community and academics in other departments, and I agreed to do an informal lecture with discussion. Surprisingly, 60 people showed up, and I could not have had more responsive, intellectually curious interlocutors than these clinicians and these professors in the creative writing, anthropology and political science departments. Bion speaks so directly to people in extremis. The university library happened to have a single copy of *The Long Weekend*, which had not been borrowed for decades, but now had a long line of holds placed on it. During my week-long visit, I received many thoughtful responses by email, from the audience, and have subsequently received heartfelt appreciative reviews of the *Memoir*, for the great work of literature that it is.

The twelve-member cohort had undergraduate degrees in either clinical psychology or counselling, and were in their first year of a Master's programme, which can theoretically be completed in one year, though many of them continue with the research component of their degree into their second, the internship year. Their didactic curriculum is so intense, it is difficult to imagine that such complex bodies of thought could be metabolised in the short time allotted. It is based on the work of Alessandra Lemma, with Mary Target and Peter Fonagy (2003, 2011), mentalisation being viewed as a concept that is located within psychoanalytic thinking but draws on cognitive ideas and attachment theory. The director informed me that though only one seminar is spent on Klein and object relations, unconscious processes, the transference–countertransference and object relations are very much the core of what is taught, and what is required of students' case formulations and process, in supervision. She added that the psychoanalytic therapy seminars are introductory, and that students also learn other modalities, such as narrative therapy and cognitive behavioural therapy, while also completing assessment modules, community psychology modules, and an ethics module. All this in two years?!

Most conspicuously absent in this training is the dimension of mandatory concurrent therapy that we hold indispensable in our tripartite training programmes. Very few students were currently in therapy, let alone psychoanalytic psychotherapy; and most had not been in therapy as undergraduates either. Their response to my teaching was emotional and experiential to a degree I have rarely experienced in didactic teaching: it more closely resembled group therapy. I believe this was a particular chemistry between my natural pedagogical style, which is casual, experiential and immediate, rather than linear, and the rapidly-formed group unconscious, filled with profound need for expression and containment. The clinical cirector made several attempts to rein the process in and return to a more didactic discussion of concepts. But this horse would not be corralled.

The outpouring of deeply personal responses, including accounts of their gut-wrenching personal gross trauma and how Bion's thinking illuminated it, was unprecedented. This process is very close to Bion's heart: 'I am not very interested in the theories of psychoanalysis or psychiatry or any other theories: the important point is what I call the 'real thing,' the practice of analysis, the practice of treatment, the practice of communication' (Bion, 2005a, p. 16).

Among the outcomes was that this group came together as an intimate work group, which I have since heard has significantly deepened both their subsequent learning experience and their clinical work. It was in the course of this process that I learned how few of them had been in therapy, and also that several of them realised their need for it, and were intending to obtain it through the university counselling centre.

In his remarkable essay *The Shape of a Pocket* (2001) John Berger offers a fascinating array of ideas, many of which are deeply resonant with Bionian perspectives on psychoanalysis. He writes for example – albeit in a different context, that of artistic seeing – that we have to overcome 'the existent', that which by convention appears self-evident, if we are to 'see' things in novel, fresh and transformational ways. He also shares the belief, and has always lived it, that in the face of dehumanising socio-political circumstances that could crush us, we have the option to join with like-minded others to create acts of resistance against inhumanity, which he describes as 'pockets of resistance, instigating hope'. More powerfully than ever, I experienced psychoanalysis in South Africa as one community that could potentially offer this resistance in the face of devastating and demoralising dehumanisation. Hope was palpable in our experiences of feeling and thinking together about each individual's personal trauma and about their patients, as well as about the outrageous fanning of the flames of violence throughout the country. Whether this taste of resistance through dream-thinking, and hope for maintaining communities that can resist, survives and grows, remains to be seen.

In the end, 'teaching Bion' is a necessary start, an overture, equivalent to teaching the alphabet or heralding an opera;

but quite insufficient for any personal grasp of Bion's radical re-visioning of the lifelong process of 'becoming psychoanalytic'. It is the challenge of transmitting a sensibility, one that defies imitation, but requires resonant sensibilities to interpret and transform it. I am reminded of Grotstein's (2007) dedication: 'To Wilfred Bion: my gratitude to you for allowing *Me* to become reunited with *me* – and for encouraging me to play with your ideas as well as my own.'

CHAPTER SIXTEEN

Teaching Bion through clinical example

Dorothy Hamilton

My patient Sarah sat the doll up on the spare chair. The doll was her mother: she spat hard at its head. Later she told me that as she did so, she had an image of cutting her own synapses. It was the perfect metaphor for an attack on linking. Sarah's capacity to think had been damaged in its earliest stages, and she could barely experience herself as separate from her mother, or from me. Here are some of the things she used to say:

'I don't know what you're thinking, because I'm not thinking it. I don't know what you mean till you say it.'

And as she sat with head averted, staring toward the wall: 'If I turn to you to be closer to you, I won't like you … or you won't like me … or I won't like myself.'

When I spoke of the despairing baby turning toward the wall because she could not get what she needed, she said: 'The wall doesn't give me anything.'

I spoke about the baby's need to interact, speak with, look at mother, and she said: 'I couldn't get what I needed because my mother put her face right up to me ... so I had no face. I couldn't like her face.'

And then: 'It's like I don't exist except to reflect you ... to make you feel good. That's what I had to do for my mother.'

Sarah was expressing, graphically enough, the emotions that tormented her. But she was severely handicapped in her efforts to process them, to link them up, to make them into self-knowledge. Most tellingly, she expressed the fracturing that was somatically embedded in her: 'My thoughts hurt my body. My head doesn't like my body.'

The work with Sarah was a revelation to me of what it feels like to 'know' so much, to have so many thoughts and indeed be able to 'name' them, yet to be unable to use them to *think*, and therefore be able to arrive at real knowledge. My experience was of our hovering constantly at the edge of alpha process (raising hope in the therapist), but relentlessly driven back into the obstinacy of beta. When I describe all this to my students, it is a revelation for them too. They have been introduced to Sarah as a person, and felt her reality through her relationship with me: her peculiarly frustrated mental pain is vivid to them. To hear the words of people living these states in the relationship with the seminar leader they know is so much more illuminating than the accounts in the textbooks.

All seminar leaders know this, but probably few have had the privilege, as I have, of being able to teach almost entirely through the medium of their clinical work. This has come about through teaching with Meg Harris Williams, who takes a series of fortnightly theoretical seminars presenting Bion's core ideas, while I follow in the intervening weeks, illustrating those ideas from my work. It is a combination I can recommend from my own viewpoint: that of having the luxury of engaging the students almost entirely through the lived experience of the patient, so that Bion is learned through that experience. The inevitable drawback, as in all clinical illustration, is the potential distortion: not only through the mirror of the teacher's recollection, but also through the necessary selection and adaptation of what is transmitted. This is especially true where the students are new to Bion, and, in five brief introductory seminars, must be shown some of the extraordinary wealth of new concepts he introduced, in a way that can be reasonably readily apprehended. There is a tendency to choose the more dramatic moments in the therapy that seem best to illustrate the point. One can only trust that the truthfulness of one's intention is sufficient to avoid actual 'lies'.

K link

The example I used to introduce this chapter was not chosen randomly. The drive to know, and therefore the need to think, is a theme so central to Bion's theory that it must be the driving idea of the seminars. The one text I use is Meg's paper 'Oedipus at the crossroads' (Williams, 2005b),[1] based on Sophocles' great 5th century BC dramas. This is a seminal paper for me, both in its development of Bion's key ideas and in its interest for the students. Oedipus is a good story in itself, with strong connotations in drama and history; but more than this, it is understood to be the central myth of the students' chosen profession. That this is so does not mean, however, that they are always very familiar with the wider implications of the tale, beyond its familiar sexual configurations. In my experience, the complex is cited less frequently in psychoanalytic discourse than it used to be (Bion suggests it belongs in the category of 'Freud's tomb furniture'). Meg brings the story alive again, setting its sexuality in the broader scope of the quest for knowledge, Bion's 'need' for truth.

To teach Bion is to be continually and usefully prompted to revisit Freudian and Kleinian theory. Freud's ascription of the origins of the 'epistemophilic instinct' to the Oedipal conflict, though he relegates it to part-instinct status, nevertheless reaches toward the greater significance it has gained since Bion. The students re-evaluate Freud's concepts – the primal scene, curiosity about the new sibling, exclusion from the mystery of the parental couple – in the light of Bion's K link. Likewise, we see that Klein's more developed recognition of the infant as epistemophile laid the ground for Bion's decisive move to put

---

1   Revision of 'A man of achievement: Sophocles Oedipus plays' (Williams, 1994).

Knowledge on a par with Love and Hate, using the metaphor of truth as food, an absolute necessity for mental growth.

Preparing for my first seminar, I turned to the deepest roots of Bion's ideas on thinking, the protomental life of the foetus (the experiences of 'what I later heard was 'me'), and thence to considering how far each of my patients had succeeded in moving from that early state into the realm of adult thought. I found I could construct a graph on which to plot them – which I did rapidly, with little thought, as it were 'dreaming' their places on the graph. But those places held on further reflection, and faithfully accumulated related ideas: of 'dream' and 'waking' states, of living in a primarily somatic state or having emerged to mental life. Sarah, who lived in a (fairly paranoid) dream state, trapped in an alienated body, was far to the 'unborn' side of the graph. I found it a helpful tool, a measure for presenting my patients' emotional states.

I then constructed a second graph, this time according to those patients who desired, desired less, or hated knowledge: a chart from K to –K. This was still more useful in interpreting what was happening in the work with them. I was even able to show, for those patients no longer in therapy, a correlation between their place on the graph and the outcome of their therapy. In retrospect, this may seem a fairly obvious conclusion, but it was eye-opening at the time.

In this context, Sophocles' Oedipus emerges as a veritable role model:

> I must see my origins face to face ...
> That is my blood, my nature – I will never betray it,
> Never fail to search and learn my birth. (*Oedipus Tyrannos*,
>   cited in Williams, 2005b, p. 113)

Here is a relentless desire for the truth, and an ancient one. We ponder the Eden myth, wherein Adam and Eve, if they were not to starve mentally, *had* to know. And by illuminating the discussion with reference to Jung's 'Answer to Job' (like Bion, Jung recognised that the 'human urge to knowledge asserts itself again and again ... with necessity' [Jung, 1969, p. 355]), we have now placed Bion's thinking about K in relation to the theory of the three 'parents' of psychoanalysis.

Containment

A key factor in the capacity for the K link is the experience of the original containment. Michael, another placed well to the 'unborn' side of my chart, had experienced non-containment to an exceptional degree, as we discovered when he actually regressed to the womb during a session. He relived the experience of having been pressed against his twin, and said in a frightened tone: 'my foot's gone numb'. He was acutely aware of how he had felt: crowded out, crushed (his foot) – but above all, not *entitled* to the space he took up: his twin had had the right to the space, and he had not. This profoundly affected the state of expectation with which he was born: he did not expect good containment subsequently, and did not find it. Indeed the twins' mother, unable to cope with the burden of two babies, used to feed them while she lay flat on her back, one on each breast, feeling imminently in danger of falling off. Early in Michael's therapy, he went all round the walls of the consulting room, carefully placing his palms along the wall, one touching the other, until the whole room had been encircled by touch, a solemn ritual to render the room a safe containing space.

Michael's adult body visibly expressed his inner state: head permanently lowered, body held as though he wished not to exist, since he could not believe in his entitlement to do so. The somatic elements of his womb experience were overwhelming. The symptoms were of being all in pieces, feeling dizzy, with 'part' of his head feeling bad, a sensation of rictus through his spine. He had 'stopped feeling' for fear he would have a fit, be taken seriously ill, or die – and thought: 'If I can't hold myself together, could Dorothy hold me instead?' He was far from convinced that I could. From this enactment of a dread that threatened to become nameless, with little faith that the fear of dying could be safely put into mother, Michael could only rescue himself by 'stopping feeling'.

It was Michael too who demonstrated for me the experience of a bizarre object, a rare occurrence in a consulting room where patients are not often so vulnerable to phenomena associated with extreme pathologies. Michael was not psychotic in the obvious way, but sometimes, of course, the very 'unborn' experience psychotic phenomena. He was gazing at me from his chair when I saw his expression change. It was as though I could see the blood draining from his face – he suddenly became a figure of shock and paralysed fear. Without warning, I had become a large black rat. The experience was far too intense to be described by the term 'projective identification' in the ordinary way. His expelled beta fragments had become horribly real to him.

In confronting such intense states of uncontainment, I have found the words of a wise supervisor invaluable, and pass them on to my students. He quoted his aunt, who hailed from a remote northern village, as often using the expression 'sitting sat'. It is the sort of phrase that calls out to be accompanied by a bodily enactment. I sit myself well back in the chair, broaden my shoulders, arms dropped to my sides, hands easy on the knees – a comfortable, ready, accepting position. For me, this is the physical representation of the maternal reverie.

Moral judgement

Most patients, however deep their feelings of worthlessness, will realise that they cannot think of themselves as actually born bad. Michael believed he was, that badness was intrinsic to his nature. He exemplified the extreme moral judgement passed on the self. This concept – the quintessential example of the failure, or refusal, to do the work of thinking – is for me one of the most important contributions Bion has given us. The Sophoclean character who most obviously embodies it is King Creon, who 'with his rigid splitting of "patriot" and "traitor", limits his knowledge to that within the narrow bounds of his own authority', and who, 'afraid of development ... would like to fossilise the *status quo* and be on the safe side' (Williams, 2005b, p. 106).

No therapist can be short of examples of the manifold ways in which the moral judgement manifests itself. Aside from my clinical illustrations, though, I find the most telling for students is that given me by that same supervisor: the late bus.

It is late, and you are waiting for the last bus. Your frame of mind is calm, you're thinking comfortably in alpha mode, musing on the pleasant evening with friends just passed, anticipating a warm bed. Time passes, and your mind turns to questioning. What has happened? What's going on? It's uncomfortable, but you can produce thoughts, and link them: there must be reasons for the delay, what are the probabilities? If it's this reason, it will come soon; if that, it will be later, etc. You duly make the bridge of thought over frustration. Then it begins to rain. Your attention is becoming focussed exclusively on the state of affairs at the bus station. Soon come the first sparks of irritation, and the internal maternal reverie begins to fail. Anger grows, and your thoughts become increasingly condemnatory: they can't sort themselves out, they're incompetent. As blame intensifies, it becomes hard to sustain a rational line of thinking. Such 'thoughts' as you have become jarring and jumbled, no longer thoughts at all but mere beta fragments. By the time the bus arrives (hopefully before the stage of total anomie), you are reduced to a poor mental state, indeed a little mad. But the arrival of the bus, the driver's apology and explanation, wonderfully restores the alpha-function. It is a place we have all been, and is greeted with warm recognition by the students.

Catastrophic change

> Oedipus' quest is not only for the 'facts' of his birth but for the mystery of his growth and identity. What is put to the test is his capacity to think through an overwhelming emotional turbulence, which will shake the mental constitution to the core. (Williams, 2005b, p. 109)

John was tall, spare, intelligent, and believed himself to be in a state of constant search for the truth in his therapy. His search was indeed an insistent one, and there were times when he reminded me of nothing so much as a big, dark bird pecking at me. He wanted to understand what I knew, to access the information about him I somehow possessed. It was a stance extraordinarily difficult to work with in a way that did not threaten to break into argument. Every so often though, he provided a visible example of what I could only describe as a 'catastrophic moment'. The authorities on Bion, I have discovered, differ in their interpretations of Bion's distinctly under-developed concept of catastrophic change, and I am glad not to be called upon to teach the theory, only to illustrate it – while being careful to stress that what I am describing is merely an outward appearance of something that seems to be happening within the patient. My blanket definition for clinical purposes is that of change, however small, which occurs in relation to the deep centre of pain that it is believed must at all costs remain unvisited.

With John, on the rare occasions where I managed to make a successful interpretation – one, that is, that was actually heard by him – a remarkable physical change took place in him. He fell silent, and his aggressive 'pecking' posture disappeared. He seemed to dwindle in his chair, his head shrank back on his shoulders and turned upward, and his eyes began a rapid blinking, while he looked from side to side with small head movements. He looked for all the world like a small, blinking fledgeling. Irresistibly, this suggested the unexpected swallowing of a large worm of knowledge that would take some digesting.

Suffering

At the beginning of her article, Meg quotes Bion: 'The patient may say he suffers but this is only because he does not know what suffering is and mistakes feeling pain for suffering it' (Williams, 2005b, p. 103).

Sophocles' Oedipus endures great suffering in his search for truth, and is rewarded with a self-knowledge that is redemptive for others as well as for himself. Such readiness to face mental pain gives us a yardstick for understanding our patients' capacity for K. John did gradually digest his 'worms': his search for truth, though mistaken in its form, was essentially a genuine one, and he proved eventually to have the strength to suffer internal change. By contrast, for Sarah the threat of change was too much known and feared. As with so many of her accurate perceptions, she was able to tell me that she feared her 'life system' would be 'broken' by the new thoughts that emerged in the exchanges with me.

The parallel with Piaget's (1952) concepts of assimilation and accommodation is an obvious one, and helpful for many students. Piaget, like Bion, uses the analogy of physical digestion for mental processes, suggesting that babies' minds assimilate information as their bodies assimilate milk. His concepts give us a model for how mental food actually behaves. The refusal to suffer change, to accommodate, produces the mental indigestion so graphically described by Sarah: 'My thoughts hurt my body.' But how difficult such accommodation is when truth has been the least of values in one's background. To my near-incredulity, Michael actually asked me, some months after the event, whether I had made up the story of his womb experience, in order to 'make him believe' he was not born bad! He found it hard to imagine that I had any real concern for the truth, his family having given him an opposite model.

Minus K

Where truth has to be rejected from an early age, a system must be constructed to maintain an alternative worldview. James approached me for psychoanalytic therapy late in a career spent working as a psychiatrist, using another therapeutic modality. He had experienced an apparently very 'traditional' psychoanalytic treatment in the past, and felt he wanted to return, both to see if it would help with certain symptoms and avowedly as a matter of professional interest. It took me some time to be able to formulate what was really happening, which was in fact an elaborate and sustained attack on psychoanalysis itself.

This was perhaps the closest I have come to encountering what I would call an almost 'pure' form of minus K. In the circumstances, it brought powerfully to mind the question: Can a liar be psychoanalysed? James practised before me technique after technique from his own tradition, and set out to seduce me into using them myself. I was asked to recite a relaxation technique, dialogue with his sub-personalities, place my hand on his head, and so on. The process reached its apogee when, having asked me to open up the (futon-style) couch to enable him to move about in a less 'restrictive' space, a request with which I complied willingly enough, he then lightly mentioned that he sometimes found it helpful for his patients if he lay down on the floor-cushions beside them!

Declining his various proffered invitations, I was accused of being afraid to experiment, unready to dare new ways of working, effectively stuck in the psychoanalytic mud. I remember suggesting at one point that my daring might be found in my interpretations; at another that I was in fact 'experimenting' where I had not planned what I might say before speaking. These comments were ignored, along with most of my offerings. On one memorable occasion when I felt I had made a particularly telling interpretation, one that gathered together extensive evidence and I felt would be hard to ignore, he became very quiet, and I felt hopeful. I looked more closely, and he had fallen fast asleep! My interventions, though he kindly acknowledged them as well-intended, were felt to be largely irrelevant to the – preferably uninterrupted – flow of his associations and dialogues, which he explained were 'free association', a requirement of psychoanalytic therapy. Only at the end of a session would he ask me to give what would have been in effect a summary of what had transpired in it, claiming this was what his analyst had done. In effect, I was being asked to enact a travesty of my own way of working, becoming a useless pseudo-analyst, whilst simultaneously required to become an altogether different kind of therapist.

In Bion's sense of lies requiring a thinker to formulate them, whereas truth does not, James was operating a 'lie' of some magnitude, extremely hard to penetrate. Not that he had the least intention that any of it – including the underlying attack on his mother – should ever be penetrated. He claimed to have come to learn from me: in fact, he was determined that I should learn from him. This was a cogent demonstration of the way in which minus K flourishes in a profoundly narcissistic system. James' example is a revealing one for the students, because of their expectation that so enclosed a system would produce a personality somehow 'bad', selfish and unhelpful. This was hardly the case: James was zealous in the pursuit of a reparative drive that was no doubt manic in its origins, but which had enabled him to help many people as a therapist. He had a reputation for being creative, and even inspiring. It became clear that any real opening to K in his therapy was out of the question, not least because, as Bion says of such patients, they have 'the sense that their wellbeing and vitality spring from the same characteristics that give trouble' (Bion, 1965, p. 144) so that loss of the 'bad' parts of the personality is inseparable from the loss of all mental health. He says further of this kind of narcissism:

> Thanks to the patient's capacity for satisfying all his needs from his own creations he is entirely independent of anyone or anything other than his products ... but the evidence of his senses belies his own predeterminations; he is *not* satisfied'. (Bion, 1965, p. 137)

James was indeed not satisfied: his tragedy was of his own unfulfilment as he grew older. Ironically, this surfaced most obviously in the 'dialogues' in which he appeared to listen to his child self, but consistently failed to fulfil any of his promises to him. This was a relentless resistance to giving his own self any real attention. And I have to convey to my students, with almost a sense of my own shame, the terrible boredom eventually created in me by being controlled in a system of 'lies' against which I found myself powerless.

From K to O

My patient Jane was shocked by the degree of pain she felt as the result of an intense positive transference, accompanied by extreme separation anxiety and rage. As I perceived it, the intensity of the pain she felt was a direct reflection of her refusal to compromise with the truth – in Bion's terms, to lie about my importance to her. Again and again she went through harrowing distress, faced the reality of it, and listened desperately for help from my words.

Insight visibly shocked and hurt her, but she would, or could, not allow herself to evade it. Her alpha-function, trapped in a fierce prohibition against going to the source of her pain, had during her life been exercised in so many creative ways for other ends that it would not allow her the luxury of denial.

The intensity of the transference situation sometimes caused me to react in ways I did not expect. One day I blurted out: 'I'm not your mother!' and then thought with dismay: Why on earth did I say that? It turned out to have been a less-than-conscious instance of Neville Symington's (1986) 'therapist's act of freedom', a phenomenon that has many resonances in the context of Bion's 'O'. Jane gave a slight gasp, and became very quiet. It transpired that my words had been heard by a part of her of which her conscious self had been unaware. My more usual interpretations, however accurate, had not been able to reach her as my crude exclamation did.

Bit by bit, and holding herself in a hard-won state of negative capability, Jane transformed her own internal states. As Meg says: 'The truth is *in itself* noble and civilising, whatever its content, if it can only be endured, "suffered"' (Williams, 2005b, p. 122). As Jane and I worked together, and she increasingly found herself able to free up for her own use her well-developed alpha capacity, she became able to say, with Oedipus; 'My troubles are mine / And I am the only man alive who can sustain them.' And at last: 'I am innocent.'

The meaning, the 'T-beta' manifestation, of such a moment of O the students must apprehend for themselves. Arising as it does from the unknown and unknowable, it is not transmissible without the active intuition of the hearer. I don't attempt to 'teach' students much about O, and 'becoming O' in the therapy: I rely on stories like Jane's.

CHAPTER FIFTEEN

Teaching theory in the context of child analysis: a case study

Gertraud Diem-Wille

Teaching Bion's theory becomes vivid when we use clinical material to illustrate the concepts in the arena of the here–and–now in the analytic process. Many of his key concepts have been directly assimilated from Klein – projective identification, splitting, death instinct, paranoid-schizoid and depressive positions – but he used them in the service of a different outlook, a new metapsychology. In this paper I want to show how Bion's key concepts such as the dynamic relationship between $Ps \rightleftharpoons D$, the container–contained, and the theory of thinking, have enriched our clinical understanding. This will be described through vignettes of analytic work with a three-year-old child, whom I call Patrick, focusing on observing his oscillation between $Ps \rightleftharpoons D$ and on the analyst's experience of being drawn into playing a special role in Patrick's inner world. I would like to illustrate the fruitful thinking about transference and countertransference in noting how our patients act on us to feel things they have experienced earlier in their lives.

Assessment: from a bombardment of beta-elements

Patrick[1] was brought to analysis aged three and a half. He refused to go to nursery, had no friends and was very aggressive. At night he awoke from nightmares shouting desperately and was difficult to pacify. He could express himself well with words, but only scribbled when drawing. His parents often did not know what to do with him. He is the oldest son and has a younger sister aged two.

At the first assessment session Patrick could not separate from his mother, but at the second session his mother explained that she would collect him 50 minutes later and he agreed to stay with me.

> Patrick sat down at the table and tried to draw, that is, he scribbled. He then discovered the glue, picked it up, and, looking at me, squeezed some onto the drawing paper. When I described how he wanted to put a lot of glue onto the paper, and perhaps even glue himself to me, he pressed even more glue onto the page, smearing it with his fingers in obvious enjoyment. He then deliberately and violently broke off the tips of the coloured pencils with a ferocious expression in his face, first breaking off the tips of the new pencils and throwing them around the room, then stamping on them. I suggested to him that he wanted to show me how easy it was to make useless broken pencils out of the beautiful new pencils, and that he perhaps felt broken himself. He seemed not to hear my voice, became more and more excited and ferocious, not stopping until all the pencils had been broken.
>
> When I told him that he wanted to see whether I would turn away from him and not allow him to come back if he made such a mess, he suddenly changed his behaviour. As if accidentally, he came up close to me, leaned trustingly on my leg. I told him that this was his way of showing me that he felt touched by my words and you come close to me and touch me. He looked deep into my eyes so that I added, 'now you feel understood'. I told him that I would

---

1   I have also described the case of Patrick in my book *Young Children and Their Parents* (Diem-Wille, 2015).

speak to his parents and suggest that he come regularly three times a week.

The parents informed me at the next meeting that Patrick had told them I had pulled his T-shirt and slapped him when he was naughty.

Patrick showed his chaotic inner world, by turning the consulting room with cruel destructiveness into a messy world in which he had no hope of making himself understood. For me as his analyst it felt like a massive attack. I felt bombarded by him. My first impulse was to transform his projections of beta-elements into words, to show him how desperate he was and that he urgently wanted to push these unbearable sensations into me. I hoped that this would stop his destructive actions. After my first interpretation I could hardly believe how he went on with a cruel expression to 'kill' each of the twelve brand-new colour pencils without mercy. He obviously corrected me by showing that it was worse than I had described it. I had to struggle to believe what I experienced, how can such a small boy with caring parents be so full of destruction and sadistic joy. My impulse was to stop him or to run away – as Bion describes it in his autobiography *The Long Weekend* and in *The Italian Seminars* when he compares the situation of an analyst being exposed to massive projections with his wartime experiences. He stresses how difficult it is to 'think under fire' in a literal sense in a tank in wartime and in a symbolic way in the analytic session (2005b, p. 40).

I was wondering whether Patrick was retaliating to a world that has destroyed him or parts of his body. He made me feel his helplessness and aggression. I had to bear the uncertainty not to know what had happened to him except that his mother had been pregnant and got a new baby a year ago. He had also symbolically tried to glue himself to me so that would be no separation. Being able to contain the violent outburst gave him the opportunity to show the extent of his chaotic inner world. He seemed to experience me as somebody who did not distract him or tell him lies but who can endure to face him as he is – with his terrible inner world and destructive impulses. When I made a link between his testing whether I would send him away, never allowing him to come back – a hypothesis about his inner conviction that nobody really wanted to be with him – he changed his behaviour. Bion asks 'What is the evidence' in the *Tavistock Seminars* (2005a, p. 17). The evidence of the accuracy of the interpretation is the way in which the patient responds. After my intepretation Patrick walked by me and touched me with his legs which I took this as his way to communicate with his body that he felt understood. Now we both knew that we had differentiated lies from truth and got a perspective on his psychic reality.

Betty Joseph has described how patients 'act on us to feel things for many varied reasons; how they try to draw us into their defence systems; how they unconsciously act out with us in the transference ... experiences often beyond the use of words, which we can often only capture through the feelings aroused in us' (Joseph, 1985, p. 447). Bion says that 'somehow we do observe things that are often not observed in the ordinary course of social intercourse' (2005a, p. 14). I think it is not only the observation but feeling the significance of a particular mode of behaviour; thus, when Patrick touched me apparently casually when he passed by, it was not incidental but a meaningful communication with me, showing him moving towards the depressive position when he felt understood. I was deeply touched by the way his face and his whole body became soft and he was able to connect with me. One could say his 'pre-conception' of a link between a breast and a mouth was 'mated' with an emotional experience felt to be realisations of them (Bion, 1970, p. 16). Two minds coming together for a moment, since thinking can only take place through the mediation of another individual, a 'you' mother (Bion, 1962a). This is what Bion referred to as 'alpha-function' leading to emotional growth.

Patrick's analysis

Patrick's psychoanalysis helped him sort out the problems of his inner world. In the first months, it was important for Patrick to orient himself. The temporal structure of the sessions, which took place on three consecutive days, was of great significance. A calendar I made for him acquired a central meaning for him during the first three months. At the beginning of each session, he took it out of his drawer and made a circle around that session. The weekends and interruptions were difficult for him.

Patrick assumed I was exactly like him. When he left the room a mess and then found it clean in the next session, he assumed that I would also forget everything that had passed. He seemed to be saying to me that nothing was of significance since it could always be cleared away. He could then make another mess and the entire world was stupid, without meaning or structure; in such a world, the significance of his actions would be ignored. But when he found that I as his analyst would clean up his mess and put his playthings away safely from the other children, but could still reflect on his motivation for making the mess and keep emotional contact with it, he too began to ponder the matter. He began asking questions and expecting answers. It seemed to calm him that I saw how often he was completely overwhelmed by something terrible, and at the same time could see how vulnerable he was and how angry he became when he was laughed at or humiliated.

In a meeting four weeks after the beginning of his analysis, both parents were deeply impressed how Patrick's fits of rage had completely vanished. He now participated in kindergarten without any problems. Visibly moved, Patrick's mother related how he now could talk about his feelings when he was sad or joyful. She tried to prepare him for decisions now instead of manipulating him as she did before. Patrick came to her, put his arms around her neck and said, 'Mummy, I love you'; that was the first time this had happened. He had less trouble parting from her. He also played 'loving his sister', where he would embrace his little sister, although so tightly that she quickly broke away.

From the very outset, his phantasies about new babies played a key role, whether they came from his mother or ostensibly from me. When Patrick for the first time felt his feelings were taken seriously, with his hate and jealousy of other children and of my husband, he was then able to talk about them. He showed me how the next child after him would fall on the wet floor and hit his head; demonstrating this, he himself fell to the floor as if in punishment. At the same time, he could also show me how important the sessions were for him, how cold he felt and how cosy it was in the room.

Step by step, he gained more access to his feelings of insignificance and panic over his self-perceived stupidity and powerlessness. Often he was afraid that the absence of something meant it was gone forever. In play, he was the father who should 'help' me, who was the small child or baby. But this help consisted in telling me what to do with a threatening voice, and he was quick to become impatient and pressure me, saying, 'Come on, let's go!'; then, without any warning, he would scream at me until I was cowering. In these cases, his face turned completely red and he roared in a loud voice. When I asked how I was to react, he told me to be afraid and cry. My reactions seemed to increase his rage and shouting, until he then stopped.

I should like now to describe in more detail two sessions from Patrick's psychoanalysis.

The provoking of feelings

The special quality of Patrick's relationship to his father unfolded through further play. Here some scenes from a therapy session:

> First, we were fishing, then his mood changed and he became aggressive. He demanded that I insult him: 'Shitty Patrick, he shits in his pants!' When he was unable to do something, he said 'shit'; when something exciting occurred, he had to go to the toilet. Later he became the small baby who had dirtied his pants; I was the father who changed his nappies. Patrick played this scene quite realistically, lying down on a baby's changing table; I was supposed to say: 'Lift your bottom' and put something under it as a nappy, then fastening it. I was supposed to put him to sleep as his father, his mother being dead. In play, he climbed out of the bed in the middle of the night. I as his father should find him, yell at him and punish him. This game was laden with great intensity. Patrick was not satisfied with my mere simulation of yelling and hitting him. He became excited, took my hand and tried to

hit himself with it. 'You have to hit me hard, harder!' Since I did not do this, instead expressing verbally how I (as his father) was upset, he began to hit himself with his own hand. 'That's how to do it', he said.

In his play Patrick let me experience the threatening quality of his paranoid-schizoid feelings. He tried to put me in the position not only of the sadistic father who unconsciously felt pleasure in such fights, but also of Patrick being stuck in these intense struggles where he felt powerful. He wants to repeat them again and again. For the analyst it is hard to let the patient provoke these feelings – but as Bion said 'If you cannot bear the heat, refrain from the kitchen' (2005b, p. 40). In numerous sessions, he demonstrated how successfully Patrick upset both himself and his father, drawing his father into his cruel games. His phantasised couple consisted of a man and a child who were bound together in a pleasurable yet intimately cruel way. The child was in control: Patrick had in his power to provoke his father to a state of extreme rage and indeed to complete helplessness. He derived great satisfaction from this. My goal was to make it clear to him that he was the active agent in this, able to make his father punish him. He did the opposite of what his father demanded, or acted as if he had not heard him. In a role play, he showed me how he did this: 'Don't you hear me?' he screamed, as his father. Sometimes he sat in the car ready to drive off, and I as the child was supposed to nag him until he really seemed about to drive away. I then had to scream in horror and run after him in terror. His pleasure at inducing rage in his father was thus quite obvious. Patrick succeeded often in tempting his father into acts of violence.

In the next meeting, Patrick's parents told of his hospital stay when he was one and a half years old, where it was necessary for four men to hold him down in order for the doctor to give him an injection. Due to a serious intestinal infection, he then had to wear nappies. His explosive diarrhoea had so scared him that he fell into panic and would not stop yelling. He was very ashamed to have to wear nappies again. He imitated his father, who then called him 'Shit-Patrick'. The birth of his younger sister, at this same time, irritated him, as if it were a confirmation that he was unwanted due to his badness and dirtiness – as if this were the reason his parents had wanted a new baby. That was the point at which his frightening dreams had begun.

Towards alpha-function

In the ensuing sessions, ghosts from his nightmares came to life. I was supposed to be the small child who woke up in the middle of the night and heard strange noises. I must then be completely petrified with fear, and he a ghost who scared me. I should then call for Mummy. Or, we sat close together and listened to the threatening noise that he imitated. When I then linked these noises to what Daddy and Mummy do at night (sexual inter-course), he agreed and said that was dangerous. But he wanted to go into the bathroom to see what they do. Making noises and listening were of great importance, bound up with his fear and the ghosts.

His traumatic hospital experiences became the focus of one therapy session:

> Patrick had kneaded blue, red and green plasticine into a brown uniform mass. He then turned a radiator next to the table all the way up and asked me to come with him into the house, i.e. under the table. Patrick climbed on the table, put little pieces of the brown plasticine on the radiator, and watched how it began to run down the radiator as it slowly melted. When I then interpreted his wish to fill the whole room with pooh-pooh so that everything would stink of him, he nodded and said: 'Yes, that's how it should be.' He took bigger pieces for melting. He demonstrated how it should grow bigger and bigger and then asked me to stop it with a paper towel. However, since I was not fast enough, he himself took a piece of paper and demonstrated how I should do it. He emphasised how important it was not to touch the plasticine in any way. I linked this to his fear that this 'diar-rhoea' could be dangerous. He became more and more excited, laid large amounts on the radiator and demanded

that I stop it, in which I was only partially successful: I was meant to see what it was like to be unable to stop this mass of diarrhoea. I asked whether this could be similar to the time when he was in the hospital with this dangerous, unstoppable diarrhoea. 'It was like an explosion', said Patrick ominously. I interpreted that his explosive diarrhoea could have made him afraid of becoming completely broken. He nodded. When I asked him what it was like back then in the hospital, he said in an emotional voice that it had been very painful. Perhaps he had considered it a punishment for his angry thoughts over his sister in his mother's belly, I added. After a short pause for deliberation, he said in a calm voice that we could now turn down the radiator. Patrick took out clean paper towels and put together the larger pieces of plasticine for me to make a ball out of, since he would need this later. He cleaned up the radiator meticulously, at first asking me to help him, but upon reconsideration deciding to do it alone. He worked at this with great concentration. Since I had made him conscious of his interconnected phantasies, he felt understood and also felt he understood himself. After this, he was able to clean everything up with great care.

In the second year of his analysis he was able to set up the traumatising situation of his illness, where the analyst could emotionally be with him following him into the helpless situation. This containment and putting it into words enabled Patrick to grow. As Bion says: 'A central part is played by alpha-function in transforming an emotional experience into alpha-elements because a sense of reality matters to the individual in the way that food, drink, air and excretion of waste products matter' (1962b, p. 42). If emotional growth took place it must show in the relationships in the outer world in the relation to his parents. With children these changes occur more rapidly than in the work with grown-ups.

In the next discussion with the parents, the father told me that he had now distanced himself from disciplinary questions, leaving this to his wife. Patrick had now begun to build houses with his sister, with his father assigned the role either of mailman who brought the two of them their mail, or policeman.

The parents thought Patrick was already cured; in kindergarten, he played with more sense of phantasy than most of the other children. Despite this, they let him still come to analysis for his inner changes to become stabilised, as I suggested.

At the beginning of psychoanalysis, Patrick was an awkward child, often teary-eyed, with a dull facial expression that rendered him rather unattractive. He slowly became livelier. In the sessions, he began to climb up on the table, to take it into his possession along with the room. He climbed from one window-sill to another, wanting at first to be held by me, but was soon able to manage this without help. He jumped from the table onto the floor and became more and more skillful. In kindergarten and on the playground, too, he had shed his timorousness. He was now one of the ones who climbed all the way to the top of the jungle gym, which pleased his mother greatly. By clearly naming and sensing thoughts and feelings, he discovered solid ground and a method of overcoming obstacles.

He was now able to use his intelligence, which had often been shrouded by his inner chaos, and he was attentive, perspicacious and quick on the uptake.

Final remarks

His serious infection – necessitating a hospital stay – together with the birth of his sister, seem to have hurled Patrick into a crisis at the age of one and a half. Although he was already toilet-trained, it was necessary for him to use nappies. His inability to control his bowels transformed his body and himself into a dirty, repulsive hull of which he felt ashamed. Patrick apparently saw his illness as a punishment for his feelings of jealousy. Mockery from his father – who saw him more as a younger brother than as a small son – caused his fragile ego to temporarily collapse. He was seized by rage and panic, screamed and raged to such an extent that almost nobody could pacify him. His guilt feelings led him to phantasise a punitive world of ghosts and monsters, added to the threatening sounds coming out of his parents' bedroom and bathroom, which he linked to his aggressive phantasies. He was continually withdrawing into an anal, destructive phantasy world. He derived the greatest pleasure from the provocations of his father, who willingly played the role of the evil, sadistic, mocking punisher. His faeces constituted a powerful instrument; his full nappies, which he often did not want to surrender, were for him laden with pleasure. Patrick's father, who was excellent at sketching, felt compelled to outdo his son in their competition; Patrick had no confidence that he could ever learn to draw as well as his father. The father also always sought to win when they played ball. Only slowly did Patrick develop a certain amount of self-confidence that he was allowed to do things his own way.

At the same time, there was a healthy part of his personality which psychoanalysis was able to build on. Patrick could build on the positive experiences in his first year of life: his world retained its essential structure; he had not had a psychotic breakdown, and did not withdraw into a private world like an autistic child. He tried to see if he could find security with his analyst. Through my steady patience with him, I represented a world where there was somebody concerned for his well-being. Patrick had the concept of an inner object, someone who could think of him. As soon as he could use analysis as an environment where he was free to show his terrible fear, describe the ghosts who haunted him, and exhibit his explosive jealousy, he could continue on at home and in kindergarten without attacks of rage and frightening dreams. A loving relationship to his mother seemed to soon outweigh his previously distorted image of her. Patrick now no longer needed to defend himself against his own feelings with attacks of rage, but could express his sadness or joy, longing or disappointment in a differentiated fashion. Although he still often burdened himself with the exorbitant demands of an exacting conscience, his ego had become stronger. He began to show concern for other people. Since his fears had lessened and he could counter the image of his repulsive body with a positive self-image and increased self-confidence, he now became much better at having friends and resolving conflicts through negotiations instead of through violence and blows.

Although Bion did not have any direct experience of child analysis his ideas can be well adopted to child analysis as Martha Harris describes in 'The individual in the group: on learning to work with the psychoanalytic method'. She first quotes Bion's remark that 'the intelligence one has [as an analyst] must be available for use "under fire"'; and then goes on to say: 'Baptism under fire at some point is an essential part of the development of a child psychotherapist' (Harris, 1978), p. 37). In child analysis an analyst has not only to be able to think 'under fire' but also to protect herself and the child by stopping the attacking child physically. Elements of destructiveness and jealousy emerged continually with Patrick, where he spat on me, kicked me, tried to tear the spectacles from my face in a fury and wanted to break them. His mood could swing harshly. I always had to be on guard to protect him and myself. However, he got more control over his hitting and pushing. When I could understand his mood swings and link them to his experiences, his aggression was transformed into gentleness; he put his head in my lap.

In this case study I wanted to show how clinically useful is Bion's concept of container–contained are, and how important it is to follow from moment to moment the oscillation within the $Ps \rightleftharpoons D$ positions. As a very distressed child he showed his inner conflict in a concrete way, often wanting me actually to perform the same cruel punishments and mockery as he provoked his father in doing. Patrick learned from the emotional experience of his analyst being able to take in his projections, suffer their impact, and put them into words. Pursuing the emotional truth even in very disturbing areas enabled him to acquire a knowledge that enriched his personality.

CHAPTER SEVENTEEN

The living mind – Bion's vision

Meg Harris Williams

'Will psychoanalysts study the living mind?' (Bion, 1979)

I have two different frameworks for teaching Bion: one with groups of students or colleagues, and the other by means of writing. The first is based primarily on Bion's theory and the second on his autobiographical writings. Both however have the same aim: to try to present a picture of the 'living mind' and its struggles for development; and this takes into account not only Bion but other thinkers who in my view have contributed to refining the modern psychoanalytic model.

I am not a clinician, and writing has always been first and foremost my personal means of exploring psychoanalytic ideas and conveying my response to others; and so in one sense I first began to teach Bion when I read and then wrote about his *Memoir of the Future*, my first contact with his publications when I was a literary student in the 1970s (Williams, 1983a). During the same period I also watched Donald Meltzer formulate his own struggle with Bion in the context of the lectures recorded in *The Kleinian Development* (1978), and his subsequent pioneering attempt to expound the relevance of Bion's ideas in clinical practice in *Studies in Extended Metapsychology* (1986). This was a time when what was subsequently dubbed 'late Bion' was regarded by much of the psychoanalytic community as evidence of dementia, and was split off from his previous 'respectable' works. Meltzer however held that his essential vision did not change, merely his metaphors – circulating through biological, chemical, mathematical, mythical, religious, and aesthetic – and eventually came to see the *Memoir* as its most advanced and complete expression (Meltzer, 1994).

For some years I have also been teaching Bion as a theory component of an MA course at the Tavistock and of the clinical training at AGIP (Association for Group and Individual Psychotherapy) in London, and before that, to psychotherapy students in the Wessex area under the heading 'The psychoanalytic attitude'. The AGIP course has been taught in conjunction with a clinical colleague, Dorothy Hamilton, who interweaves case material with the theoretical picture, in alternate seminars. The Bion segment of all these courses is short and the approach has had to be designed accordingly, though I think I would maintain the basic scheme in each setting even if there was world enough and time. Probably the type of setting where (outside writing) I feel most free to explore with others the post-Kleinian model and its context, especially its relation to art and literature, is with the Psychoanalytic Study Group of Biella where I have been speaking regularly for many years and where all the members, psychoanalysts and others, are steeped in the thinking of not only Bion but also Meltzer, Harris, Bick and the Tavistock model of psychoanalytic training through infant observation.

The idea of psychoanalysis

Bion preferred the term 'model' to 'theory' and my approach is always to focus on the model of the mind. A model is the underlying working picture of the mind and all its operations; it is worked with and thought with, not just verbally (or mathematically) formulated. It is unconscious as much as conscious and affects the way we do and relate to everything, inside and outside psychoanalysis. It is necessary to try to describe our models, but also necessary to realise that these formulations will be inadequate and approximate, and will not have the durability of poetic language.

The idea of an evolving model implies a view of psychoanalytic history that, as Meltzer describes, has an internal rationale in its development, following a series of 'logically necessary propositions' (Meltzer, 1978, I: 4). Bion, Meltzer believed, saw psychoanalysis as a Platonic idea that awaited discovery by Freud, then to be developed further by others. It is not a pluralist but an essentialist view, given that only time will tell what is the most advanced thinking, closest to the poetic spirit of psychoanalysis.

So it is the model – the current evolution of the Platonic idea – that is interesting and useful, not the poorly expressed theory. There is no need for this to pretend to be a body of authoritative doctrine, and these days, it is rarely taken as such. The model evolves along with our improving capacity for observation, in psychoanalysis and other related disciplines, and for making cross-comparisons between these disciplines in order to assess the 'truth' of the current state of the model.

As Bion asks at the end of his last talk, 'Making the best of a bad job':

> Will psychoanalysts study the living mind? Or is the authority of Freud to be used as a deterrent, a barrier to studying people? The revolutionary becomes respectable – a barrier against revolution. The invasion of the animal by a germ or 'anticipation' of a means of accurate thinking is resented by the feelings already in possession. That war has not ceased yet. (Bion, 1979, p. 256)

He was aware of the possibility of being invested with authority himself, like Freud, and of his own contribution towards realising the Platonic idea of psychoanalysis thereby becoming disempowered. As Martha Harris has written of the 'dependent group structure' that manifests itself in a 'crystallised selection' of the theories of its particular saints, such theories

> ... are suitably selected and presented to eliminate the essential questioning, contradictions and progressions inherent in

the formulation of pioneers who are constantly struggling to conceptualise the clinical observations they are making. Bion's postulation about the impossibility of knowing or describing truth, about the existence of thoughts which do not require a thinker (and of psychoanalysis as one of these thoughts) may help us to relinquish the idea of owning our own particular brand of psychoanalysis. (Harris, 1978, p. 32)

In the light of the above, when I teach the post-Kleinian model, I am well aware that it is my own understanding of the model, and that Bion, more than many, offers vital links with several schools of psychoanalytic thought. Truthfulness (not absolute truth) is sensed when as Bion puts it there is a feeling of 'confidence' or 'security' in seeing the truth, through a congruence between vertices. I find the most 'truthful' psychoanalytic model of the mind is that which finds a congruence with both the 'deep grammar' of poetic literature and with the internalised knowledge inherited from my parents and true teachers. Bion quoted Prince Andrei's feeling in *War and Peace* – 'that is sooth, accept it' (Bion, 2005a, p. 24). This congruence of vertices comes with a passive sense of the disclosure of already-existing knowledge: of something that was always there, latent, awaiting symbolic shape, as in the Platonic theory of *anamnesis* – we remember our innate ideas, rather than constructing them. Finally, after much strenuous relaxation of our 'cleverness', we 'get it'.

Learning to teach

On a personal level, I met Bion several times and discussed my PhD thesis with him (*Inspiration in Milton and Keats* [1982]), and he encouraged me to keep both my artistic and literary interests going, and to keep trying to interconnect them; he asked me to do a pen and ink drawing of his old Oxford College, Queen's, and even suggested I offer my thesis in an illustrated version to Thames and Hudson – advice which I didn't take as I thought he was being unrealistic and couldn't have known much about the difficulties of publishing in a single medium, never mind a double one. I went to the seminars which my mother Martha Harris arranged on his visits back to England from California, both privately and at the Tavistock. I found his presentation style riveting, and the expectant atmosphere in the packed rooms, and the whole show, very entertaining. I was grateful for his sense of humour when on one occasion I was engaged to drive him to a seminar and got lost, coming to a halt in a dead-end street. I am uncertain whether he said this, or whether I 'remembered' it later, but one way or another the episode became associated in my mind with his statement 'my tank stopped' in the war, just like the 'full stop' of tiger punctuation in the *Memoir*. It was during that seminar that he declared nobody was ever going to publish the third volume of his *Memoir*, upon which my mother leaped up and said 'Can we do it?' So, I thought, perhaps he understood the difficulties of publishing after all.

The *Tavistock Seminars* (Bion, 2005a) are still, together with other of his talks, amongst my favourite ways of introducing Bion's thinking to students. The texts that I select for reading vary over time, since I have found that there is no 'best' curriculum; but it seems reasonable to take advantage of Bion's presentational mode when he is making a particular effort to communicate to others, as he did especially in his later years when oppressed by a sense of urgency that time was running out – not just for himself but for humanity: 'Wisdom or oblivion?' For the same reason I do not put on the reading list writings not intended by Bion himself for publication, as this communicatory element may be lacking and there may even be a risk of falling into the illusion of seeing behind the scenes of the great man's head. Bion often insisted he was always saying the same thing and that he was sick of repeating himself. We can choose, or dip into his works at almost any point, to find evidence of his model of the mind.

I recommend to students that especially when trying to access his more 'difficult' works, they follow Bion's advice to read straight through, marking the bits they like or that arouse interest and passing over the bits that don't, and leave the whole thing to stew unconsciously. I hope that by focusing on the model of the mind, and regarding this as an unconscious vision which he was continually seeking to portray more clearly and communicatively, whilst lamenting his own inadequate powers of expression, we can achieve a basis from which students can at their leisure dive into a personal tussle with whichever of his metaphors they find most empathic or rich in potential.

As we go along we discuss some of Bion's tricky terms and signs, including his punning (though not unique) usage of 'at-one-ment', 'common sense', or 're-membering', and his 'unsaturated' categories of alpha-function (symbol-formation), beta-elements (a term which he uses ambiguously), C (dream-level in the Grid), F (faith) and O (the neoPlatonic noumenon). This extension of the Kleinian picture into the realms of meta-psychology is probably what Bion is most admired and hated for – the idea that the analyst is being analysed whilst analysing, and hence internally accountable; this constitutes a significant shift in the way psychoanalysts view their own countertransference (another term whose usage has changed).

In the last seminar if there is time I go over a list of Bion's concepts and formulations, with a view to showing how they all fit together as part of the same model. I prefer to do it this way round, rather than starting with the names of the concepts and building these into a model. Hopefully, most of these concepts will have already made their way into class discussion in a natural way; but if not, the aim is to detoxify the offputting effect of too many unsaturated formulations so that students are not intimated when they continue reading by themselves.

My courses, of whatever length, follow this same basic structure: namely, what is a psychoanalyst; how does the mind grow; and what hinders development.

What is a psychoanalyst

We begin with a brief introduction to the idea of the 'post-Kleinian', based on Meltzer's (1978) description of the move from Freud's neurophysiological model, through Klein's geographic-theological model, to Bion's epistemological and metapsychological model. Meltzer considered Klein's three-dimensional picture of the concreteness of psychic reality to be a necessary foundation for Bion's investigations into psychoanalytic intuition, the non-sensuous parallel to sensuous reality. This leads us to consider Bion's picture of what it is to be a psychoanalyst – what it feels like, what is a useful psychoanalytic attitude, what sort of thing is the mind, and what is the use of psychoanalysis as a thing-in-the-world. The idea is not to answer these questions but to bear them in mind, since they underlie everything else we shall be looking at. Many of my students are doing Applied Psychoanalysis, and awareness of links with other disciplines helps to define the possibilities and limitations of doing psycho-analysis, whether as analyst or analysand.

In addition to some extracts from Meltzer, the advance read-ing for the first session generally includes 'Making the best of a bad job' (1979), Francesca Bion's (1995) 'The days of our years', and Martha Harris' (1980) 'Bion's conception of a psychoanalytical attitude', which summarises succinctly all the important features of Bion's idea of a psychoanalytic discipline: the toleration of turbulence until a pattern emerges; the need to avoid covering facts with paramnesias; the commitment to developmental catastrophic change rather than being 'seduced into carrying on that unsatisfactory imitation of an analytic encounter in which the truth of an immediate experience is bypassed' (p. 48); and the view of psychoanalysis as (citing Bion) 'an attempt to introduce the patient to who he is, because, whether he likes it or not, that is a marriage that is going to last as long as he lives' (*ibid.*).

We also take note of another post-Kleinian feature that Bion helped to bring into focus (though others, Money-Kyrle in particular, have clarified this): namely the fact that the main therapeutic tool of the psychoanalyst is his own thinking process, rather than his (maybe muddled) thoughts. Hence Bion's emphasis on the observer–observed, or the 'third' person in the room, and other indications that the psychoanalytic process is a specialised variant on inspired teaching in general, in which two or more partners both feel themselves to be under benign scrutiny, essentially by their own internal objects. (I say 'benign' scrutiny since the severe superego has no place in teaching or learning, only in disciplinarian and basic assumption control.) The teaching object is itself in evolution, and this is crucial to its efficacy. The required tools are attention and interpretation, which on closer definition, means observation and intuition. Last but not least, a psychoanalyst is someone who, according to Bion, 'believes that a mind exists' – a simple definition with complex implications in practice.

How does the mind grow

The main part of the course consists in considering how the mind learns from experience, through the structure and growth of thoughts. I point out that a feature of the post-Kleinian evolution is the increased awareness of the complexity of 'normal' development, which grew out of Melanie Klein's work with children and the realisation that apparently psychotic processes were disturbances in the quality of necessary functions such as projective identification, and that these functions were dramatic transactions actually taking place between internal objects in psychic space. Without a clear picture of normal mental development, the space in which it occurs, and the child's normal struggles in negotiating its challenges, it is hard to locate the nature of developmental problems; yet up till this point in psychoanalytic history the psychosis had always been put before the psyche.

The readings for this section usually include Bion's 'A theory of thinking' (1962a); the introduction of alpha-function and LHK in *Learning from Experience* (1962b); passages from *Attention and Interpretation* (1970) on the container–contained, catastrophic change, and memory and desire; and chapters on these topics from Meltzer's *The Kleinian Development* (1978); the 1976 paper on 'Emotional turbulence'; the last chapters of *Bion in New York and Sao Paulo* (1980); selections from *A Memoir of the Future* (1991); and the 'Denouement' to Meltzer's *Studies in Extended Metapsychology* (1986) which neatly summarises the post-Kleinian expansion in terms of the move to understand symbol-formation as the foundation for mental development. Meltzer states:

> To view [the container–contained] as if the analyst were the container misses the point that it is the fitting together of the

analyst's attention and attitudes to the cooperativeness of the patient that forms and seals the container, lending it the degree of flexibility and resilience required from moment to moment (Meltzer, 1986, p. 208)

When we discuss Bion's container–contained model of thinking, based as it is on mother and infant communication, I make sure to link up with Esther Bick's parallel work on the nature of the 'skin' in infancy, and her systematic method of practical observation, since Bion's philosophy is speculative rather than experiential. Greater scientific understanding of infant development also enhances the validity of Bion's speculations about prenatal life and parts of the personality, which push the beginnings of object relations back in time into foetal life.

Also, in relation to the philosophy of early development, I point out the link with Roger Money-Kyrle's 1968 paper on 'Cognitive development', which lists three prototypal preconceptions, namely the good breast, the parental intercourse, and death. All these investigations were 'in the wind' at the time as Meltzer puts it (1994, p. 523). Meltzer (1986) also noted the move from 'phase to field' that is indicated by Bion's $Ps \rightleftharpoons D$ oscillation, which brings normal projective identification, as well as introjection, into the dynamics of mental growth.

The overall picture of how the mind grows is summarised thus: in the beginning, a potential thought or pre-conception, appropriate to that stage in an individual's mental development, starts to press on the psyche in the form of a 'feeling'; this is uncomfortable as it threatens the status quo with some kind of structural ('catastrophic') change, so may be resisted, or embraced if love and hate (of the impinging object) link up with curiosity ('kill it or find out about it'). We note Bion's repeated depiction of 'turbulence' at the point at which the thought impinges, and his fondness for the metaphor of latency to describe the smooth surface that disguises the hidden turbulence. If it is not confronted and contained, this may then become catastrophic-disastrous. Hence the need to improve our powers of observation; but also, the requirement to harness our innate vitality in order to work through the turbulence.

When the new thought is assimilated, finding 'psyche-lodgement', the mind's structure is irrevocably changed. This is the moment of symbol-formation, the piece of self-knowledge achieved by communion between self and object (alpha-function/ reverie) – for as Bion always stresses, in every situation it is the relationship, the link (caesura), that counts. Meltzer calls this 'aesthetic reciprocity' and observes (1986, p. 204) that this aesthetic quality is itself a 'new idea' of, and in, psychoanalysis, that came into prominence through Bion (although, he points out, it was also always clear in the work of Adrian Stokes, the Kleinian art critic who was part of the same circle).

The mind grows this way with or without psychoanalysis; psychoanalysis is merely a mode of investigation which, if itself a genuine learning from experience ('becoming'), helps to develop that which it is investigating. What is distinctive in Bion's vision, and links it with that of the philosopher-poets, is the conviction that a true symbol is both primitive and sophisticated, sensuous and abstract, and contains within its final form all the Grid-levels of its evolution, like the mediaeval Chain of Being or the neoPlatonic ladder. Every new or future thought is rooted in the 'fishy origins' of our *present* prenatal selves, the island of psychic reality where Caliban meets Ariel.

Hindrances to development

The hindrances to development are many but are more easily kept in view once it is recognised that they are all in some way negatives of the process of accepting and digesting thoughts. The life-force is debilitated by the killing of curiosity – by 'Yes I know', the already-known, motivated by 'envy of the growth-promoting objects' (1970, p. 129). This sort of envy often takes the form of an 'outraged moral system' implanted by the pseudo-objects of worship or obedience. The mind can 'parasitise' itself, and the protomental level take over, in the form of somatic symptoms or basic assumption allegiances, reacting against the 'suffering' and 'patience' required in learning from experience.

In Meltzer's (1988) elaboration of –LHK, this is 'retreat from the aesthetic conflict' that is aroused by the ambiguity

of the knowledge-containing object. Students have been especially interested in one form of retreat, autism, where a two-
dimensional relation to the object prevents symbol-formation:
a description which, though not in Bion, was made possible
through Bion's 'key of alpha-function' when applied to the 'lock
of two-dimensionality' (Meltzer, 1986, p. 207).

The other major hindrance to development concerns the
tyranny of the basic-assumption systems which function like
a type of protection-racket sheathing the vulnerable self in an
exoskeleton which actually prevents the endoskeleton from growing. They are produced by 'pseudo' objects since such objects are
really projections of the self; they are not internal objects in the
true sense of the most advanced aspects of the mind – interces-
sors or mediators capable of 'intersecting with O'.

This intersection is always a 'falsification' of O (in the sense of
absolute truth), but such a falsification is nonetheless truthful, in
line with O, and not a lie. It is the same falsification as occurs in
artistic forms, which are imaginative not illusory, 'symbiotic' not
'parasitic'. They are representations of truth. The liar however
has a premonition or glimpse of the truth, and reacts against it,
covering it with what William Blake calls the 'conglomerations
of the selfhood', 'disorganised' substitutes for truth.

Whereas lies are manufactured, truths are discovered. It
is possible to 'be a lie', says Bion, and this applies also to the
psychoanalytic relationship when it becomes a *folie à deux*, as
may be the temptation when the observed facts are intolerable
and the desire for cure is too strong: the patient doesn't need
resistances of his own, he just activates the analyst's. Bion always
warns against the ingenuity of the human animal who is intelligent but incapable of being wise.

The reading I usually recommend to illustrate the negative
movements of the mind includes the sorting of basic assumptions in *Experiences in Groups,* together with Meltzer's (1978)
commentary which brings out the crucial new distinction
between the mental and the protomental; the sections on lies
and morality in *Attention and Interpretation,* with Meltzer's
(1978) chapters '"Learning about" as resistance to "becoming"'
and 'The bondage of memory and desire'. If there is time and

interest we look at some examples from *A Memoir of the Future* which illustrate the attempt to emerge from a basic-assumption exoskeletonous condition and to create a thinking work-group from conflicting elements of the personality: passages such as the prenatal scene, the otter hunt, or the escape from the tank.

I like to draw attention to the quotation from Plato's *Theaetetus* with which Bion concludes 'Making the best of a bad job'; here Socrates explains his 'art of midwifery' during the travail of the birth of the soul:

> *Socrates:* The highest point of my art is the power to prove by every test whether the offspring of a young man's thought is a false phantom or instinct with life and truth. I am so far like the midwife that I cannot myself give birth to wisdom, and the common reproach is true, that, though I question others, I can myself bring nothing to light because there is no wisdom in me. (Bion, 1979, p. 257)

Bion too seems to have seen his mission as a 'questioner' who hoped to be a midwife to thoughts and help others distinguish between those 'instinct with life' and 'false phantoms', that is, no-thoughts. He is one of those whom Money-Kyrle (1968) defines as a Platonic 'realist', that is, who believes in the non-sensuous reality of the mind. In his later seminars in particular, Bion declares repeatedly, and almost despairingly, his difficulty in getting across his conviction that the mind 'exists' and is not merely a figure of speech (2005a, p. 40; 2005b, pp. 30, 70): the implication being that psychoanalysts need to constantly scrutinise themselves to be sure they are real and not just playing a game.

The Memoir *and the aesthetic–depressive mentality*
of the work group

I would like to conclude this chapter with a note on my adventures in teaching with *A Memoir of the Future*, Bion's ultimate metaphor for his thought-processes. In addition to various writings on Bion's autobiographies (Williams, 1983a, 1983b,

1985, 2005, 2010a), I was involved in an attempt made in 1983 to produce a film of the *Memoir*. Meltzer (1986, p. 204) said that only in the *Memoir* does Bion's aesthetic orientation find an 'unambiguous place' in his thought. *Transformations* and *Elements* might indeed be regarded as unsuccessful attempts to formulate an aesthetic theory of psychoanalysis. The nearest is perhaps his (1970) formulation of the 'language of achievement', or certain passages in his late talks, such as the metaphor of the 'sleeping beauty' of truth which can only be glimpsed after fighting through the surrounding brambles of basic assumptions (see Williams, 2010b).

Yet it is clear that Bion's interpretation of the Ps$\rightleftharpoons$D oscillation of Kleinian value systems is given a specifically aesthetic colouring, in which the D (depressive) position is one of an aesthetic harmony or reciprocity, and the Ps (paranoid-schizoid) is one of inevitable disintegration, as the road opens up towards the next thought on the horizon; for each aesthetic 'truth' is followed immediately by a new set of problems that were not previously perceptible, in an oscillating pattern that ends only with the cessation of life. The Ps position offers a choice of directions, depending on the capacity to tolerate the new unknown: hence the 'patience' required in allowing the internal object to aesthetically organise the new shape of the personality.

This is the 'underlying pattern' of learning from experience that Bion presents in the *Memoir*, at the same time trying to evolve a tailor-made genre for its expression. This is constructed via a fictional conflict between internal characters as they veer between various basic assumption alliances and a search for reciprocity and integration through the 'depressive' orientation of a work-group, across the caesura between pre- and post-natal parts of the personality. At the end of his life, like Socrates with his desire for 'live' characters not empty 'phantoms', Bion seems to have relinquished his efforts to achieve an unsaturated mathematical notation for psychoanalysis, and instead turned to the traditional imaginative means of formulating abstract psychological truths: that is, through the interaction of fictional characters in a semi-autobiographical narrative.

Each character is realistic and yet the truth they represent is not historical but abstract.

Hence Bion writes in his preface to *The Long Weekend:*

> By 'truth' I mean 'aesthetic' truth and 'psychoanalytic' truth: this last I consider to be a 'grade' of scientific truth. In other terms, I hope to achieve, in part and as a whole, the formulation of phenomena as close as possible to noumena. (Bion, 1982, p. 8)

He states expressly that he is not writing about those people from his past, but about himself in the present: 'I write about me.' It is the same in fiction as in psychoanalysis: the idiosyncrasies of the individual (if truthfully presented) acquire a universal application which goes well beyond the saturated notation of its characters. We need some sensuous realism to hang our imagination upon. The proper reaction of the reader is not 'Now I know a lot more about Bion', but 'Now I know a lot more about myself' – we have been offered a tool for insight. We only talk 'about Bion' (somebody who is not us and whom we do not and cannot know) as a kind of shorthand, a writing convention. He presents his way of thinking about himself, his self-analysis, to help us with our own. This is even more true of the *Memoir*.

The unfinished film was intended to be used as a teaching aid, not just for the *Memoir* but for Bion's thinking as a whole. The plan was drawn from a streamlined version of the *Memoir* taken in conjunction with scenes from *The Long Weekend*. The method of presentation is one in which images from childhood recur in different forms, interwoven with fantasies shaped by later experience, to form an internal drama. The film borrows biographical events from the life of the author, not in order to inform us of facts about his life (which are of no interest to anyone who has not lived them), but in order to use the vividness of childhood and youth as a matrix for the development of his later philosophical ideas, which are relevant to everyone.

Bearing in mind Bion's own stress on the necessity for learning to observe the experience of the moment, the progression of the film is not chronological. Instead of showing the passage from one event to another, the film explores Bion's idea of imaginative 'remembering', through repetition with a difference, as the characters strive to emerge from the strictures of a basic assumption mentality, or oscillate between Ps and D. Internal conflicts are dramatised by means of central metaphors enacted by figures from Indian and English religion and history: hence the Tiger Hunt, the Train and 'electric city', the Run; hence Krishna and Christ, the Devi and the Virgin, the 'green hill' of sacrifice. These conflicts represent the positions and processes defined by Bion as pairing, dependence, and fight–flight, and the movement towards K (Knowledge) or away from it to –K.

The conflicts become manifest at key 'caesuras' or points of catastrophic change which, within the film, include: birth; the transition between India and England made at the age of eight; and the First World War – all of which contribute to Bion's metaphor of 'invasion' of the self. The film begins and ends with an image of the birth of its subject, Wilfred Bion – the first caesura. The temporal circularity emphasises another kind of progression – the development of the relationship of the internal characters, in a way which also evokes the intuition of their origins in prenatal experience.

Given the Bionic perspective of 'grouping' within the mind, the film is also in a position to explore afresh the drama of groups larger than the individual: of institutions and communities (the family, school, army); and to examine from a new viewpoint political and social themes (such as war, colonialism, cultural clashes) which already have a significant tradition in cinematic representation.

The film was born of the inspiration of a young Bombay psychoanalyst, Udayan Patel, and his friend Kumar Shahani, who was already known for his film *Maya Darpan* as a brilliant formalist art-film director. In 1979 Bion had agreed to do a documentary interview-style film with them in India, where he intended to return for the first time since his childhood; however he died shortly before this planned visit. But owing to the publication of his autobiographies, the idea of a fictional film continued if anything more enthusiastically than before. Help was requested from the British Society but Bion's post-London writings were regarded with disapproval at that time, and the

Melanie Klein Trust refused to support what was considered a dubious venture. Donald Meltzer and Martha Harris (who had taught in India) were interested however, as were a number of their students, some of whom had film connections and helped to gather the acting cast on the English side. Money was raised from the Roland Harris Educational Trust and private subscriptions in the UK and abroad, and sets were built in India, including a lifesize plaster replica of the British Museum for the 'party of times past'.

As I was the only person to have written anything about either the *Memoir* or *The Long Weekend*, I was asked to co-write the script with Kumar Shahani. A first version of the script was simplified for cost reasons, meaning that the war sequences were to be narrated rather than enacted, with the aid of footage from the Imperial War Museum, where I went with Kumar to watch archival material. This turned out in fact better, more dreamlike and introspective. Many an hour, too, was spent in the British Library researching the First World War and Indian scriptures.

Owing to a series of accidents on top of the establishment disapproval the film was never completed, despite many attempts over the years to resurrect it, and remains as a collection of unedited rushes. However, with the passage of time attitudes change, and interest in the *Memoir* has grown. The unfinished film was recently shown by Michael Eigen, one of the original sponsors, and put on YouTube, followed by a version with Portuguese subtitles by Estanislau Alves da Silva, and other groups have asked to see and discuss it, including Ambedkar University in Delhi (its original location), and the Psychoanalytic Center of California; so altogether it began to seem worthwhile preparing the script for publication. It will be accompanied by a commentary, including an e-book format incorporating video sequences from the film, which may even fulfil in part the original teaching purpose of the film as it was first projected.

CHAPTER EIGHTEEN

The individual in the group: on learning to work with the psychoanalytical method[1]

Martha Harris

T his paper attempts to convey some of the ways in which I see Dr Bion's work as raising questions and throwing light upon problems of organising training in psycho-analytical method and attitudes. His thoughts on this topic are most cogently but, as always, often obliquely stated in *Attention and Interpretation*. There he pursues further his ideas about the relationship between the container and the contained; the nature of the transformations effected by the quality of their interaction; the subtle proliferation of mythology and lies which in differing degrees obstruct the search for truth. There he continues the preoccupation which runs throughout his writings, with the relationship between the individual and the group, and, as befits a historian, the relationships between different groups.

It is hardly possible to be complacent about the history of psychoanalytic groups or of psychoanalysis in groups. The tension between the pressures of the group and the thrust of the individual for development, is a theme which runs throughout Bion's

---

1 Written 1978; first published in J. S. Grotstein (Ed.), *Do I Dare Disturb the Universe? A Memorial to W. R. Bion* (1981).

work: between man as a social animal dependent upon, and with obligations to society; and man as a developing individual with a mind that grows through introjecting experiences of himself in the world, impelled to think in order to retain internally relationships with needed and valued objects in their absence.

Those of us who are concerned with training and the establishment of psychoanalytic work cannot afford to neglect his ideas. The vertex from which I shall be speaking is that of one who has been concerned for over twenty-five years with the practice and training in psychoanalysis in public institutions as well as privately, and in particular with the expansion of the Tavistock training in psychoanalytical psychotherapy with children, parents and young people. This is a four-year training based upon ongoing work and is divided into two parts. Part One is concerned with the development of psychoanalytical observation and attitudes in various settings while Part Two is specifically concerned with learning to apply the method of psychoanalysis to treatment, ranging from once weekly to five times weekly. This training qualifies people to become members of the Association of Child Psychotherapists and to join what was initially a somewhat nebulous and almost unrecognised profession, which has now expanded to achieve a salary and career structure within the British National Health Service. This professional respectability carries with it the necessity of conforming to certain minimal criteria changeable only by the agreement of the appropriate committees. These are by definition bound to be fairly conservative in their operation and undoubtedly inimical to 'catastrophic change'. And yet change and expansion need to be facilitated so that psychoanalytic ideas and attitudes can travel and take root among workers who are ready to receive them, so that their usefulness may find homes in which to flourish.

So how does one keep the mystical idea of psychoanalysis alive within such a formal structure? How can a structure remain adaptable and be used to protect, perhaps even to promote the development of the individual worker within it? How can one create a group of professionals, of psychoanalytic workers who are able to function with and among other groups of professionals in a way that reduces interference (is 'commensal' in Bion's terms), and may even be beneficial? To quote from *Attention and Interpretation*:

> In the symbiotic relationship there is a confrontation and the result is growth-producing though that growth may not be discerned without some difficulty. In the parasitic relationship the product of the association is something that destroys both parties to the association. The realisation that approximates most closely to my formulation is the group–individual setting dominated by envy. (Bion, 1970, p. 78)

The 'envy' does not arise from one partner or the other but is 'a function of the relationship.' He continues with the contrast between the symbiotic and parasitic relationships:

> In a symbiotic relationship the group is capable of hostility and benevolence and the mystic contribution is subject to close scrutiny. From the scrutiny the group grows in stature and the mystic likewise. In the parasitic association even friendliness is deadly. An easily seen example of this is in the group's promotion of the individual to a place in the Establishment where his energies are deflected from his creative–destructive role and absorbed in administrative functions. (*Ibid.*, p. 78)

He speaks of 'the dangers of the invitation to group or individual to become respectable, to be medically qualified, to be a university department, to be a therapeutic group, to be anything in short, but *not* explosive.' And again, of the dangers and responsiblities of the establishment group:

> The institutionalising of words, religions and psychoanalysis – all are special instances of institutionalising memory so that it may 'contain' the mystic revelation and its creative and destructive force ... the function of the Establishment is to take up and absorb the consequences so that the group is not destroyed. (*Ibid.*, p. 82)

Perhaps one could transpose this into a lower key and say that the function of the psychoanalytical training group or establishment is to provide a sufficiently protected and organised place in the world within which students are given the opportunity, facilitated by their own personal analysis, to study and to experience development and change, in themselves and in their patients; to study and to work with the elements and configurations which impede that process. If psychoanalytic work, transcending the urge to cure, has an appeal for them, this will be prompted by the emotional impact of the close scrutiny of the children and adults with whom they are concerned.

As described by Bion in *Elements of Psychoanalysis*, the evolution of the transference in the psychoanalytic relationship, involving passion rather than violence (as for example in the form of action by either analyst or patient) is essentially creative–destructive for them both: destructive of existing states of mind and constantly creating others. It may not always be apparent whether the new state of mind is – so to speak – a step in the right direction. It is hard for the teachers and establishment of any group that begins to meet with some success in the world, to bear in mind that they may not know the right direction, that there may not be a right direction, without being formless and disintegrated. It is difficult to allow the individual workers to find their own style and voice in a language and in a setting which enables them to carry on some meaningful discourse.

Some of the applicants for the Tavistock course have already sought analysis for their own personal problems. They may be motivated to become psychotherapists themselves partly through projective identification with their analysts, fundamentally still children who believe that to have children/patients will make them grown-up like mummy and daddy. This is a ubiquitous phenomenon and we all probably retain vestiges of it within our personality. Others, however, may wish to learn to work with patients, following some more genuine introjection and appreciation of the attention and understanding from which they have benefited and which they would like to share with others.

Observation as a prelude to analysis

As Part One of the course is concerned not with the application of the psychoanalytic method to the patients, but with the development of psychoanalytic modes of observation and thinking in varied settings, students are not required to have had some experience of analysis themselves before they begin.

We attempt to give them a disciplined experience of close observation of the week-by-week development of an infant in a family, of a young child or children. Such detailed observation has inevitably an emotional impact upon the observer which is likely to disturb complacency and to lead to the kind of self-questioning that evokes an interest in personal analysis in those whose desire to get at the truth of themselves is likely to be stronger than their wish to preserve the status quo. The same kind of closer observation of the details of interaction and the responsibilities involved in the work with children, families or young people which students are also doing in this first part of the course, also alerts them to the mental pain as well as to the developmental thrusts in their charges. It enables them to be more receptive of the projections of this which come their way and to see that personal analysis leading to self-analysis is a method for being able to bear this better.

These infant observation seminars were initiated by Esther Bick in 1949. They now form part of the curriculum of the British Psychoanalytical Society and have proved to be one of the best preparations for developing those qualities of perception which Bion describes as essential in the psychoanalytic consulting room. The mother–baby couple, initially the baby–breast, can be perceived as a model for the psychoanalytic couple, exemplifying the relationships, for instance, which he categorises as parasitic, symbiotic or commensal. The discussion of these observations within a small group in which theoretical preconceptions ar relegated as far as possible to the background, can be a model for the work group where the task is to study the aspects of material described and to look at them from different angles until some pattern emerges which speaks for itself. The discussion relates to a situation in which the observer has no responsibility other than to notice what there is to be seen while remaining unobtrusively friendly and receptive. As the impulse to action has to be noticed and restrained, the task of the group is to follow, imagine and think about the observations, including the role and effect of the observer, and notice the difficulty sometimes in refraining from taking action to 'improve' the situation.

Thus one has the leisure to note how relationships develop and change without interpretation or formal intervention. This helps towards the orientation described by Bion in which the analyst realises that he is observing phenomena from which it is possible to construe mental processes. If one is truly observing configurations which are there and is describing them well enough, unimpeded by theoretical preconceptions, other people with a different theoretical background may, if they can also free themselves from their preconceptions, make similar findings. As it is difficult to free oneself from one's background and the expectations and modes of thinking established by that, it is a help in seminars which focus on detailed observation to have members who come from different backgrounds. There is no university course which prepares one for psychoanalytical thinking and observation. People may be facilitated, but are also limited, by the vertex from which they begin to describe human behaviour and interaction. To have in a seminar people who approach it from different vertices is an enrichment, even if at times one has to reckon with those whose previous training may have positively blocked their spontaneous vision.

Let us assume that detailed observation, and that the increase in awareness of the children's emotional life in their work settings which ensues, brings the student into greater contact with mental pain and the devices used to avoid experiencing this. He may feel the urge to understand the turmoil and disturbances evoked him himself, a state of mind which is likely to prompt him to seek analysis for himself. This may be necessary for his training and is essential for those who wish to proceed to Part Two. The link between analysis and training is, however, an unfortunate one. Experience indicates that the more the former can be seen as an entirely private matter, a process which will hopefully give the analysand a new experience of hitherto unapprehended parts of himself, the freer he is likely to be to have such an experience, which will incidentally add to the equipment he can bring to his work. If the analyst is required to make judgements about his progress, this undoubtedly encourages the analysand to keep an eye on the expectations of analyst and teachers, to make transformations

in K (learning about) rather than in O (becoming). It is difficult enough to become the person one is without positive
encouragement from the establishment towards conformity
and deception.

Relationship between student and teaching group

To recount a personal recollection of Dr Bion when confronted
with the anxieties of a candidate with a first training case: 'What
do I do if the patient asks me if I am a student?' 'What *are* you
when you *cease* to be a student of psychoanalysis?' Every teacher
must be continually learning or he has no immediate experience
to share. Every therapist must be learning something in the heat
of every session or he has nothing of interest to say. One of the
ways in which senior practitioners can continue to learn, apart
from their own direct experience, is by trying to share the experience of younger people and by trying to look at material from
their vertices.

In a psychoanalytically oriented framework, the work must
be done by the individual on his own, whether he be concerned
with the meaning of the behaviour of another individual in an
intimate individual, family, or small group setting. In order to
work well, to think about relationships involved, most people
for a while do need the support of some group of colleagues as
well as of teachers and supervisors, who are learning from them.

According to Bion's premises, all groups are subject to basic
assumption activity which interferes with the capacity of the
members to work severally and together. We must assume that
no training group or society of psychoanalytical workers is
going to be free from these phenomena, or that one can ever
afford to relax one's vigilance in trying to spot their recurrences.
Perhaps the pairing groups produce the messianic hopes whether
substantial or false, which tend then to become invested in a
dependent group or groups relying on these new or apparently
original messages. Then in turn these are inclined to become the
fight-flight groups ready to flee from or to attack enemy ideologies. The dependent group structure so often manifests itself
in the reliance upon a crystallised selection of the theories of

Freud (the original Messiah), sometimes pitted against a similar extrapolation from Melanie Klein (a latter day saint). Bion is unlikely to escape the same fate. Their theories in such a climate of polarisation are suitably selected and presented to eliminate the essential questioning, contradictions and progressions inherent in the formulation of pioneers who are constantly struggling to conceptualise the clinical observations they are making. Bion's postulation about the impossibility of knowing or describing truth, about the existence of thoughts which do not require a thinker (and of psychoanalysis as one of these thoughts) may help us to try to relinquish the idea of owning our own particular brand of psychoanalysis.

One can hope to promote a relationship between fellow workers, students and teachers which might be described by Bion as symbiotic for some, and for the rest at least commensal: co-existent if not mutually profitable. Thus the therapist's relationships with his patients, objects of study, may take place within a framework of teachers or colleagues who are all dedicated to the task of enlarging their field of observation and of self-scrutiny. In such an atmosphere, hopefully, senior colleagues instead of being content to rest upon positions earned by past achievements, or longevity, may be able to continue or to allow others to continue that process of mental and emotional growth whose infinite possibilities are released, according to Bion, by putting aside memory and desire in order to have a better apprehension of the present moment.

Recruitment for training

A group or training is either kept alive or ossifies, by virtue of the quality of the new members it recruits. These may be attracted by the power or status which membership is supposed to confer upon them; they may be attracted by the possibility of participating in some interesting learning experience connected with the work which they are already doing or which they would like to do. The senior members forming the establishment which selects the new trainees tend to become increasingly exclusive as a training acquires a reputation and attracts more applicants. Sheer numbers may make exclusion necessary. The tendency in a genuinely well-meaning establishment concerned with preserving standards of work is to use experience of past mistakes to play safe. The establishment of a group in which envy predominates, as described by Bion, may attend, under the guise of protecting standards, to proliferate regulations which do the choosing and end up by including a preponderance of people who have come to join an elite profession which they have a vested interest in restricting.

If one has to limit recruitment, how can this be effected without producing an elitist atmosphere? The best way of selecting would seem to be to give candidates an experience analogous to the work which they wish to do, which will also allow them an opportunity for self-selection, and place the decision as far as possible in their hands. The most obvious course is to encourage prospective students to have a personal analysis. If they find they can stay with that and with the revelations of themselves which unfold in its progress, then hopefully they should have a better basis for supposing they may be able to help others to undergo a similar experience. This is the usual procedure in most psychoanalytical societies and in principle can hardly be bettered as an initial method of selection.

One must allow, however, for the likelihood that some analysands will return having fairly successfully resisted a real experience and grasp of their more unpleasant parts (the unwanted O), perhaps having learned *about* them and become cleverer consciously or unconsciously in disguising them. These may return filled with enthusiasm about analytic work and training, having achieved some sort of collusion of mutual idealisation with their analyst – enthusiasm about analysis for others, not for themselves.

If one can sometimes deceive one's analyst and go on deceiving oneself, one can surely also deceive one's tutors and teachers. It seems necessary throughout training to allow work and study experiences which as far as possible encourage students to test the results and capacities which they have. It seems important not to collude in the idealisation of being a psychoanalyst or a psychotherapist. For that reason we hope that students in Part One will already be working professionally with children, families and young people in a job that may be seen as valuable in itself and potentially more interesting and rewarding as the worker's perceptions increase. The aim is to make it easy for students to leave after the first part of the training, or to develop more satisfactory roles and methods of working in the fields where they are already employed. The basic aim of the course is not to create a certain number of trained professionals, labelled 'child psychotherapist', but to offer an education in psychoanalytical attitudes and ideas which will lead to some people learning to practise the psychoanalytical method, and to others learning to practise these attitudes and modes of thought in related fields: as in social case work, pastoral care in schools and colleges. The present Part Two of the course is likely in the future to be one alternative, alongside others which may be devised to try to meet the need for further development in related fields.

Teaching methods and continued self-selection

Students who do proceed to the second part of the course – the application of the psychoanalytic method, in the playroom and consulting room – need support to bear the exigencies of the work, but also sometimes towards selecting themselves out of it if the burden seems likely to be greater than the pleasure and profit derived from it. The attitude of the teaching group can surely do much to promote or discourage honesty in the individual.

If seminars are used too much for monitoring and judging the progress of cases or of the students presenting the cases, their potential usefulness can be obscured by the evocation of feelings of inferiority, defensiveness and the urge to produce less than honest work: to bring to a seminar, for instance, only those sessions in which the therapist thinks he appears to advantage. The primary function of a seminar leader, as of a supervisor, is surely to help the therapist after the event to think about the experience of clinical interaction which he is describing, and to recapture imaginatively the events described. Thus he may be able to think about them better and become more able to shoulder the burden of clinical responsibility and more open to receiving the patient's projections. This, I imagine, is an aspect of what Bion is describing when he talks of experiencing O, involving always a further penetration in the direction of the unknown. I would be inclined to think that thte most fruitful seminar or supervision is one in which participants are left, not just satisfied with a piece of good work done, dazzled by the brilliance of pupil, teacher or patient, but with the impetus for further exploration in their own work, and encouraged to persevere in the face of difficulties.

In supervision (surely one should try to discard the name and concept of 'control'), the tendency of the non-omnipotent student who is anxious to learn and who respects his supervisor, is to look for explanations, clarifications and good interpretations which he is sure the greater expert can offer. Bion has repeatedly emphasised that however inexperienced and uncertain the candidate, no knowledge and experience on the part of the supervisor can equal the actual experience of being with the patient in the session. The supervisor is always working with the student's reports.

This perhaps brings us to the usefulness of Bion's advocacy of the abdication of memory and desire. It is a difficult concept for the inexperienced student to grasp. When one is conscious of having so little information about psychoanalytic theory and personality development to remember, it is particularly difficult to put that aside rather than to cling tenaciously to the scraps that one has. But it seems to me essential to proceed and to encourage students to proceed on two fronts: they need to acquire and evaluate information which I suspect must mean in earlier learning days the writing of some very detailed notes on cases and observations as an exercise in remembering and in producing something which can be studied sufficiently closely in seminars or supervisors to throw into relief what is not there. But yet the encouragement towards the putting aside of memory and desire, that 'willing suspension of disbelief' as described by Coleridge, would seem to me a state of mind essential to try to cultivate in the psychoanalytic sessions. When achieved it can, for instance, relieve the boredom and frustration of apparently interminable unchanging sessions with a latency child who sits

everlastingly drawing similar geometric patterns. The recollection that so it was yesterday and the desire – somewhat hopeless
– that it should not be thus tomorrow, can so cloud one's perceptions that they are unable perhaps to receive some intimation of
anxiety or emotionality peeping out from the confines of the
pattern today.

It is perhaps especially difficult for people working analytically in clinics to achieve the necessary state of sequestration to
direct the 'beam of darkness' on the here and now: to put aside
expectations arising from yesterday's session together with whatever information may have percolated from some other worker
about the family or crises at school. It is helpful as an exercise
in studying what may be drawn out of the immediate session to
concentrate occasionally in clinical seminars upon the presentation of a session in detail without any history, to work in the
dark to find out how much food for thought there is when not
flooded with information.

If one has to guard against institutionalising psychoanalysis,
one must beware of using past experience in training to limit
future as yet unthought-of developments. Bion's comments on
the limitations of relying upon memory and desire have some
applicability to the field of training as well as to the consulting room; to one's wish for instance to keep up standards which
may alas tend towards reproducing paler copies of oneself. The
more one has to delegate to committee judgement the more one
is likely to flatten out into a group of social and well-adjusted
banality consisting of those who have learned to adapt successfully to the system.

However, as a tutor or supervisor one cannot abdicate entirely
the responsibility which greater experience confers, both to the
patient and to the student, for trying to see that some reasonable match of capabilities takes place between a particular case
and a particular student with regard to his stage of development.
Experience is likely to bear out the fallibility of these assessments
and certainly one cannot judge from the apparent progress of the
treatment alone the capabilities of the worker who is undertaking
it. Some patients have such an urge to grow and to understand,
that they do well with attention but limited comprehension on

the therapist's part. Others need infinite patience and test to the limit the therapist's capacity to bear negativism and the projection of frustration and pain.

It seems to me that during training one must allow situations which give students the opportunity to test and live through some of the stresses to which they must inevitably be subjected sooner or later in psychoanalytic work, to find if they can struggle with them and even enjoy that struggle. As Dr Bion once remarked: one may not necessarily have to be outstandingly intelligent to be a psychoanalyst, but such intelligence as one has must be available for use 'under fire'; and this is especially true in work with certain children. Baptism under fire at some point is an essential part of the development of a child psychotherapist, and it can be a help towards recognising the same configurations occurring in a subtler form in the adult.

If we cannot and should not protect our students from difficult and frustrating experiences and we should probably be loath to rescue them too soon even when the going becomes very rough, yet support may be necessary and required: support of the kind that shares the burden of thinking and worrying. This may alleviate but can never remove the loneliness in difficult clinical situations, for no supervisor can relieve one of the burden of deciding how to respond in the immediacy of the session.

As obviously, in this field, teachers must continue to be practitioners, continued experience with patients – especially when these are not at all aspiring analysts or psychotherapists – keeps one closely in touch with the pains and unpredictabilities in becoming an individual, and more able to empathise with the problems of fellow practitioners who are less experienced in years. The humility which this should engender is the only way of hoping to create a profession that will not be idealised as an elite, and of hoping that it will not attract recruits for this reason.

Written work

In the Tavistock training we have found that it helps students to think about what they are doing and learning, by writing accounts of their work at different stages. We seem likely to extend this as an additional method of self-selection: to ask for descriptions and distillations of sequences of observations, work experiences, case presentations and comprehension of theory. Encouragement to present honest accounts of experience, rather than scholastic essays including references to all the right authorities, may contribute to producing a group of workers who do not proliferate the kind of theories described by Bion as characteristic of the lying group dominated by envy. Probably one of the ways of mitigating the envy of the achievements of others, the passively dependent attitude which sees the strength and expertise in others, and which is moreover unable to differentiate between true and false achievement, is the attempt at least to do and to take stock of what one is managing to do oneself – to use language as a prelude to further achievement.

Theory

There is a question as to how to teach theory in a course which aims to encourage students to learn from a genuine experience of themselves in close contact with others. The collection, the manipulations, the evaluation of theories are traditionally used in the field of mental health as bulwarks against disturbing uncertainties endemic in the work. But yet one needs theories and 'models' – to use Bion's term – as a notation or mythology to bind constant conjunctions. They are necessary as tools to help one to organise thinking about experiences in order to proceed further. In Bion's definition: theory not as a solution but as a model which may prove convenient and useful.

Over the years with the help of Donald Meltzer, a selection of reading has been evolving which aims to orient students to the study of psychoanalysis as a developing art-science of a descriptive kind, essentially useful as it illuminates the experiences and furthers the method of working with the transference within the consulting room. It is studied from a historical point of view as a series of pioneering adventures in the mind. We begin with Freud's attempts to free himself from a nineteenth-century physiological view of the mind, to evolve theoretical models which could account for the phenomena he encountered in his patients. We follow the development of his theories of psychopathology as he attempts to reconstruct from his patients their childhood neurosis and to account for what went wrong. The work of Melanie Klein centering round the *Narrative of a Child Analysis*, is studied from the point of view of her attempt to observe how the child builds up from infancy his inner world, and the way in which this influences the kind of adult that he will become. Finally Bion's work is studied as an attempt to evolve a model of the mind providing a method of studying linkages between emotionality, truth and lies – an attempt which is in the vanguard of psychoanalysis.

Working in institutions

The emphasis in all of this has been on how the establishment may foster the development of individuality and individual responsibility. Yet we are training people to work in institutions that are likely to contain rival groups and forces that are inimical to psychoanalysis. We must hope to create a friendlier climate in some of these institutions.

The practice of the psychoanalytic method requires a degree of sequestration so that the patient may be protected from the impingement of unnecessary external intrusions which could interfere with the evolution of the transference. The therapist himself needs to find a place in his institution so that he too can deploy his attention during the treatment in a relatively uncluttered way.

This sequestration and preoccupation lends itself to being perceived by other less psychoanalytically involved colleagues as a mystique and as a claim to special consideration and position. Therapists in a clinic can attract to themselves only too readily an ambivalent transference, as to parents who evoke curiosity by obtruding evidence that they are engaged upon some mysterious intercourse, but who tantalise by performing it behind doors. They may take refuge from the attacks of the critical by forming a close-knit little group, a mutual protection society which, however much in possession of the truth it may feel, is bound to be essentially persecuted at core;

or they may try to deal with these transference phenomena by denial and placation of differences. The tendency to revert to basic assumption behaviour enters into and between every group formation, in an institution or clinic which can readily split itself, and give up the task in hand in favour of defending respective positions or ideologies.

The most pervasive basic assumption perhaps in work with children is the dependency one. Close work with children in pain, and accountability to rivalry with their parents, tends to bring out feelings of inadequacy and unresolved infantile dependence in ourselves. If we cannot manage to deal with those by introspection, and introjective identification with valued internal parental figures, how can we deal with them in the children we treat? Surely there must be someone who can provide a better answer than we can? Our supervisors, our analyst, or – supporting these – some excellent theoretical formulation into which all clinical data must ultimately fit? There are tendencies even (perhaps particularly) in the most progressive groups to rely upon the latest findings and formulations to provide the answer for every problem. Hence the polarisation in so many psychoanalytical groups between adherents to different psycho-analytical theories, rival loyalties to the different flags where unresolved hostility and envy underlying the dependence is split off on to the rival group. There is something to be said for working in an institution which contains a section of workers who are simply ignorant of or hostile to psychoanalysis. This gives one the impetus to have another look at essentials.

Dr Bion's studies of group behaviour have continued to be the germinal impulse for the recurrent group relations conferences held by the Tavistock, an impetus to institutional groups to study themselves and their behaviour to one another. There is one psychoanalytical tradition that regards the study of group behaviour as almost disloyal to psychoanalysis which is concerned with the internal world, the internal grouping. Yet the study of the transferring of this internal grouping to the therapist in the psychoanalytic couple is surely complemented by the study of the behaviour of the individual in a group, of the impingement of group pressures upon him. The departure from analytic attitudes occurs when the study of group behaviour becomes the kind of group therapy in which a cure is effected through an abdication of responsibility, by fragmenting and losing parts of oneself in the group, by regressing to protomental activity, carried along by the stream of unconsciousness or the mythology jointly engendered.

Work groups and establishments

To return to that early distinction made by Bion between the basic assumption and the work group. Without continual and rigorous examination of group activities in the realm of training and of practice with colleagues, the activities of the establishment group are only too easy to talk about when one is an outsider but to overlook when one becomes a member. Knowing about groups and being aware of the nature of one's emotional participation in a group activity are two different things; again instances of the distinction between transformations in K and becoming O, where experience is transformed into growth and learning through experience takes place.

In order to prevent oneself from becoming the spokesman of some 'advanced' psychoanalytic group, perhaps one should consider the following quotation from *Attention and Interpretation*:

> The individual himself must be able to distinguish between himself as an ordinary person and his view that he is omniscient and omnipotent. It is a step towards recognition of a distinction between the group as it really is and its idealisation as an embodiment of the omnipotence of the individuals who compose it. Sometimes the separation fails and the group is not only seen to be ideally omnipotent and omniscient but believed to be so in actuality. The individual's realisation of a gulf between his view of himself as omnipotent and his view of himself as an ordinary human being must be achieved as a result of a task of the group itself as well as in individual analysis. Otherwise there is a danger that a state of mind is transferred (by projective identification) to the group and acted out there – not altered. (Bion, 1970, p. 76)

Despite all the emphasis upon training people to be as far as possible individuals within their group it seems likely that for most of us the continuance of a group or an establishment within which we can work is a necessity. 'The function of a group is to produce a genius; the function of the Establishment is to take up and absorb the consequence so that the group is not destroyed' (Bion, 1970, p. 82). The International Psychoanalytical Association is the establishment within which the work of psychoanalytic geniuses – rare as always, but including surely Bion – must be preserved and utilised. But when an establishment becomes too vast and monolithic the tendency is to increase committees and legislation in ways that do not allow for individual developments and eccentricities:

> Dislike of the onus of decision, or awareness of responsibility for the decision, contributes to the formulation of selection procedures by which selection, like dogma and laws of science, is made to act as a substitute for judgement or a scapegoat for the guilt attendant on overtly acknowledged exercise of responsibility. (Bion 1970, p. 123)

There is room and, it seems to me, a necessity to allow for a number of establishments within which the psychoanalytic ideas of genius are contained and within which students may become acquainted with them and learn to apply them from different vertices. The vertex from which one looks when nourished by close observation of child and of infant development would seem to be a fruitful one for discerning later on the presence of the child within the adult, an essential nucleus of analytic work with adults.

How does a parent who wishes to have his child psychoanalysed or a person who wishes to have a psychoanalytic experience himself, know how to set about it? Bion in *Experiences in Groups* indicates that in this field, the label on the bottle can be no guarantee of the contents. 'Psychoanalyst' like 'psychotherapist' is a trade name: the former more exclusive than the latter and carrying with it probably the guarantee of a more formal training. But neither name is any guarantee as to whether the individual in the role designated has some competence and capacity to go on struggling to improve that competence by practising the psychoanalytic method. Prospective clients or patients will have to continue to use their other known professional advisers, their friends, the grapevine, and sometimes – if available – their own intuition in the last resort when they wish to find their way to having psychoanalytical treatment. But a variety of training establishments which are attempting to cultivate a psychoanalytic attitude and to follow the psychoanalytic method must, hopefully, make this more available to patients – who exist everywhere, and not only in our capital cities. To quote Bion's comments about the growth of the personality, applicable also to institutions which are concerned with this: 'What is required is not the decrease of inhibition but a decrease of the impulse to inhibit; the impulse to inhibit is fundamentally envy of the growth-stimulating objects' (Bion, 1970, pp. 128–29).

Aguayo, J., & Malin, B. (2013). (Eds.). *Wilfred Bion: Los Angeles Seminars and Supervisions.* London: Karnac.

Berger, J. (2001). *The Shape of a Pocket.* New York: Vintage.

Bergson, H. (1911 [1896]). Matter and Memory. Transll. N. M. Paul & W. S. Palmer. London: Sonnenschein.

Bion. F. (1995). The Days of Our Years. *Journal of Melanie Klein and Object Relations,* 13: 1–29. Also at: http://www.psychoanalysis. org.uk/days.htm.

Bion, W. R. (1950). The imaginary twin. In: *Second Thoughts,* pp. 3–22. London: Heinemann, 1967.

Bion, W. R. (1952). Group dynamics: a review. *International Journal of Psychoanalysis,* 33: 235–247. Reprinted in *Experiences in Groups.* London: Tavistock, 1961.

Bion, W. R. (1954). Notes on the theory of schizophrenia. *International Journal of Psychoanalysis,* 35: 113–118.

Bion, W. R. (1956). Development of schizophrenic thought. International Journal of Psychoanalysis, 37. Reprinted in *Second Thoughts,* pp. 36–42. London: Heinemann, 1967.

Bion, W. R. (1957). Differentiation of the psychotic from the non-psychotic personalities. *International Journal of Psychoanalysis,*

38: 266–275. Reprinted in *Second Thoughts*, pp. 43–64. London: Heinemann, 1967.

Bion, W. R. (1958a). On hallucination. International Journal of Psychoanalysis, 39. Reprinted in *Second Thoughts*, pp. 65–85. London: Heinemann, 1967.

Bion, W. R. (1958b). On arrogance. International Journal of Psychoanalysis, 39: 144–146. Reprinted in *Second Thoughts*, pp. 86–92. London: Heinemann, 1967.

Bion, W. R. (1959). Attacks on linking. International Journal of Psychoanalysis, 40: 308–315. Reprinted in *Second Thoughts*, pp. 93–109. London: Heinemann, 1967.

Bion, W. R. (1961a). *Experiences in Groups*. London: Heinemann. Also at: http://www.p-e-p.org/books.htm.

Bion, W. R. (1961b). The conception of man. Unpublished.

Bion, W. R. (1962a). A theory of thinking. *International Journal of Psychoanalysis* 43: 306–310. Reprinted in *Second Thoughts*, pp. 110–119. London: Heinemann, 1967.

Bion, W. R. (1962b) *Learning from Experience*. London: Heinemann. Reprinted London: Karnac, 1984, and *Seven Servants*. New York: Aronson, 1977. Also at: http://www.p-e-p.org/books.htm.

Bion, W. R. (1963). *Elements of Psychoanalysis*. London: Tavistock. Reprinted in *Seven Servants*. New York: Aronson, 1977. Also at: http://www.p-e-p.org/books.htm.

Bion, W. R. (1965). *Translformations*. London: Heinemann. Reprinted in *Seven Servants*. New York: Aronson, 1977. Also at: http://www.p-e-p.org/books.htm..

Bion, W. R. (1967a). Notes on memory and desire. *The Psychoanalytic Forum* 2 (3): 271–180. Reprinted in Spillius, E. B. (Ed)., *Melanie Klein Today*: Vol. 2: *Mainly Practice,* pp. 17–21. London: Routledge, 1988. [See also *Cogitations*, pp. 293–296.]

Bion, W. R. (1967b). Reverence and awe. In: *Cogitations*, pp. 284–292. London: Karnac, 1992.

Bion, W. R. (1967c). *Second Thoughts*. London: Heinemann.

Bion, W. R. (1970). *Attention and Interpretation*. London: Tavistock. Reprinted in *Seven Servants*. New York: Aronson, 1977. Also at: http://www.p-e-p.org/books.htm.

Bion, W. R. (1975a). *Brazilian Lectures 1973–1974*. 2 vols. Rio de Janeiro: Imago.

Bion, W. R. (1975b). Brasilia, a new experience. In: *Clinical Seminars and Four Papers*, ed. F. Bion. pp. 121–130. London: Karnac Books, 1987.

Bion, W. R. (1976). Emotional turbulence. In: *Clinical Seminars and Four Papers,* ed. F. Bion, pp. 223–233. Abingdon: Fleetwood Press, 1987.

Bion, W. R. (1977a). *Seven Servants.* New York: Aronson, 1977.

Bion, W. R. (1977b). *Two Papers: The Grid and Caesura.* Rio de Janeiro: Imago.

Bion, W. R. (1978). São Paulo clinical seminars. In: *Clinical Seminars and Other Works.* Abingdon, England: Fleetwood Press, 1994.

Bion, W. R. (1979). Making the best of a bad job. Reprinted in *Clinical Seminars and Four Papers*, ed. F. Bion. London: Karnac Books, 1987.

Bion, W. R. (1980). *Bion in New York and Sao Paulo.* Perthshire: Clunie Press.

Bion, W. R. (1982). *The Long Weekend 1897–1919.* Abingdon: Fleetwood Press.

Bion, W. R (1985). *All My Sins Remembered and The Other Side of Genius.* Abingdon: Fleetwood Press.

Bion, W. R. (1987). *Clinical Seminars and Four Papers.* Abingdon: Fleetwood Press.

Bion, W. R. (1991 [1975–1979]). *A Memoir of the Future.* Single volume edition. London: Karnac.

Bion, W. R. (1992). *Cogitations.* London: Karnac.

Bion, Wilfred R. (1997). *War Memoirs 1917–1919.* London: Karnac.

Bion, W. R. (2005a). *The Tavistock Seminars.* London: Karnac.

Bion, W. R. (2005b). *The Italian Seminars.* London: Karnac.

Bion, W. R. (2014). *The Complete Works of W. R. Bion,* ed. C. Mawson & F. Bion. 16 vols. London: Karnac.

Bléandonu, G. (1994). *Wilfred Bion: His Life and Works 1987–1979.* Transll. C. Pajaczkowska. New York: Guilford Press.

Borges, J. L. (1962). *Ficciones.* Transll. A. Kerrigan. New York: Grove Press.

British Institute of Psychoanalysis (2012). Meeting Ron Britton. *Encounters through Generations.* Audiovisual Project.

Britton, R. (1992). Keeping things in mind. In: Anderson, R. (Ed.), *Clinical Lectures on Klein and Bion,* pp. 102–113. London: Routledge.

Britton, R. (1998). Belief and psychic reality. In: Britton, *Belief and*

Imagination, pp. 8–18. London: Routledge.

Britton, R. (2001). Beyond the Depressive Position: Ps (n+1). In: Bronstein, C (Ed.), *Kleinian Theory: A Contemporary Perspective*, pp. 63–76. London: Whurr.

Britton, R. (2010). The pleasure principle, the reality principle and the uncertainty principle. In: Mawson, C. (Ed.), *Bion Today*. London: Routledge.

Brown, L. J. (2012). Bion's discovery of alpha function: thinking under fire in the battlefield and in the consulting room. *International Journal of Psychoanalysis*, 93 (5): 1191–1214.

Buber, M. (1994). *The Way of Man*. New York: Citadel Press.

Caper, R. (1999). On alpha function. In: *A Mind of One's Own: A Kleinian View of Self and Object*, pp. 127–137. London, Routledge.

Castel, P.-H. (2008). Bion, épistémologue. In: Bion, W. R., *La Preuve et Autres Textes*, pp. 61–120. Paris: Ithaca.

Carroll, L. (1970 [1872]). *Alice's Adventures in Wonderland*. London: Dent.

Costantino, A. N., et al. (2000). *Los Sueños de la Humanidad*. Presented at APdeBA Symposium.

Costantino, A. N., et al. (2001). *Psicoanálisis y Psicoterapia*. Presented at APdeBA Symposium.

Costantino, A. N., Ginocchio, V., & Spector, R. (2009). D4: radar turbulences. Presented at *Bion in Boston* conference.

Diem-Wille, G. (2015). *Young Children and Their Parents: Perspectives from Psychoanalytic Infant Observation*. London: Karnac.

Dilthey, W. (1883). Introduction to the Human Sciences. In: Dilthey, W. (1985–2002). *Selected Works*, Vol. 1 (1989), ed. R. A. Makkreel & F. Rodi. Princeton, NJ: Princeton University Press.

Eigen, M. (1986). *The Psychotic Core*. London: Karnac. London: Karnac.

Eigen, M. (1996). *Psychic Deadness*. London: Karnac.

Eigen, M. (1998). *The Psychoanalytic Mystic*.

Eigen, M. (2001). *Ecstasy*. Middletown, CT: Wesleyan UP.

Eigen, M. (2007). *Feeling Matters*. London: Karnac.

Eigen, M. (2009). *Flames from the Unconscious: Trauma, Madness and Faith*. London: Karnac.

Eigen, M. (2010–2011). *Eigen in Seoul*. 2 vols. London: Karnac Books.

Eigen, M. (2011). *Contact With the Depths*. London: Karnac.

Eigen, M. (2012). *Kabbalah and Psychoanalysis.* London: Karnac.

Eigen, M. (2014). *A Felt Sense: More Explorations in Pychoanalysis and Kabbalah.* London: Karnac.

Ferro, A. & Basile, R. 2009. *The Analytic Field: A Clinical Concept,* London: Karnac.

Freud, S. (1900). *The Interpretation of Dreams. S.E.* 4–5.

Freud, S. (1911). Formulations on the two principles of mental functioning. *S.E.* 12: 213–226.

Freud, S. (1912a). The dynamics of translference. In: *The case of Schreber, papers on technique and other works. S.E.* 12: 99–108.

Freud, S. (1912b). Recommendations to physicians practising psychoanalysis. *S.E.* 12: 111–20.

Freud, S. (1914). Remembering, repeating and working-through: further recommendations on the technique of psychoanalysis. *S.E.* 12: 147–156.

Freud, S. (1915). The unconscious. *S.E.* 14: 161–215.

Garvey, P. (2010). Found in transllation: Ukraine is not dead yet. *Teaching the psychoanalytic approach in Ukraine.* http://www.melanie-klein-trust.org.uk/worldwide_events?item=31.

Gittings, R. (1970). (Ed.). *Selected Letters of John Keats.* Oxford: Oxford University Press.

Green, A. (1998). The primordial mind and the work of the negative. *International Journal of Psychoanalysis,* 79: 649–665.

Grinberg, L., Sor, D., & De Bianchedi, E. T. (1971). *New Introduction to the Work of Bion.* Northvale, NJ: Aronson.

Grotstein, J. S. (1981). (Ed.). *Do I Dare Disturb the Universe? A Memorial to W. R. Bion.* Beverly Hills, CA: Caesura Press.

Grotstein, J. S. (2004). The seventh servant: the implications of a truth drive in Bion's theory of O. *International Journal of Psychoanalysis,* 85: 1081–1101.

Grotstein, J. S. (2007). *A Beam of Intense Darkness.* London: Karnac.

Grotstein, J. S. (2009). *But at the Same Time and on Another Level.* Vol. 1 and 2. London: Karnac.

Harris, M. (1978). The individual in the group: on learning to work with the psychoanalytical method. Reprinted in Williams, M. H. (Ed.), *The Tavistock Model: Papers on Child Development and Psychoanalytic Training by Martha Harris and Esther Bick,* pp. 25–44. London: Harris Meltzer Trust, 2011. Also at: http://www.p-e-p.org/books.htm.

Harris, M. (1980). Bion's conception of a psychoanalytical attitude. Reprinted in Williams, M. H. (Ed.), *The Tavistock Model: Papers on Child Development and Psychoanalytic Training by Martha Harris and Esther Bick*, pp. 45–50. London: Harris Meltzer Trust, 2011. Also at: http://www.p-e-p.org/books.htm.

Hinshelwood R. D. (1991). *A Dictionary of Kleinian Thought*. London: Free Association Books. In Russian: Moscow: Cogito-Centre, 2007.

Hinshelwood, R. D. (1994). *Clinical Klein*. London: Free Association Books.

Hinshelwood, R. D. (1992). Brazilian Lectures: 1973 Sao Paulo, 1974 Rio De Janeiro/Sao Paulo. *International Review of Psychoanalysis*, 19: 123–126.

Hinshelwood, R. D. (2013). Bion's nomadic journey. In: Torres, N., & Hinshelwood, R. D. (Eds.), *Bion's Sources: The Shaping of his Paradigms*. London: Routledge.

Hopper, E. (2009). The basic assumption of incohesion. *British Journal of Psychotherapy*, 25(2): 214–229.

Isaacs, S. (1939). Criteria for interpretation. *International Journal of Psychoanalysis*, 20: 148–60. Reprinted (1948) in Isaacs, S., *Childhood and After*, pp. 109–121. London: Routledge & Kegan Paul, 1948.

Jacobus, M. (2005). *The Poetics of Psychoanalysis: In the Wake of Klein*. New York: Oxford University Press.

Joseph, B. (1985). The translference: the total situation. *International Journal of Psychoanalysis*, 66: 447–454.

Joseph, B. (1989). *Psychic Equilibrium and Psychic Change: Selected Papers of Betty Joseph*, ed. M. Feldman. London: Routledge.

Jung, C. G. (1969 [1939]). Answer to Job. In: *Collected Works of C. G. Jung*, vol. 11: *Psychology and Religion: West and East*, transl. R. F. C. Hull, pp. 355–470. London: Routledge & Kegan Paul.

Junqueira, L. C. U., Jr. (1985). A obra (pré)-concebida por 'Bion'. *Jornal de Psicanálise*, 18 (37): 5–23.

Karnac, H. (2008). *Bion's Legacy: Bibliography of Primary and Secondary Sources of the Life, Work and Ideas of Wilfred Ruprecht Bion*. London: Karnac.

Kernberg, O. F. (1992). *Aggression in Personality Disorders and Perversions*. New Haven, CT: Yale University Press.

Klein, M. (1946). Notes on some schizoid mechanisms. *International*

Journal of Psychoanalysis, 27: 99–110. Reprinted in *Envy and Gratitude*, pp. 1–24. London: Hogarth. Also at: http://www.p-e-p. org/books.htm.

Klein, M. (1952). The origins of translference. *International Journal of Psychoanalysis*, 33: 433–438. Reprinted in *Envy and Gratitude*, pp. 48–56. London: Hogarth. Also at: http://www.p-e-p.org/books. htm.

Levine, H. B. (2011). Myth, dream, and meaning: reflections on a comment by Bion. Presented at the International Bion Conference, Porto Alegre, Brazil, November.

Levine, H. B. (2012). The analyst's theory in the analyst's mind. *Psychoanalytic Inquiry*, 32: 18–32.

Levine, H. B., Reed, G., & Scarfone, D. (Eds.). (2013). *Unrepresented States and the Creation of Meaning*. London: Karnac.

López Corvo, R. E. (2006). *Wild Thoughts Searching for a Thinker.* London: Karnac.

McGuire, W. (1974) (Ed.). *The Freud–Jung Letters: Correspondence between Sigmund Freud and C. G. Jung.* Princeton, NJ: Princeton University Press.

Meltzer, D. (1978). *The Kleinian Development.* 3 vols; single-volume edition. Perthshire: Clunie Press. Also at: http://www.p-e-p.org/ books.htm.

Meltzer, D. (1983). *Dream Life.* Perthshire: Clunie Press. Also at: http://www.p-e-p.org/books.htm.

Meltzer, D. (1994 [1985]). Three lectures on Bion's *A Memoir of the Future.* In: *Sincerity and Other Works: Collected Papers of Donald Meltzer,* ed. A. Hahn, pp. 520–550. London: Karnac.

Meltzer, D. (1986). *Studies in Extended Metapsychology: Clinical Applications of Bion's Ideas.* Perthshire: Clunie Press. Also at: http:// www.p-e-p.org/books.htm.

Meltzer, D., & Williams, M. H. (1988). *The Apprehension of Beauty.* Perthshire: Clunie Press. Also at: http://www.p-e-p.org/books.htm.

Money-Kyrle, R. (1968). Cognitive development. *International Journal of Psychoanalysis,* 49: 691–698. Reprinted in *The Collected Papers of Roger Money-Kyrle,* Perthshire: Clunie Press; and in Money-Kyrle, *Man's Picture of His World,* pp. 209–228. London: Harris Meltzer Trust, 2015. Also at: http://www.p-e-p.org/books.htm.

Noel-Smith, K. (2013). Thoughts, thinking and thinker: Bion's philosophical encounter with Kant. In: Hinshelwood, R., &

Torres, N. (Eds.), *Bion's Sources*, pp. 124–136. London: Routledge,

Ogden, T. H. (1997). Reverie and interpretation. *Psychoanalytic Quarterly*, 66: 567–595.

Ogden T. H. (2001). Conversations at the frontier of dreaming. *Fort Da*, 7: 7–14.

Ogden, T. H. (2003). On not being able to dream. *International Journal of Psychoanalysis*, 84: 17–30.

Ogden, T. H. (2004a). An introduction to the reading of Bion, *International Journal of Psycho-Analysis*, 85: 285–300.

Ogden, T. H. (2004b). This art of psychoanalysis: dreaming undreamt dreams and interrupted cries. *International Journal of Psychoanalysis*, 85: 857–877.

Ogden, T. H. (2007). On talking-as-dreaming. *International Journal of Psychoanalysis*, 88: 575–589.

O'Shaughnessy, E. (1981). A commemorative essay on W. R. Bion's theory of thinking. *Journal of Child Psychotherapy*, 7: 181–192.

O'Shaughnessy, E. (1999). Relating to the superego. *International Journal of Psychoanalysis*, 80 (5): 861–870.

O'Shaughnessy, E. (2005). Whose Bion? *International Journal of Psychoanalysis*, 86. Reprinted in Mawson, C. (Ed.), *Bion Today*, pp. 33–39. London: Routledge, 2010.

Piaget, J. (1952). *The Origins of Intelligence in Children*. New York: International University Press.

Poincaré, H. (1946 [1913]). *The Foundation of Science: Science and Method*, transll. G. Halsted. Lancaster, PA: Science Press.

Quinoidoz, J.–M. (2008). *Listening to Hanna Segal*. London: Routledge.

Rather, L. (2001). Collaborating with the unconscious other: the analysand's capacity for creative thinking. *International Journal of Psychoanalysis*, 82: 517–532.

Rather, L. (2010a). Playing with Bion: dreaming life into theory and practice. Workshop for *Waking Dream*. Oklahoma Society for Psychoanalytic Studies. Norman, OK.

Rather, L. (2010b,). Importing psychoanalysis to China: the function of critical pluralism as a container. Conference paper for *Freud and Asia: Psychoanalysis in the Asian Context*. IPA, Beijing.

Rather, L. (2010c). Fundamentals of the psychoanalytic process. Lecture for East China Normal University Department of Psychology and Cognitive Science. Shanghai.

Rather, L. (2013a). Playing it by ear: analytic listening as a creative process. Workshop for Peninsula/SouthBay Year-Long Psychoanalytic Studies Series. Menlo Park, CA.

Rather, L. (2013b). Psychoanalysis from Freud to Ferro. Two-day workshop for Griffin Memorial Hospital Psychiatric Residency, Oklahoma Society for Psychoanalytic Studies. Norman, OK.

Rather, L. (2013c). Everyday psychotic states in our patients and ourselves: using Bion to understand primitive mental states. *Hayden H. Donahue Seminar Series,* Oklahoma Department of Mental Health and Substance Abuse Services. Norman, OK.

Rather, L. (2013d). All the world's a stage: dream-work-alpha and the waking dream. Workshop for Oklahoma Society for Psychoanalytic Studies. Oklahoma City, OK.

Romanov, I. (2002). Thinking, experience and communication in the works of Wilfred Bion. In: *Philosophical Peripeteias*. V. N. Karazin Kharkiv National University Bulletin: Philosophy Series, pp. 54–61 [in Russian].

Romanov, I. (2006). In the rhythm of the soul's movements: a few observations on the evolution of Kleinian psychoanalysis. *Journal of Practical Psychology and Psychoanalysis*, 1: http://psyjournal.ru/psyjournal/articles/detail.php?ID=2669 [in Russian].

Romanov, I. (2009). Extension in the area of thought: Bion's ideas and contemporary psychoanalysis. In: Bion, *Elements of Psychoanalysis*, Russian transllation, pp. 7–10. Moscow: Cogito-Centre.

Roper, M. (2012). Beyond containing: World War 1 and the psychoanalytic theories of Wilfred Bion. In: Alexander, S., & Taylor, B. (eds.), *History and Psyche: Culture, Psychoanalysis, and the Past.* London: Palgrave Macmillan.

Rosenfeld, H. (1981). On the psychology and treatment of psychotic patients. In: Grotstein, J. S. (Ed.), *Do I Dare Disturb the Universe? Memorial to Wilfred R. Bion,* pp. 167–180. Beverly Hills: Caesura.

Sartre, J.-P. (1949). *What is Literature?* New York: Philosophical Library.

Segal, H. (1978). On symbolism. *International Journal of Psychoanalysis*, 59: 315–319. Reprinted in *Psychoanalysis, Literature and War*. London: Routledge.

Segal, H. (2001). Changing models of the mind. In: Bronstein, C. (Ed.), *Kleinian Theory: A Contemporary Perspective,* pp. 157–164. London: Whurr.

Steiner, J. (1993). *Psychic Retreats*. London: Routledge.

Stitzman, L. (2011). *Entrelazamiento: un Ensayo Psicoanalítico*. Buenos Aires: Promolibro.

Stokes, A. (1965). *The Invitation in Art*. London: Tavistock.

Strenger, C. (1997). Hedgehogs, foxes, and critical pluralism: the clinician's yearning for unified conceptions. *Psychoanalysis and Contemporary Thought*, 20: 111–145.

Symington, N. (1986).The analyst's act of freedom as agent of therapeutic change. In: Kohon, G. (Ed.), *The British School of Psychoanalysis: The Independent Tradition*, pp. 253–272. London: Free Association Books.

Tabak de Bianchedi, E. T. & Costantino, A. (1987). *Resistencias a salir del Edén*. Presented in APdeBA Symposium.

Tabak de Bianchedi, E. T. (1991). Psychic change: The becoming of an inquiry. *International Journal of Psychoanalysis*, 72: 6–15.

Tabak de Bianchedi, E. T. (2005). 'Whose Bion? Who is Bion?' *International Journal of Psychoanalysi,s* 86: 1529–34.

Talamo, P. B. (1981). Ps⇌D. *Rivista di Psicoanalisi*, 27: 626-628.

Talamo, P. B. (2007). Perché non possiamo dirci bioniani. *Gruppo e funzione analitica*, 8 (3): 279–285. Reprinted in *Mappe per l'Esplorazione Psicoanalitica*. Rome: Borla, 2011.

Torres, N. (2013). Intuition and ultimate reality: Bion's implicit use of Bergson and Whitehead's notions. In: Torres, N., & Hinshelwood, R. D. (eds.), *Bion's Sources: The Shaping of his Paradigms*. London: Routledge.

Vonofakos, D., & Hinshelwood, R. D. (2012). Wilfred Bion's letters to John Rickman (1939–1951). *Psychoanalysis and History*, 14 (1): 53–94.

Wallerstein, R. (1988). One psychoanalysis or many? *International Journal of Psychoanalysis*, 69: 5–21.

Williams, M. H. (1982). *Inspiration in Milton and Keats*. London: Macmillan.

Williams, M. H. (1983a). 'Underlying pattern' in Bion's *Memoir of the Future*. *International Review of Psychoanalysis*. 10 (75): 75–86. Reprinted in Mawson, C. (Ed.), *Bion Today*, pp. 381–405. London: Routledge, 2010.

Williams, M. H. (1983b). Bion's *The Long Week-End*: a review article. *Journal of Child Psychotherapy*, 9: 69–79.

Williams, M. H. (1985). The tiger and 'O'. *Free Associations*, 1: 33–55.

Online:http://human-nature.com/free-associations/MegH-WTiger&O.html.

Williams, M. H. (1994). A man of achievement: Sophocles' *Oedipus* plays. *British Journal of Psychotherapy*, 11 (2): 232–241.

Williams, M. H. (2005a). *The Vale of Soulmaking: the Post-Kleinian Model of the Mind*. London: Karnac. Also at: http://www.p-e-p.org/books.htm.

Williams, M. H. (2005b). Oedipus at the crossroads. In: *The Vale of Soulmaking: the Post-Kleinian Model of the Mind*, pp. 103–124. London: Karnac.

Williams, M. H. (2010a). *Bion's Dream: A Reading of the Autobiographies*. London: Karnac.

Williams, M. H. (2010b). *The Aesthetic Development: The Poetic Spirit of Psychoanalysis: Essays on Bion, Meltzer, Keats*. London: Karnac. Also at: http://www.p-e-p.org/books.htm.

Winnicott, D.W. (1954). Metapsychological and clinical aspects of regression within the psychoanalytical set-up. Reprinted in *Through Paedeatrics to Psychoanalysis*, pp. 278–294. New York: Basic Books, 1975.

Wisdom, J. O. (1981). Metapsychology after forty years. In: Grotstein, J. S. (Ed.), *Do I Dare Disturb the Universe? Memorial to Wilfred R. Bion,* pp. 601–626. Beverly Hills: Caesura.

Wisdom, J. O. (1987). Bion's place in the troika. *International Journal of Psychoanalysis*, 14: 541–551.

Yalom, I. (1980). *Existential Psychotherapy*. New York: Basic Books.